AFTER EXPERIENCING the *Waveman*, Robert Redenbach returned to Australia to establish an independent publishing company. A regular guest speaker at corporate events, Rob offers business audiences unique insights into leadership, teamwork and benefiting from change. He lives with his wife and their five children.

www.redenbach.com

WAVE MAN

WAVE MAN

ROBERT REDENBACH

COURTNEY
BALLANTYNE

Courtney Ballantyne Publishing
PO Box 201 Bond University
QLD 4229 Australia
Email: info@cbpublishing.org

First Edition August, 2006
Reprinted March, 2007

Retail Distribution by
Macmillan Publishing Services
Level 4, 627 Chapel Street
South Yarra VIC 3141

National Library of Australia
Cataloguing-in-Publication data:

Redenbach, Robert P.
Waveman

ISBN 978-0-646-47039-9

1. Australia – Biography. 2. Australia – Social life and customs.
3. International – Travel. 4. Martial Arts – Self Defence. 5. Iraq – Security.

For *Natasha, Reilly, Cuan, Liam, Blake* and *Brontë*

With special thanks to
Peter Drake

Contents

GOING FOR BROKE 1992–1998

DUAL WORLDS 1999–2005

THE SHARP END

1996

I WONDER IF THAT MIGHT HAVE BEEN
THE TIME WHEN I REALISED THAT
ONE WORD MIGHT BE THE KEY TO
MY ENTIRE LIFE.
CONTROL. OR THE LACK OF IT.

CHAPTER 1

Los Angeles

SOMETHING MOVED at the edge of my vision and I turned my head, slowly. It was a bead of sweat. For a moment I watched it rolling down Jerry's deeply lined face, around the rim of the eye-socket and over the broad, tanned cheekbone, gathering momentum towards the line of the jaw.

Sitting next to me, hunkered low in the driving seat of the Buick, Jerry caught my eye and gave me a quick, quizzical glance. Twitching my lips into what I hoped was a smile I turned back to the windscreen and focused once again on my breathing.

In these moments — which I knew could stretch into hours — I needed the regimen of deep breathing to help dissipate my fear, clear my mind, maximise the acuteness of my hearing — and give me the widest possible field of vision.

Out of the corner of my eye I saw Jerry give me a troubled look.

'I'm not happy about this,' he growled.

'It's my arse, mate,' I murmured.

'Yeah, but if you get shot, then it's *my* ass. It'll be okay for you. You'll be dead.'

I chuckled. I loved the dark, mordant humour of the guys in the Bureau. I turned my eyes back to what Jerry called the vacant lot. The ground was scattered with the burnt-out hulks of cars; littered with abandoned refrigerators and washing machines and the nameless parts of car engines which, rusting in the bright sunlight, were silhouetted starkly against the bright blue of the Californian sky.

The breeze was wafting a few pathetic tufts of wispy grass and

1

straggling weeds and I made the conscious decision not to let my mind dwell on what might lay hidden there … broken needles, used condoms, dead … no, stay focused.

'You can always let me have a gun,' I said. 'You've got a spare SIG in the boot.'

'The what?' Jerry said.

'The trunk. You have a spare SIG-Sauer in there.'

'Yeah, and that's where it's staying, buddy. I give you a handgun and something goes wrong in there, we'll have an international incident on our hands. You getting shot is bad enough but one of those clowns getting shot by an Aussie who's only supposed to be here as an observer is even worse. It would compromise the arrest. Those badasses might walk. Besides which it could start a war between Australia and the United States.'

'Nice to know I might be remembered for something after I'm gone.'

'Yeah? Well, it's not going to happen. Not on my watch. When this goes down you keep your Aussie ass the hell out of the way. Way, way back. Way out of the line of fire. You hear me.'

'How far back you reckon I should be?'

'New York would be good.'

Jerry was top value.

'No, I'm going to be right behind you. All the way.'

'And supposing I get shot?'

'Then I'll pick up your gun and shoot the mongrel who did it.'

'Yeah, you do that. But don't say I said so, okay? It's not Bureau policy.'

I studied the rueful face beside me. 'It'll be fine, Jerry. No worries.'

'If I hear "no worries" or "she'll be right" one more time today, I'll shoot you myself.'

I laughed, turning once more to contemplate the decaying, windowless warehouse two hundred metres across the lot that was our target.

There was always banter before action but the fact was — Jerry *did* have plenty to worry about.

It had started as a simple stake out. The Bureau had an informer on the inside of a heroin deal planned to go down in a plain panel van in the parking lot of a shopping mall. Bureau agents were meant to watch the deal completed and then move in; some of the fifty-man SWAT team would be in attendance as backup, just in case anything went wrong.

After I conducted my training session with the team, which had started before dawn and lasted almost nine hours, Doug Able, the team commander, had suggested I go along as an observer. He often did that. But within hours, both the place and the play had changed: the deal had escalated with over a quarter of a million expected to change hands; the location switched to the vacant lot. Far worse, there were new players in the game.

'These men are dangerous,' Able had announced. I was sitting on top of an old school desk next to Jerry in the cramped, ramshackle SWAT team briefing room in the FBI building on Wiltshire Boulevard.

'What he means is these guys are some of the meanest mothers alive,' Jerry whispered.

I smiled, quietly impressed by the nonchalance of the men in the room; men I knew from long hours of training with them to be totally professional, completely dedicated to their task.

'There are four of them,' Able continued. He shuffled through his notes and recited a list of names that meant nothing to me, though from the movement and undercurrent in the room it was clear they meant something to everyone else. Guys casually leaning against the battered sports lockers straightened up.

'These guys are strong, criminally aggressive and highly motivated,' Able said. 'All are known to carry firearms, especially when a drug deal is going down, and the word is that instead of the usual crap weaponry of your average dealer, these badasses have got their hands on at least two Ingram MACs. Maybe more.'

3

The atmosphere in the briefing room took on the quality of a collective indrawn breath as the SWAT team thought about it. A MAC fires over a thousand rounds a minute, which means the full thirty-round 9mm magazine could be coming at you in less than two seconds. The fire-power of just one Ingram MAC was devastating; but two or more … well, no one wanted to go there.

Because the nature of the raid had so radically changed, Able announced that the entire fifty-man SWAT team would now be the primary force in the raid. It was SWAT who would move in, SWAT who would make the arrests.

'We'll take them on the vacant lot. The moment the van arrives we hit them. We won't give them a chance to react or mobilise. Take 'em down before they get time to think.' He glanced at me from his perch on a desk next to the coffee urn, holding eye contact long enough to let me know he was serious.

'Red, if you want to sit this one out, that's okay. It could turn into a shitstorm.'

'She'll be right,' I said. 'I want to come. Hell, I've got nothing better to do.' I was single and in my early thirties; there wasn't anywhere else I wanted to be.

'Okay, but if it starts getting out of control, I want you to pull out. Jerry, that's your responsibility. If there's gunplay, get his ass out of there. You gottit, Jerry?'

'Yeah, I gottit. I'll baby-sit him. *Naw warrice mate.*' It was a terrible impression of an Aussie accent, and funny because of it. We all laughed.

But almost as soon as we'd arrived at the vacant lot and positioned the vehicles, things had started getting out of control.

As I write this account a decade later, I wonder if that might have been the time when I realised that one word might be the key to my entire life. Control. Or the lack of it.

Though there was supposed to be radio silence until immediately before the bust, Able had come on the radio, his voice distorted by the static. 'Heads up. The deal has changed. It's happening *inside* the warehouse. Targets are arriving separately; we can't take them in the van. If we want to nail these guys we have to take them as the deal goes down. Inside.'

'This thing is turning into a crocka shit,' Jerry had moaned.

I could never make up my mind whether Jerry and the others deliberately parodied Hollywood, or whether Hollywood script-writers tuned in to these guys and immortalised their idiom. Either way I knew what Jerry was thinking. The same thoughts were occurring to me. Outside, going up against a quartet of well-armed, highly motivated criminals was exceptionally dangerous; inside, it was something close to lunacy.

A female agent dressed as a bag lady and pushing a supermarket trolley crossed the vacant lot, sidling up to the car to push a crudely drawn map of the interior of the building through the driver's window. The deal was set for the second floor, in a storage room towards the back. Two flights of stairs then a narrow passage of about fifty metres before a sharp left and another passage of thirty metres to the room. One man with a MAC could hold off the entire team all day.

Together we studied the floor plan, Jerry muttering that it would be more use as toilet paper than an item of criminal intelligence.

The SWAT team had been split into three squads, plus a squad in reserve with the command and control unit. Charlie Squad, commanded by Jerry and comprising me plus the nine agents sitting in a couple of battered UVs thirty metres away, were slated to go in first.

Yes, I thought, Jerry had a lot to worry about. Which, I supposed, meant that I did too.

The radio crackled.

'Target vehicle in sight.'

We watched a dusty Trans Am bounce onto the lot and stop close to the door of the building. Two men got out, taking a moment to stare around the lot. Jerry and I hunkered further into our seats as Able's voice came over the radio.

'They're the targets. The short one, he's our man.' We watched the men pull open the door and disappear inside the building.

About a minute later a white panel van slewed onto the lot, fishtailing slightly and kicking up clouds of dust. Three men piled out, rubbernecking the surroundings. They were wearing unfastened cotton windcheaters, just right for concealing a lightweight submachine gun.

The radio traffic was frantic about where the hell the fourth man was.

'We don't want that scum in back of us,' someone wailed. 'He's the most dangerous of the whole goddam crew.'

Seconds later Able's voice came over the radio, his tone sharp and authoritative: 'We can't hang here all afternoon waiting for him. We either go now or stand down. If he shows we'll take him outside. All squads wait for my order to go.'

Somewhere on the other side of the building Bravo Squad was readying to enter the building from the street, while the guys from Alpha Squad were finding themselves high elevation in neighbouring buildings to set up with their sniper rifles.

Pulling my Bureau baseball cap firmly on to my head, I breathed deeply and deliberately.

'Go, go, go.'

I was out and running while the final monosyllable was still echoing inside the car, my dark blue Kevlar body armour with the big, yellow FBI across its back bouncing tightly against my chest. Within seconds Jerry and the rest of the squad were up with me, their M16s at high port, their boots pounding the rubble; all of us racing towards the building, desperate to reach the lee of the warehouse wall. The vacant lot was a killing ground; from any of the smashed windows someone with a submachine gun could shoot at least four of us before we made the door.

We made it, smacking into the wall with our impetus, all of us breathing in rasping, staccato bursts. The guys were superbly fit and I knew their erratic breathing was as much to do with the sudden surge of anxious energy as with the explosive dash in the heat of the afternoon.

We regrouped on either side of the battered metal door, taking a moment to calm our breathing as every member of the squad focused on his role in the team.

Jerry held up fingers, pointed, and made various unequivocal gestures. Two of the biggest guys moved to the door, one holding a large body shield, the other a short battering ram. Six of the others, their shoulders hunched, cheeks pressed into the stocks of M16s raised in firing position, moved into place behind them. All were wearing Kevlar body armour; the guys at the front in dark blue combat helmets. Jerry and the radioman, who had taken up position at the rear, had turned their Bureau caps around backwards. I did the same.

Jerry signalled, and SWAT Charlie Squad went into Entry Against Armed Assailant mode, one of the guys at the front easing open the heavy door which scraped and grated fit to bust, Jerry quietly cursing as, in an instant, the front men were inside, their M16s moving: arcing around in fields of fire.

Nothing.

I slipped inside behind Jerry, the radioman checking our rear. We were in a stairwell. It was stained, covered in graffiti, smelled of piss and shit and had a rusty iron balustrade and crumbling concrete steps that disappeared into a murky gloom. We moved swiftly up the stairs and yet again I was amazed at how quietly big men could move.

Two floors; four flights of stairs; up in twenty seconds; no sound, no opposition; no hopped-up pushers leaning out and spraying our faces with a lethal blizzard of 9mm Parabellum. We reached the second landing. The passage was to our left.

This was the moment of maximum danger.

Fifty metres of narrow passage with no cover other than an insanely brave guy with a big, bulletproof shield. If, halfway along the passage two MAC carrying gunmen stepped out and opened up, there would be no place to go; nowhere to hide; it would be the equivalent of a fire-fight in a telephone booth. And I didn't have a gun.

The instant after the point man sneaked a look around the corner, Jerry signalled to move out and we shuffled tentatively into the passage, everyone's eyes riveted on the place fifty metres ahead where the other passage intersected; the corner around which violent death might be waiting.

The squad moved slowly; ten metres, twenty, thirty, thirty-five … then stopped, muscles tight, trigger fingers slowly squeezing, at a movement at the far end of the passageway, beyond the intersection. What the hell was happening? Nothing was supposed to be down there.

A flash of colour; blue cloth and white skin; a face taking a quick peek around the corner at the end of the passage. Above the face, a blue combat helmet.

Bravo Squad.

I caught the unanimous sigh, the relief almost palpable as shoulders relaxed, trigger fingers eased off an iota.

We continued on, both squads stopping just short of the intersection of the passage on the left. Jerry moved forward and, after a flurry of signals between him and the boss of Bravo a man from each squad peeked around the corner. Two thumbs jerked up. The passage was clear. Both squads slid around the corner simultaneously, each file of men hugging the wall on their own side. Thirty metres away, facing us at the end of the passage was a door, slightly ajar, from beyond which came a low murmur of voices. The front men, assault rifles trained on the door, stepped delicately towards it, while I found myself the number four man in the file moving along our side of the passage. Whether Jerry was aware of my presence so far up front I had no idea. But even if he knew, there was nothing he could do about it now.

The squads halted a couple of metres from the door. The voices from beyond it had risen; clearly the deal was not proceeding smoothly and it occurred to me that if we waited long enough maybe the bad guys would shoot each other. No, it'd never happen; that wasn't the way the Bureau did things. But whatever was happening, it was clear the men in the room were unaware that the wrath of God and Uncle Sam, in the shape of twenty fully armed members of the Los Angeles FBI SWAT team, plus one Aussie unarmed combat instructor, was about to descend on them.

Jerry raised a hand, the front men turning for the count. Five fingers.

Each man counted off to himself ... five, four, three, two, one ...

'FBI. GET DOWN. GET DOWN. FBI. GET DOWN.'

The squads erupted into the room; a score of men piling in, boots booming on the scuffed timber floor, their weapons trained, their voices bellowing that single, insistent, command. 'GET DOWN.'

The noise, bouncing off the bare concrete walls was shocking.

Three of the men dropped immediately, streetwise enough to instantly place their hands on top of their heads. One man thought about it for a second but with the muzzles of at least four M16s in his face he gave up on thinking and threw himself to the floor. The last man, the one nearest me, hesitated, his hand shooting towards his open windcheater.

I moved in, readying for a takedown.

Luis got there first. Little Luis, barely an inch over the minimum height for the Bureau, but always the hardest worker in my training sessions, the most dedicated; pound for pound the toughest in the whole team.

It was perfect. Just like we'd practised in our training sessions, Luis shifted his weight to his front leg as his lead elbow shot forward, the gloved hand moving so fast it was no more than a black blur, the heel of his palm connecting with the point below the man's nose. The guy shot backwards in shock; you could almost see his brain blink its confusion. Luis closed the gap like a leopard going in for the kill. Wildly, the guy swung a heavy right fist. It hit nothing but air. Luis had wrapped one arm around the attacker's torso as his other grabbed a large handful of hair. In the half-a-heartbeat that followed,

Luis yanked down with one hand as his rear leg swept through and executed a simple yet devastatingly effective takedown.

'Nice one, Luis,' I murmured. 'Where'd you learn that?'

Luis's dark face broke into a grin. 'Just something my Mom taught me.'

'Yeah? That explains a lot.'

Luis laughed, the sound lost in the noisy cacophony of the room. Relief was everywhere, like a sudden leak of happy gas, the tension pouring out of the men like sweat after hard training; the room filled with raucous laughter and loud banter, in among it the sound of the men on the floor being cuffed and cautioned.

Able had appeared and was in a corner with a couple of the team, intently questioning the little guy he'd ID'd as the Bureau's snitch.

In the centre of the floor was an arsenal of weaponry; two of the feared MACs, what looked like an early model Steyr GB and a battered 9mm Beretta. Along a couple of the walls were stacked cardboard boxes covered in a fine white dust — distemper, and maybe a little chalk. Unlike the rest of the building, this room didn't harbour the overwhelming smell of urine and excrement. It smelled of cardboard and dust and reminded me of something familiar yet long gone.

'We've got a chance to take down Ramon.' Able's voice jerked me out of my reverie.

'What?'

'Ramon. We can take him. If we move quickly.'

I had no idea what he was talking about and glanced at Jerry, standing close by.

'Ramon's the one who didn't show,' he explained.

'How do you know where he is?' I asked.

'My man,' Able jerked his head at the snitch being led away by a couple of the team, 'says Ramon is going ahead with the original deal. In the parking lot of a shopping mall in Westwood. It's going down in about thirty minutes.'

'We'll never make it,' Jerry moaned.

'Try.' Able's tone was uncompromising. 'Your squad will be enough. I need Bravo to take these guys into custody. Three vehicles, lights and sirens. Get going.' Jerry pivoted, yelling for Charlie Squad.

'Wait,' Able ordered. 'Take the van.'

Jerry turned back to him. 'What?'

'It's evidence. And it's Ramon's. He sees it arriving at the parking lot he's going to feel relaxed. Like the deal here went okay. He won't be expecting a bust. Here, take the keys.'

Jerry took them reluctantly. 'Who the hell am I gonna get to drive it?'

I watched his eyes cut to me before a broad grin spread across his face. He tossed the keys and I snatched them out of the air. 'Keep up, Aussie, we're going for a drive.'

Charlie Squad exited the building in a vastly different mood to the one in which we had entered it. We pounded out of the door, racing towards the vehicles on the far side of the vacant lot.

Gleefully, I leapt into the nearby van, my excitement dying the moment I gunned the engine and put it in drive. It was a heap of junk. The steering was spongy and unresponsive; the vehicle had no acceleration and the brakes — hell, what brakes? Putting my foot on the brake pedal was like stepping in cow shit: the pedal went all the way to the floor before I could get the thing to slow down.

Bouncing across the lot I called Jerry a mongrel bastard. Behind me, in the back, things crashed and banged against the metal walls. It was like driving an iron foundry.

I took up position at the rear of the convoy as the vehicles roared off the lot; one Buick and two beaten-up utility vehicles whose appearance was deceptive. Their engines had been tuned to deliver speed. Which was what they were doing.

Within seconds, heading west towards Harbor Freeway through early rush-hour traffic, the convoy was travelling at sixty miles an hour, each UV only inches from the proceeding rear bumper. In the lead Jerry had attached a magnetic red light to the roof of the Buick and, with its siren wailing, the car was slicing through the traffic. We hit the Harbor Freeway; rocketing up the on ramp at over seventy. The Freeway was busy but Jerry cut his way across to the outside lane and within seconds we were doing eighty. I did the conversion — bloody hell, I was travelling at close to a hundred and thirty kilometres an hour. If we should have to suddenly stop? — in this heap I'd be screwed.

Yet the sensation of racing down a busy LA freeway was exhilarating. Bouncing crazily in my seat, I gripped the juddering steering wheel, almost oblivious to the shattering racket of metal behind me.

Tyres squealing we rocketed off Harbor, speeding around the enormous cloverleaf loop west onto the even busier Santa Monica Freeway. Here the convoy was forced to a crawl.

From my elevated position in the van I could see six lanes of vehicles, all moving at the velocity of cold porridge. And then, as I watched, the solid mass of traffic ahead parted. I stared as it separated — opening like a zip — and suddenly I felt the rush as six lanes of freeway traffic opened up for me.

I shoved my foot to the floor as Jerry accelerated, the convoy parting the traffic like a scalpel opens flesh. I pushed the van towards eighty, enjoying the heady, invigorating thrill of watching the road open before me.

It didn't last.

We came off the Santa Monica at La Cienaga, onto a boulevard filled with people and parking lots and cross streets and traffic lights. Suddenly the traffic was no longer parting like waves in the Red Sea. It was more like herding cats.

Cars pulled off out of the way of Jerry's Buick and immediately tried to re-enter the traffic, narrowly missing being sideswiped by one of the speeding UVs or my van. People stepped off the sidewalk; cars crossed late on the green and all four of us were suddenly in the business of chicaning around vehicles slowing in the middle of intersections. Swerving the van was like trying to manoeuvre a pregnant hippo. Somewhere along La Cienaga we made a left and then it happened. A car pulled out in front of me and I hit the brakes, hearing the banshee screech of metal clamping metal, the smell of burning. I pressed my hand hard to the horn but the idiot driver remained in front. I watched the convoy speeding away.

I pulled out into the oncoming traffic and pushed my foot as far to the floor as it would go, scarcely noticing the gap closing. I frantically pulled back into the kerb. After what seemed like a week I passed the car. The convoy was over two hundred metres ahead, crossing a set of lights turning to red.

Oh shit. Stop? No, go. No, stop.

No, go. Go, go, GO.

I kept my hand on the horn and rocketed into the intersection glancing to my right to see a dark brown Plymouth going into a full side slide.

And then I saw it. Way beyond the end of the cross street, high up Mount Lee to the north, the crooked letters of the sign — HOLLYWOOD. I burst out laughing: here I was, in an FBI cap and body armour, driving a drug dealer's vehicle through the streets of Los Angeles in hot pursuit of an FBI car with a flashing light and wailing siren. If that wasn't pure Hollywood, what the hell was? I didn't even have an American driver's licence.

Was this living or what? It just doesn't get better than this.

Still laughing, with my hand held down on the horn, I caught up with the convoy, which, after a couple more minutes, slowed and pulled alongside the kerb. I got out of the van, ignoring my quivering legs and walked as casually as I could to join the others gathering on the sidewalk.

'You okay?' Jerry asked.

'Yeah, I'm fine. Thanks very much for letting me drive that heap of crap. I almost killed myself.'

Everyone laughed.

Jerry prodded my body armour with his finger. 'Take off your Kevlar and cap for me will you.' Beneath the body armour I was wearing a check shirt and slacks. 'Yeah, you'll do.'

'What do you mean, I'll do?'

'I mean you don't look like a cop or Bureau. Apart from that bent beak you call a nose, you look perfectly ordinary. Like John Q Citizen.'

'So?'

'So when we've figured where Ramon is, I want you to drive the van real slow to where he's at and stop and get out.'

'Yeah? And then what? What do I say before the mongrel shoots me?'

'Tell him José sent you.'

'José sent me?'

'Right.'

'And then he shoots me.'

'He won't shoot you. You get close enough you can take him down yourself.' He shrugged. 'It goes without saying you're not as good as someone from the Bureau but you're okay — for an Australian.'

It was getting a bit predictable how he brought up the Aussie thing at every opportunity. 'Gee, thanks for the compliment.'

'You're welcome, just don't let it go to your head.'

'Okay, but don't you think this Ramon is going to be a mite curious as to who I am and what the hell I'm doing with his van?'

'Exactly.'

'What do you mean?'

'While he's trying to figure out all that, we'll be sidling up his blind side to nail his ass.'

'So I'm the decoy. To distract him.'

'Right.'

I stared into Jerry's open face as long as I could draw it out and then shrugged. 'Okay. So long as I know.' I tried to sound cheesed off, but in fact the plan appealed to me. It sounded like fun.

Minutes later I was easing the van on to the parking lot of a huge shopping mall, looking for a big, silver Mercedes with two men in front and one in the rear. I spotted the car in seconds and drove the van at walking pace towards it. One of the men got out of the Mercedes and stood with his back to it, eyeing me and the van suspiciously. He was short and stocky, with black hair and dark, reptilian eyes. Like his buddies, the man was wearing a loose, unzipped windcheater.

I parked opposite the Mercedes and slowly got out of the van, strolling across the asphalt with my hands in full view and my shirt tucked into my slacks to show, as best I could, that I wasn't carrying a concealed weapon. I got to within a couple of metres of the man before I stopped and said, pleasantly, 'G'day.'

'Who the fuck are you?' the man demanded.

'Banjo Paterson, mate.'

'Who?'

'José sent me.'

The man frowned. 'So? Where's Emilio?'

'That's it, mate. José sent me.'

The frown deepened. 'But who are you, man? You ain't from around here. So who the hell are you?'

'I told you. I'm Banjo, the man from the lucky country. The sunburnt country. The land of golden soil and wealth for toil, the land that's girt by sea. And José sent me.'

'Are you shittin' me? What the fuck is this?'

Silently a large, blue-armoured figure appeared behind the man, pointing a handgun at the back of his head. Then another appeared, and another, all armoured and all pointing M16 rifles at the occupants of the car.

'Hello Ramon,' Jerry said. The man spun around to find the muzzle of the Glock about half a metre from his forehead, just outside the reactionary gap. Jerry smiled at the man. 'If there's H in that car, Ramon, then your ass is grass and you're looking at twenty-five years in the Federal Pen.'

It took a couple of hours to process Ramon and the others at Wiltshire, after which we all retired to the local Ribs and Beer joint to celebrate the victory. After about an hour, Jerry disappeared to make a call. Returning he said, 'My wife says to come on over for a couple of beers and a barbecue. You want to come?'

I nodded. 'I'd like that.'

Driving towards his home in Glendale, Jerry buttoned down the windows to let in the night air. It was a perfect LA evening; the sky indigo, the breeze, coming in off the ocean cooling the city and wafting the fronds of the tall cotton palms along the boulevards.

Jerry sighed contentedly. 'You know, a lot of days in this job are pure hell. If it's not bureaucratic bullshit it's legal bullshit. Sometimes I wonder why I do the goddam job. And then, along comes a day like today and I know. Trouble is, you don't get that many days as good as this. But when you do … boy … don't it just feel great.'

I smiled in the darkness. 'Yeah.'

'I always wanted to do this job. Ever since I was a kid at school, right from the eighth grade, I wanted to be a Federal agent and take down bad guys. Never wanted to do anything else. Ever. You believe that?'

I grunted, not really listening. Jerry's words had triggered something, a memory long buried and deliberately forgotten.

The smell in the room where we'd busted the dealers reminded me of my Grade Six classroom. Reminded me of a time when I wasn't even called Red.

Most of all, it reminded me of Mrs Gannon.

Starting Out

1975–1980

I WAS ABOUT AS UNREMARKABLE AS
YOU COULD GET: SMALL FOR MY AGE
AND SKINNY; SILENT MOST OF THE TIME
AND SOFTLY SPOKEN WHEN I WASN'T.

CHAPTER 2

Gippsland

IT WAS a small, austere room with a scuffed wooden floor and plaster walls, the plaster peeling in damp patches close to the ceiling or where posters had once been pinned. The place was dreary even by the standards of the school; even by the standards of the small town in the heart of Gippsland. It smelled of dust and chalk, of tedium and defeat and that vague, unwashed smell of a classroom of kids. A blackboard stretched across one wall, before it a low timber platform.

Unlike other teachers at St Patrick's, Mrs Gannon didn't have her desk on the platform. Instead, she sat with her twenty or so pupils' desks arranged in a wide semi-circle around her. For teaching a class of eleven year old boys it was an excellent arrangement. For Mrs Gannon.

Not for me. I hated it.

I wanted to be in a class where the desks were lined up in rows and I could sit at the back and not be noticed. I definitely did not want to be noticed by Mrs Gannon. Mrs Gannon was short and dark and dumpy, with a screeching, heavily accented voice. What the accent was I had no idea; but wherever Mrs Gannon was from, I wished like mad she'd go back there.

Mrs Gannon didn't like me. In fact, I was number one on her hit list. I couldn't understand it. I was about as unremarkable as you could get: small for my age and skinny; silent most of the time and softly spoken when I wasn't. In a classroom of kids I should have been almost invisible. But in Mrs Gannon's class I was made to stand out like a leper; in her book, I was stupid and lazy and recalcitrant. Yet I wasn't stupid.

I knew I wasn't, but the areas where I excelled weren't recognised in an orthodox curriculum. I could glance at a Jeff Hook cartoon each morning in *The Sun* and tell in a moment where the trademark 'hook' was hidden, but this didn't compensate for my one major problem: it was almost impossible for me to make sense of the words in my school books.

They jumped about, rearranging themselves into meaningless jumbles; whole paragraphs turned into gobbledygook and, try as I would, I couldn't make the words stand still.

Why they wouldn't stay still was beyond me; it was yet another thing I couldn't understand. It made me want to cry with frustration. Of course I held back my tears. I was eleven and eleven year old boys didn't cry.

It was 1975, and while in the Northern Hemisphere, Ashton and Lieberman were undertaking innovative research into dyslexia, here in the grey stone and concrete monolith of St Patrick's College, Sale, I'd never heard of it.

Nor, it seemed, had Mrs Gannon. And even if she had, she would have dismissed it as some academic psychologist's pathetic excuse to let lazy, stupid and disobedient kids like me off the hook.

Sitting as delicately as I could on the hardwood bench seat of my desk, with the bruises from the last beating hurting like hell, I'd wait fearfully for the day's reprisal to fall.

'Read that paragraph *properly*,' Mrs Gannon would screech. 'Do it again.'

I am conscious of the faces of the other kids in the semi-circle; some smirking, others puzzled as to why, yet again, I'd made such a mess of an easy read.

'No, Ma'am. I can't.'

'What did you say?'

'I … I can't read the letters, Ma'am. They jump around the page.'

'*They what?*' The screech goes up an octave.

'They … they jump around the page. The words don't make sense.'

'You're looking for trouble, aren't you? Didn't you learn anything from yesterday?'

'Not really, no.'

'Come out here. *Now.*'

Another day — another caning.

For Mrs Gannon corporal punishment was a way of life; beating me a banal, almost daily event. And while by law six was the maximum strokes with a cane permitted in any beating, a Gannon 'six' could amount to seven, eight, sometimes nine.

* * *

In some respects I was a typical Aussie kid: walking to and from school barefoot, hating to wear shoes even when it was cold and raining; which seemed to be the permanent state of the weather in Gippsland. Barefoot had nothing to do with poverty: my parents could afford shoes. For me it had to do with freedom … and the fact that the less I wore my shoes, the less I had to clean them.

At weekends, instead of watching sport, which I hated, I'd venture out with my Labrador Duke to collect blackberries or go swimming in the local river. Sometimes Duke and I would go rabbiting.

My loathing of cricket and football, the two greatest pursuits in the State of Victoria, was notorious. I simply had no interest in the games, and was hopeless at anything that involved a ball and eye-hand coordination. Like my inability to read words on a page, the incapacity was seen by my teachers as a serious defect in my character. No one I came in contact with thought the two might be connected, or had any idea that specific training and practice could improve both conditions.

I didn't fit: at school or at home.

The youngest of four children, my closest sibling, Sue, was three years older than me. My brother, Steve, was seven years my senior and Julie was two years beyond him. My family's life was spent almost entirely in front of the television. *Bellbird, The Ernie Sigley Show, Happy Days, Coronation Street, Aunty Jack, Upstairs Downstairs, Some Mothers Do 'Ave 'Em, Matlock Police, Steptoe & Son, Six Million Dollar Man, Class of '75* ... these shows were our life. There was no discernment; we watched whatever was dished up. Even the irreverent (and very funny) Dave Allen was allowed into our smoke-filled living room — so long as I pretended not to understand his jokes. Watching the black and white images even as we ate our meals there was something about the box that frustrated me; I liked watching it, but it suppressed rather than satisfied a hunger to experience life.

My favourite escape was when I rode my bike out to the Saturday afternoon kids' matinee at the base cinema of RAAF East Sale. It was a round trip of over twenty kilometres, though it seemed even further as the weather was almost always grey and windy and wet. Pedalling past the perimeter fence I'd eye the big, fat-bellied C130 Hercules and the strangely shaped Chinook helicopters, not long returned from Vietnam, but most of all I loved to see the F111 jet fighters, so sleek, so slim, so deadly. I felt an affinity with the base; my father's elder brother had trained as a pilot there during World War II.

When Grade Six finally dragged itself painfully to a close, I left St Patrick's convinced I'd learnt nothing. It wasn't true, although it was years before I realised what lessons I had learnt at the hands of Mrs Gannon.

Soon afterwards my family moved to Melbourne, renting a solid weatherboard house on a quarter-acre block in Murrumbeena. I was delighted to leave Sale and liked Melbourne much better, setting out every school day on the hair-raising bike ride to Caulfield Technical College. No one wore helmets in those days and it was a real thrill to feel the wind in my hair as I dashed among thundering trucks, clanging trams and whizzing cars.

Not long after the move I managed to convince my father to buy me a bow and allow me to take up archery. My father had been an archer and I was keen to try the sport. I practised every day, sacrificing my favourite television programs to retreat to the timber garage to shoot arrows in among my father's workbenches and racks of tools.

It was the first time I'd been really dedicated to anything and my practice paid off. In just over a year I won a State under-fifteen archery shoot-out along with an open invitation competition, seriously annoying many of my much older and far more expensively equipped competitors. And, curiously, in the process of practising archery every day, something even more beneficial happened. I learnt to read. The words stopped leaping about on the page; now they stayed still long enough for me to make sense of them.

I didn't know it at the time but the archery had developed my mind in a way that the researchers into dyslexia would later say was classic. I had learnt to concentrate; the Zen-like practices of correct breathing and total focus, whereby the archer, the arrow and the target all become one, had sharpened my perception, while the daily exercises of shooting arrows had given me patience, a tolerance of frustration and a much greater awareness of my state of mind.

It was a tectonic shift, and archery became an important part of my life, yet when my parents announced the family would be returning to Bairnsdale I was content to go.

It seemed to me, as it seemed to the whole family, that Bairnsdale, the small Gippsland town two hundred and ninety kilometres east on the Princes Highway, was the centre of the known world — it was where we all belonged. Not that we'd ever really moved away; throughout the family's time in both Sale and Melbourne, we'd constantly returned to visit relatives and friends.

We'd only ever left Bairnsdale because my father, a craftsman and master upholsterer, had been doing very well in a second-hand furniture store in which he also re-covered antique furniture. But in the land of tall poppies, the manager of the town's biggest department store had threatened his suppliers that he'd take his business elsewhere if they didn't stop supplying my father. Threatened with bankruptcy, we'd been forced to move.

Now I was glad to be going back, especially as a new sport beckoned. For some years my older brother Steve had been practising martial arts. Now he promised to train me and get me into a club.

I was excited. I was going home; in less than two years I could leave school, and I had a new skill to conquer — learning from the one person I admired more than anyone: my brother.

Things didn't work out as planned. Steve, once so keen on martial arts, fast became seduced by the alternative attractions of a small town. Often on the dole, he did carpentry jobs for cash, which he spent in the local pubs. At twenty he'd also discovered women. So, between getting laid and getting wasted, he was devoting less and less time to training.

Though he kept promising, he was always 'too busy' to take me to the local dojo. Finally I decided that if I was ever going to learn martial arts I'd have to arrange it myself — even though the idea of fronting up alone at a place where people were supposed to throw you from one wall to another, though exciting, filled me with trepidation.

On the next training night I summoned the courage to walk into an Aikido dojo and approach the instructor.

The first few training sessions were painful. Aikido, like archery, was about technique, but I needed to be stronger. I worked at it, training hard whenever I could and running to increase my endurance. In my bedroom I practised the Aikido moves while at another club I also started training in a Korean kicking style.

One of my instructors, sensing my level of commitment, lent me a book illustrating the techniques. It was by Morihei Uyeshiba, the founder of Aikido.

Though my word blindness had been allayed by archery, reading was not one of my favourite pastimes and I did as little as possible. Yet I studied this book assiduously, propping it on a chair in my room as I practised the moves. To my family's surprise I saved up $20 and bought my own copy.

At the back of the book was a short account of Uyeshiba's life. For months I ignored it, but as I grew stronger and gained proficiency in the art, I wanted to learn everything there was to know about Budo, the martial way of life. I wondered about the man who had founded Aikido, the path to union with *ki* (life force), and as my instructor seemed to think Uyeshiba was some god-like kind of figure, I sat down to read his story.

It was a revelation, so many facets of Uyeshiba's life resonating with my own.

In his village Uyeshiba had been a loner; a kid who didn't fit, not interested in the things the other kids were interested in, while his father had been hounded and beaten for holding unpopular political beliefs.

But Uyeshiba had made something of his life. He had become a disciplined man who worked hard, who had never lost the desire to learn. Primarily he had learnt by travelling, seeing places and meeting people he would never have met in his village.

The biography was stimulating yet vaguely unsettling, suggesting to me that there might be a world beyond Bairnsdale; a concept my family refused to entertain; a notion I found uncomfortable. Life in Bairnsdale was easy and undemanding. I was training three to four evenings a week at the club and waiting out my time at school, doing the minimum I could get away with as I counted down the days.

CHAPTER 3

Whangarei

I LEFT school in Year Ten, a month before my sixteenth birthday, glad to escape the trammels of a system hell-bent on making me read books I didn't want to read and teaching me things I didn't want to know.

I went to work immediately, getting a job at the local hardware store, feeling like King of the Hill when I received my first weekly pay packet of $82.79 (I still have the original payslip). Though I was only fifteen I found that with money in my pocket it wasn't hard to get served in one of the local pubs. Going for a beer with my mates and my older brother made me feel even more liberated. This was living.

Within weeks I was down off the hill and slowly sinking into the swamp. I hated my job, the sheer excruciating boredom of it. And all my mates hated their jobs too. There appeared no way out of it. The pattern for all of us was to spend our days doing something we despised while yearning for knock-off time and the chance to down as much beer as we could afford or hold.

I came to dread Mondays, that sinking feeling in my gut as I cycled slowly down Nicholson Street towards Alpine Ash Building Supplies and another five and a half days of mind-numbing monotony.

I moaned about life to my mates in the pub and was met with the observation that 'life was hard'. I pulled a face and shrugged in agreement; I was sixteen and I didn't know any other response.

It took me about six months to come to terms with the fact that an undemanding, comfortable life in a small town had its price.

Early one autumn morning, Frank, the store manager, called me into the dingy office at the back of the shop.

'Bad news, Robbie,' he said. 'The business has gone belly up. We're in strife.'

I didn't understand. 'What?'

'We're bankrupt. We're shutting up shop.'

Bankrupt was a word I knew from my father's business experience in the town. 'You've lost all your money?'

'That about sums it up. By tomorrow the accountants will be all over this place and we'll be off like a bride's nightie.'

'So what should I do?'

'Nothing you can do. Go home. Look for another job. Sign on for the dole. I dunno. It's all over here. You'll be paid up to yesterday but that's it.' Frank shrugged. 'What can I say?'

I got my coat and stumbled out, too shocked to go home. I made for one of the benches in the park next to the town library and sat down, stunned. After ten years at school I had worked a grand total of six months before being thrown on to the dole. I was sixteen and redundant.

I should have been comfortable on the dole yet I wasn't. It wasn't the stigma of not having a job; a lot of people in the town were on the dole, including a few of my mates. And I was always able to make a little money on the side. Steve, who was a past master at working on the black while pulling down social security, helped me get casual work for cash which meant that at least I had money for a few beers.

The big problem with the dole was that it gave me time to notice things; importantly, I didn't fit. The footy club and the pub didn't satisfy me. I played with Duke for hours and even started watching daytime television.

I was bored. I reread Uyeshiba's biography. His emphasis on learning and travel, on moving beyond the comfort zone, was like a wake-up call.

My sister Sue was living in New Zealand with a Kiwi fisherman who had a part share in a fishing boat. I wrote to her asking if I could visit. She wrote back saying that Neil, her boyfriend, was looking for a deckhand; I could stay with them and earn money. Elated I set off for NZ; my first time out of Victoria.

Neil's boat fished out of Whangarei, a small, pretty port, tucked away 160 kilometres north of Auckland on the North Island. I liked the physical work of a deckhand, liked being outside. It was adventurous; in minutes the ocean could change from a benevolent, flat blue calm to a fearsome, in-your-face world of huge, grey rolling waves. Catching fish I'd never seen before, including small sharks and manta rays, was fun and interesting.

Even more exciting was watching dolphins playing next to the boat, seeing a giant humpback breach — twenty tonnes of whale shooting out of the water with the ease of a missile. When it belly-flopped we felt the shudder a kilometre away. It stayed around for a while spraying jets of water into the air, grey and indifferent, as huge as a landmass.

But my new life had a downside. Everyone I knew or worked with, including Neil and Sue, smoked dope. I didn't like drugs and, what's more, didn't enjoy being around people who did. Even at sixteen I'd seen what drugs could do to a person's body and mind. As far as I was concerned, whether it was sniffing petrol or smoking pot, it was all the same to me — stupid.

What surprised me was how anyone could afford the stuff. None of them made much money while I, at the bottom of the heap, wasn't even being paid enough to live on.

As the months passed, I watched the gloss rub off this bright-shining adventure until I was down to subsistence living in the company of a mob of pot-heads.

I thought of my boring, unchallenged but well-fed life at home and quit New Zealand, flying back across the Tasman to the security of Bairnsdale. Back home, Steve was going through one of his intense, though usually short-lived, bouts of application in the martial arts. He'd heard of a guru in Hobart who was said to be something of a martial arts legend. There was building work in Tasmania, and Steve was about to set off. Did I want to go with him to train under the master? I leapt at the chance. I'd never met a guru before, and to train under someone close to the status of Uyeshiba was a fantastic opportunity.

The reality turned out to be a disappointment. The guru, if he'd ever been one, had long since lost any semblance of competence or discipline. All I could see was a middle-aged boozer who pontificated about how people had lost all discipline and self-respect. The training was pitiful.

Short of funds, Steve and I set off for Rosebery, a small mining town on the north-west of the island where Steve got work putting up house frames and I worked on site digging ditches. We camped down in the bush next to the local footy oval from where, every night, Steve would shoot off to the pub while I went for a run before going down to the local gym to train. Occasionally I'd catch up with Steve just before closing time.

One night, after we'd been there for a couple of months, Steve came roaring back from the pub in his battered Ford 100 pickup with a couple of drinking buddies. Drunk and noisy, they decided it'd be fun to do a few doughnuts on the oval, yelling like rodeo riders above the roaring engine as the spinning wheels churned the grass to mud and its blazing headlights sliced the night.

After about twenty minutes they got bored and eased the vehicle over to the campfire. Just minutes later a set of fresh headlights came cutting through the blackness. It was a police car. Steve and his mates bolted into the bush. I'd done nothing wrong, so I stayed exactly where I was. The police car stopped close to the campfire and two cops got out. They ordered me to stand in front of the F100's bonnet where the older of the two demanded to see my driver's licence. I told him I didn't have one; I was only sixteen and didn't know how to drive. For some reason my explanation incensed the cop. Grabbing me by the throat he called me a fucking lying prick and slammed me into the F100.

Shocked and wide-eyed I stared dumbfounded at the cop. I couldn't believe what was happening. What had I done? I'd told the truth … why was I being attacked?

My silence seemed to incense him even more. Still holding me by the throat the cop drove an open hand into my mouth, splitting my lower lip and spraying blood on to his tunic. In the headlights I saw him glance down at his spattered shirt. He swore, and then hit me again — in my ear.

The world went spinning away in a sickening hazy whirl; a very loud buzzing inside my head. Terrified, I shit myself.

If the cops didn't hear it they certainly smelled it. The old one let go of me, calling me a dirty cock-sucker. For some reason my evident terror seemed to convince the cops I was speaking the truth and from a respectable distance they told me to tell my brother that both of us were to get out of Rosebery the next day. They drove off as, hurt and humiliated, I began cleaning myself up.

Quieter and considerably more sober, Steve and the others emerged from the bush. I started to tell him what the cop had said but Steve stopped me; he'd heard the whole thing.

Tending to myself in the darkness I wondered how it was that Steve hadn't come out and admitted to ripping up the oval. How come he'd let me take a beating for it? Why hadn't he come to help? What were brothers for? It didn't make sense. Or, maybe, it did.

We left Rosebery the next day, heading back to Bairnsdale. I was quiet as I thought about what had happened. My life was beginning to take on a pattern. I would escape Bairnsdale only to discover that I was still destitute, still an outsider and, right now, an assaulted and humiliated outsider. And because life was hard away from home, I'd gravitate back to the town.

Gravitate wasn't a word I ever used, though I grasped the natural phenomenon of gravitation; understood that I was a single biological entity struggling to exit the orbit of the small town my family called home. But always, when things got tough I'd allow myself to be sucked back into the safe, warm swamp.

Even though I'd left school at fifteen I kept my eyes open and made connections. I could see the town's ability to foster jealousy and gossip. It seemed to me that people didn't grow up in Bairnsdale; they grew complacent. Intuitively, I felt I was more susceptible than most to the dangers of the place.

I knew I needed to get away — and stay away. If I didn't, the small-town mentality would suck me under and I'd finish up like … well, it didn't matter. It wasn't going to happen.

Uyeshiba had explained in his biography how, in order to obtain knowledge and ability, he'd forced himself to go out into the world. And, so that he might gain information and experience he'd joined the military; deliberately choosing to experience military life at the lowest rank, without status or prestige.

Eight weeks later I fronted up at the Defence Force Recruiting Centre in Flinders Lane, Melbourne, to sit the entrance examination for the Army.

ARMY SCHOOLING

1981–1987

MUCH OF WHAT I WAS TAUGHT WAS MINDLESS AND EXCRUCIATINGLY BORING.

CHAPTER 4

Canungra

IN 1981 joining the army was anything but fashionable. Although it had been eight years since Australia had formally declared an end to its involvement in the Vietnam war, the memory of conscription was alive and well in pockets of Bairnsdale.

When my brother-in-law heard I'd *voluntarily* enlisted he laughed derisively and quoted a popular anti-war slogan from his university days. Not that I cared. I was quietly thrilled to have passed the entrance exam and happily swore fealty and allegiance to Queen Elizabeth the Second before being bussed off to Wagga Wagga.

Not that I saw much of Wagga, even though the First Recruit Training Battalion at Kapooka was close by. Apart from four days leave at the half-way mark, every day of my next twelve weeks was spent learning to be a soldier, starting at 6am with room inspections and finishing at 10pm with polishing equipment. In between, I learnt how to march and parade, how to salute and address an officer, how to parade, how to iron my uniform, how to handle guard duty, how to march, how to make my bed, how to sweep a floor, how to parade, how to crawl through the mud, how to clean my plate.

And how to march and parade.

Much of what I was taught was mindless and excruciatingly boring, on top of which Wagga in winter was freezing, the sober, three-storey, brick-built Kapooka barracks with its bare walls and glossily polished floors as cold as a tomb. Along with everyone else I shivered — and got shouted at for shivering. Yet despite all that, I found myself enjoying my new life. The food was plentiful and good and to my surprise I found I could take the garbage the army liked to dish out. And there was plenty of it.

Standing awkwardly to attention on the damp, grey concrete adjacent to the barracks, the platoon was confronted by a Vietnam vet, his Drill-Sergeant's uniform embellished by combat ribbons, his iron-hard eyes as opaque to empathy as ball bearings.

The Sergeant surveyed us as if we were something a dog had vomited up before screaming, 'What kind of scrawny, piss-weak bunch of wankers are you? You look like a pack of longhaired schoolgirls. You, you scraggy little turd, step forward.'

'Me?' my voice quavered.

'Yes, you,' he bellowed. 'Who do you think I mean, you bloody dickhead? Are you stupid? Are you depriving some fucking village somewhere of its idiot?'

I moved forward, suddenly back in Mrs Gannon's class, conscious of the platoon's petrified eyes darting sideways to witness my humiliation.

'How old are you?' the Sergeant shouted.

'Seventeen, sir.'

'Don't call me sir, you little tosspot. I'm a Sergeant. And you're not seventeen. You look about twelve. Are you lying to me?'

'No sir ... Sergeant.'

'How much do you weigh?'

'About sixty-seven kilograms, Sergeant.'

'What? You *are* lying to me, you skinny runt. And what are those things dangling beneath your hips?'

'I ... I don't know what you mean sir ... Sergeant.'

'Those toothpicks stuck in your friggin' sandshoes. What the fuck are they?'

'My legs, Sergeant?'

'You've got to be fucking joking. What are you, a bloody comedian? They're not legs. I've seen more muscles on dental floss. They're those white wavy things hanging off fucking jellyfish, that's what they are. What's your name you little piece of fly shit?'

I told him.

'Red and what?' he screamed. 'Red and black? What are you, a flag? What kind of stupid mouthful of a name is that? I'm not calling you that. From now on you're Red. Gottit? Red. That's your name now.'

So in the beat of a scared and racing heart, I became Red.

I liked it. A new name in a new life. No one in Bairnsdale had ever called me Red, and in a land where redheads were called Bluey, it made perverse sense that the army would call a skinny frightened recruit with dark curly hair, Red.

I did six years in the army and learnt a lot, most of it beneficial, though often it didn't seem so at the time.

The main thing I learnt was discipline — not the mindless imposed discipline the army insisted upon, but self-discipline. Perhaps I always had it — those evenings in the garage in Melbourne practising archery instead of watching television; the hours spent in my bedroom practising Aikido moves from a book.

Much of my new life was learning how to live with other people, adjusting to a whole range of differing personalities. Though usually in the barracks there were four recruits to a room, in my room there were only two; myself and Ronnie Grimes.

Ronnie was a gawky hundred and eighty-five centimetres with long, sticklike limbs and a beaky Roman nose. In the tradition of the army, while I was called Red, Ronnie Grimes, who had hair as red as a Kalbarri sunset and freckles like he'd been buckshot with paprika, went by the startlingly unoriginal nickname of Grimesy.

About my age, Grimesy was one of four brothers, the son of a tough, hard-drinking miner and amateur boxer from Newcastle whose life revolved around playing rugby and drinking beer. He was a brawler from a family of brawlers, always quick with a joke but equally as quick to smack someone in the mouth if they said something he didn't much like. He was a man's man who didn't pull his punches and who, if he stayed in the army, had Sergeant written all over him.

I eyed him cautiously for the first few days we bunked together. Ronnie Grimes was exactly the kind of kid who had given me trouble at school for not liking football. I needn't have worried. So long as I was happy to go drinking on our few passes out of the barracks, and match drink for drink with him, Ronnie was my mate.

After three months of freezing in Kapooka, the platoon was dispatched to the Infantry Training Centre at Singleton in New South Wales. Though happy to be assigned to the infantry rather than to the armoured or artillery corps, I found Singo to be as hot as Wagga had been cold, the barracks of long, timber huts with sixteen Diggers in each hut like saunas set to the max.

Our three months in Singo were stupidly aggressive; the food crap, the training hard, the screaming in our ears relentless.

I understood that to turn us into fighting men, life had to be hard, but Singo was mindlessly macho, the brutality at times approaching outright cruelty. It was as if we were the enemy.

Ronnie summed it up as we were crawling on our bellies in full battle kit through a field of evil-smelling mud.

'Silver paper has come right off this fucking shitcake,' he gasped loudly.

Twelve weeks later our platoon was deemed a fighting unit and received its first posting. It was to last a year and before being dispatched we were given leave.

I'd scarcely given a moment's thought to my home town and though I'd experienced the occasional nostalgic twinge for my family, if truth be told I'd missed Duke more than any of the two-legged members.

The first thing I did on arriving home was take the dog for a long run. Then I went to the dojo, before going down to the local pub with Steve.

And that rapidly became the pattern; a cross-country run with Duke before a couple of hours at the dojo followed by a beer, or a lot of beers, with Steve. Occasionally I sat down with the family to watch television.

Drinking in a local pub with Steve near the end of my leave, I got into a fight. It was a stupid, sloppy affair, started by a mob that didn't like long-haired Steve or his crew-cut brother and finished by Steve and I, though not quickly and not well. There was no skill attached to it; merely a lot of crashing glasses, shouts and curses and waving arms and legs with strikes and punches connecting more by accident than intention and in the process I had my nose broken and a tooth chipped.

Steve was triumphant. In the car on the way to Emergency to get treatment for me he crowed over how we'd won, how we'd beaten the shit out of those bastards, his voice filled with elation. I wasn't so sure. Though I didn't say so, I couldn't see what we'd won — what the fight had changed — except that I'd gotten hurt. The fight had been pointless and meaningless; a sudden spiking of snarling, bad-tempered testosterone to absolutely no end.

Hung over and feeling like crap, the following day I took Duke on our usual run. I thought about the fight as I ran, my body on automatic, scarcely feeling my limbs, my mind back in the pub. It was a rare day, the weather was good, the sun dappling the roadway through the leaves of the eucalypts.

Picking up the pace I ran across a busy road, glancing at my watch. I was making good time and started to stride out when I heard a sudden screech of tyres and a dull thud behind me.

Even before I turned my head I knew what I was going to see. Duke had been hit by a car. He'd taken the force of the impact on his hips; his back was broken at an impossible angle.

He lay in the middle of the road, a yelping bundle of golden hair, struggling to raise himself on his front paws. I dashed back, dropping to my knees beside the dog as a crowd gathered and a half-hysterical car driver wailed at anyone who would listen that it wasn't her fault.

I clutched at Duke, clasping his head in my arms, quietly murmuring: 'It's okay, boy, it's okay.', my heart breaking, my brain telling me *none* of this was okay.

As gently and carefully as I could, I shifted Duke to the side of the road. He squealed in agony. I laid him down, bending my head close to his broken body.

The nearest vet was two kilometres away. To move Duke there would put him through unendurable torture and in any case could only result in him being put down. I wished I had a gun to finish it quickly. But I didn't. Sick to my stomach, I knew what I had to do.

I got into position and with a quick jerk tried to break the dog's neck. I couldn't do it. Duke's neck muscles, strong in any case, had gone into rigor with the shock of the broken back. It was like trying to snap a tree trunk.

I had one option left. I shifted position to face him and put a jujitsu lock on his neck, drawing the sternocleidomastoid muscles across the carotid artery, cutting off the blood supply to his brain. Sobbing, I watched as Duke's eyes filled with bewilderment at his friend and master putting him to death.

Very slowly, his eyes fogged over and he died.

Two days later I returned to my unit.

Our platoon's new posting was in South East Queensland, at Canungra, in what during the Vietnam War had been the army's jungle warfare centre. Canungra had a reputation as a hard place to train which, given my experience on leave, suited me down to the ground.

I arrived a couple of weeks before my eighteenth birthday and left a few weeks after my nineteenth. It was a good year. Assigned to Battle Wing — a specialist cadre with more decorated combat veterans than any other single unit in the Australian Army at that time — we were now part of the post staff for the succession of senior infantry command courses going through Canungra. Our platoon's role was mainly out in the bush, acting as 'the enemy'. Operating in deep rainforest, our job was to get behind the opposition's lines to harass and disrupt them. We were the only Independent Rifle Company in the regular army and it was an honest learning environment — completely free of parade ground drill — with plenty of hit-and-run tactics in bush close to the camp as well as in the tough terrain of Levers Plateau in the border ranges between New South Wales and Queensland.

I enjoyed the work, though I found irregular tactics consisted of long periods of boredom. In between conducting recons and setting ambushes I made time to sneak off into the bush, either to do a few sets of push-ups and sit-ups or to practise my *katas* so I could maintain some continuity in my martial arts training.

Even when on sentry duty I was planning and devising new training programs I could follow away from the barracks.

Back in the barracks my training took less effort to organise. As often as possible I drove to the Gold Coast to practise at different clubs, while at the barracks I worked out in the gym to improve my strength.

Inspired by a documentary I'd seen on Donald Bradman — which included black and white footage of 'The Don' using a wicket to rebound a golf ball against the corrugations of a rain-water tank — I constantly sought out different ways to improve. I experimented with everything from medicine-ball routines to sand surfing: a gruelling exercise of sprinting up beach dunes and then 'surfing' down on a piece of marine ply.

I trained whenever I could: before breakfast, at lunchtime and in the evening when I was off duty; all of which, in addition to my regular infantry training of route marches, log carries and obstacle courses, made me fitter than I'd ever been.

Yet it was easy to lose it. Without the huge quantities of food I consumed in the mess, it only took a couple of weeks back in the bush to lose the bulk of what I'd worked so hard to achieve. The calorie content of the rations in a grunt's field pack wasn't huge and it was hard enough having to march and hump a grunt's equipment through hard country without burning extra calories in additional exercises. Like everyone else, I was always kilos lighter and a lot weaker when I came out of the rainforest and back into the barracks. But I stuck to my regime as closely as I could.

Canungra was a good posting where I worked hard, trained hard and, when I could, played hard: driving, whenever I had leave, with Ronnie and my other mates to the Gold Coast, where we would get totally pissed and, with little success, try to get lucky.

I didn't go back to Bairnsdale for the whole year.

CHAPTER 5

Holsworthy

IN OUR final week at Canungra we were given a choice of battalion. I chose 3RAR, partly because I'd had an uncle serve with the battalion during the Korean War, but mainly because it was stationed at Holsworthy, south-west of Sydney. That close to the city would give me a great choice of martial arts options.

We were given six weeks leave and I decided it was about time to see my family. I still missed Duke and felt a pang whenever I thought of him and how he died, but I was a year older and I really did want to see my folks.

After a couple of days in Bairnsdale I knew nothing had changed.

Though I spent time with my family, I focused on my fitness regime, incorporating into my training a thirty-kilometre cycle sprint through the hills around Bairnsdale, cycling six days a week, pushing myself as hard as I could with the sound of kookaburras and the smell of lucerne all around me; every day timing myself; every day looking for a better result.

Three days before I was to join my new battalion I had a serious accident.

To keep my time up I'd been riding at speed across a timber bridge at the bottom of a steep valley. It was risky: the bridge was built of railway sleepers laid lengthways; the gap between the sleepers exactly the width of my tyres. One slip into a gap would shoot me straight over my handlebars.

But I'd been rocketing across the bridge using the archery technique of singular focus; committing to a line of sleepers and willing myself and the bike over them, enjoying the sensation of cheating death.

That day I was making my best time yet, hitting the bridge at top speed, when my front tyre hit a small rock and shot into the gap between two sleepers.

The bike stopped dead, crumpling like aluminium foil as I sailed forward.

It felt like forever before I finally smacked onto the deck. I felt my guts crunch, the breath bursting from my lungs as I rolled over and over along the rough, splintery surface, tucking my head into my chest, protecting it with my arm, discovering as I rolled that wooden railway sleepers are immeasurably more hostile than the mats of a dojo. I slid onto the roadway at the far end of the bridge feeling the bitumen flay the skin from my body.

I rolled for what seemed an eternity.

At last I stopped. Painfully I sat up, feeling myself limb by limb, amazed that I had no broken bones. I stared down at my body. It was a mass of scraped and bloodied skin. Worse, and far more alarming, great slivers of old timber the size of pencils were sticking out of my arms, legs and ribs; I could feel them in my back and shoulders while the arm I'd used to protect my head looked like a porcupine quill. A spigot of wood the size of a spearhead jutted from my thigh.

I groaned when I moved but managed to get up and stagger back to my bike. It was a wreck, a total write-off. That really cheesed me off: I'd built it from scratch just before I went into the army. Picking it up was agony; I moaned with the effort of throwing it into the nearby scrub.

I considered my situation. It was a lonely part of the country with hardly any vehicles and I'd probably have to walk to a farmhouse a couple of kilometres distant. I wasn't sure I could make it — the tent peg spearing my thigh was tremendously painful. Though it hurt like hell to move my arms, I finally managed to grasp it and yank it out. A thin spume of blood splashed onto the ground.

I staggered to the roadside where, bent over in pain, in my ripped

T-shirt and shorts, my flesh bloody and scraped red-raw, I began pulling out some of the more spectacular shards of timber from my body. It hurt like hell.

I will never forget the woman who stopped her car and drove me to the Emergency Ward. Considering the sight I must have looked, I would have understood if she had driven on.

I was six hours in Emergency, with a team of nurses pulling splinters ranging from small needles to the size of kitchen knives from my flesh. Their major worry was infection — the sleepers on the bridge were over a hundred years old — and they took a long time dressing my punctured and scraped skin.

Three days later I drove to my new battalion so heavily bandaged I looked like the Michelin Man. It was the worst possible time to be injured. The culture of the battalion was tremendously physical, fiercely competitive and judgemental. It is vital, when joining a new unit, to establish a reputation from the get-go. But I was scarcely able to blow my own nose, let alone function as a soldier, and after a few days I was forced to report to the Regimental Aid Post. Here the medics took a series of X-rays, which showed nothing. I noticed the medics looking at me, scepticism in their eyes. Already they were labelling me a slug, a malingerer, a Jack Bastard. I tried soldiering on but it was impossible. I went to see the battalion doctor who, after calling the medics fools for not knowing that wood doesn't show up on X-rays, examined me thoroughly and immediately sent me off to a surgeon.

The day after the operation the surgeon came to see me in my bed. He was carrying three tubs about the size of large margarine containers filled with wooden splinters.

'Son, there was more old jarrah in you than in Tasmania. I've never seen anything like it.' He frowned. 'The thing is, I don't think we've got it all out. I think some splinters may have got themselves embedded really deep in your muscles. I'm probably going to have to operate again, maybe twice. It could leave some nasty scarring, I'm afraid.' It was the first of five operations, which resulted in sufficient scarring that on future visits to a beach someone was always asking, 'Are they shark bites?'

Half-drugged in my hospital bed, I wondered if there was some message in this about returning to Bairnsdale. Since leaving to join the army my visits home seemed fated to end in disaster.

As soon as I was over my operations I threw myself into battalion life and recovering my fitness. I started running, committing to it seriously by training in my own time. Though sometimes I ran on my own it was more often with mates: Ronnie, who liked to train as hard as he liked to drink; Alan Macfarlane — Macca, and Sall, a well-respected member of the battalion who, as a State boxing champion, was a bit of a legend.

I also ran with Rick, Physical Training Instructor of a neighbouring unit. Rick was a couple of years older than most of us and, to me, seemed to have everything. He was incredibly fit, intelligent and funny; very good looking and great with women. He was popular with just about everyone, yet remained a really good bloke and definitely one of the boys.

Rick took something of an interest in me, taking the time to give me useful advice about consistency in training and the value of doing something positive every day. Like everyone else, I looked up to the PTI. He seemed the perfect example of the dedicated, professional soldier.

As I recovered from the operations, I began pushing the envelope. Though life in the battalion was filled with physical conditioning, running gave me something more. Like martial arts, running honed my competitive edge; it forced me to choose, either to endure the pain that it took to keep me out in front, or to give in to it and slow down. Every race involved making those choices.

When I wasn't running I was spending a substantial chunk of my army pay on the training and grading fees associated with the different martial arts styles I was practising in Sydney. Living cheaply in the barracks and eating in the mess, I had money to spend on the things that mattered to me.

My main problem was what to do with my dead time: those hours I was stuck on base, kicking my heels waiting for orders. The battalion had a habit of keeping us busy by first hurrying us up and then making us wait; sometimes for hours. Some in the platoon chose to kill the time by sitting around smoking cigarettes, comparing tattoos or watching television. I chose to read. Someone had lent me a book by Wilbur Smith, which I'd enjoyed. I went looking for other books by Smith, and then Desmond Bagley and Frederick Forsyth and many others. I read whenever I had a chance, discovering that reading was far more satisfying than watching television.

Unexpectedly, surprising even myself, I developed a hunger for print.

* * *

I had been at Holsworthy about six months when I gradually began to make the disturbing connection that life in the battalion was uncomfortably like life in Bairnsdale.

At first it was minor things; overhearing officers discussing their pension entitlements; noticing how frequently some of them spoke of gaining promotion through not rocking the boat. Of course there were exceptions, but generally there was a noticeable absence of inspirational role models. It was a very different environment from Canungra.

Had I really, I asked myself, left Bairnsdale for this? Part of my problem was the sheer monotony of military life. Every January the Year Planner pinned to the wall of the company HQ was a replica of the previous year's Planner; the activities never varied: range practice, duty week (mess duty and guard duties), sports carnival, Kapyong Day parade, Anzac Day booze-up, bush exercise, range practice, duty week, cross-country, bush exercise, annual fitness test, duty week, range practice … nothing changed.

It was a tedious existence, one that I could lighten only by fighting like a feral cat to get on one of the specialist courses the army offered

… or by taking a trip into Sydney with Ronnie, Sall, Rick and the guys, to visit the combination circus and zoo that was Kings Cross.

The Cross, especially in the early hours of the morning, was a noisy, neon-lit, kaleidoscopic snake-pit and freak-show of brawling drunks and screeching hookers, of drug deals and punishment beatings, of junkies high on crack and weirdos even higher on God only knew what. In the few hectares of the Cross, if you walked down the right alley you could find anything you wanted; walk down the wrong alley, and you could find everything you didn't want.

We threw ourselves into the whirling circus by getting drunk and looking for trouble, one of our favourite pastimes being to push the bouncers in the clubs to see how far they'd go before they started swinging.

One night, feeling especially formidable and making a lot of noise, I pushed a big bruiser over the edge.

'Okay mate,' he snarled, 'let's go outside and see how good you really are.'

As we stepped out into the alleyway something inside me turned cold and shaky. I thought about the fight in Bairnsdale. Even if I beat this guy I could still get hurt. Suddenly I was feeling regretful. But I couldn't back down. Not now. Maybe, I hoped, the bouncer wouldn't go through with it.

In the alley I turned. The guy was standing in the doorway, looking at me.

I heard myself shouting, 'Come on, then. Let's go.'

He considered me piteously. 'Wanker,' he sneered. He turned back into the club and shut the door.

I felt a huge surge of relief. I wasn't going to get into a fight. Now I felt good. 'What's your problem?' I screamed, and kicked the solid door. 'Coward. C'mon outside and fight, you piece of shit.'

Yet I knew that the more time I spent in the Cross the more chance I'd end up in a fight; that chance being a smack-down certainty if I kept company with Ronnie Grimes.

The inevitable happened late one night when a guy leaving an unlicensed casino grabbed a chip off the plastic plate Ronnie was holding. Grimesy called him a dickhead, whereupon the guy, along with his two mates, turned, strolled back, grabbed another chip and asked casually, 'What did you say?'

Grimesy said, 'I called you a dickhead, you deaf shit,' and whacked him in the mouth.

The fight went badly; almost immediately I found myself up against a wall with a guy trying to strangle me with one hand while slamming his other fist into my face — spreading my nose in a sudden explosion of blood. Managing to squirm my head around, I found the guy's thumb in my mouth and bit down. He screamed and I bit down harder, feeling the bone crunch, tasting the guy's blood mingling with my own. I shifted my position and began driving elbow strikes into the guy's head. After a moment the screaming stopped and the guy dropped to the ground.

Wildly, I looked around for Grimesy.

Gone.

The next instant I heard a noise. Thinking for a moment it was thunder, I turned to gape at the surreal sight of a big, blue industrial waste-bin hurtling along the pavement. Propelling it was Grimesy, the red-headed berserker, who, at the last moment managed to divert it, steering it straight through the plate-glass window of a late-night coffee shop.

The world erupted, alarms wailing and people screaming, and a car came screeching to a halt. Staggering a little I turned to see a big, brown, beaten-up Statesman Caprice with its tyres smoking rocked to a stop beside me. Inside the car were four hard-faced men who looked like they were hunting for trouble and had just decided they'd found it.

The front passenger door sprung open to the thumping beat of heavy metal and a man, snarling wolfishly at me, started to emerge. The guy had a face like a prison gate. I kicked the door hard, hearing the crunch of metal on the man's shinbone and a litany of loud curses.

Discretion was the better part of valour. I bolted, yelling at Grimesy, now mixing it with one of the original trio of chip thieves, to follow.

Ronnie was up with me in seconds as we raced across the busy road, zigzagging among the traffic.

Scared and exhilarated, with the adrenalin roaring in my blood, I shot a glance back over my shoulder and caught a glimpse of the huge, Coca-Cola sign on Darlinghurst Road. The image, along with the sound of Grimesy screaming in my ear: 'Run faster, run faster.', imprinted itself in my brain.

I laughed triumphantly as I ran.

This is living. It does not get any better than this.

CHAPTER 6

Hatyai

I BLINKED, my eyes as tired and dry as the rest of me, my eyelids practically seizing with the effort. The night was lit by stars. Earlier there had been a full moon but that had disappeared over the horizon a couple of hours after midnight and now all I had to see by was the Milky Way glowing down coldly as I blinked my eyes again and tried to figure out what baby elephants were doing in the Hunter Valley of New South Wales.

I blinked once more and watched the elephants morph into sheep and then change back into little elephants. I shook my head, trying to clear my benumbed brain.

I was four weeks into a six-week infantry Junior NCO course: on patrol with full battle pack and SLR — Self Loading Rifle. I hadn't slept for thirty-six hours, hadn't eaten for the same length of time, and was so dehydrated my urine was turning to sludge. Days earlier, in a less exhausted state, I'd decided this was a worthwhile course and I'd got a lot out of it — despite such gruesome activities as being taken to Liverpool Hospital to witness autopsies of cadavers. But since then it had degenerated into something senselessly hard.

I had read somewhere that the policy of the German Army in the two world wars had been to train hard and fight easy. It seemed to me the policy of the battalion was to train until you were completely bloody senseless.

Yet the course was so prized and fought over I'd been amazed to be nominated for it. Every day of the past month I'd thought — today will be my last day … I'm not good enough to become an NCO …

they'll see I'm not good enough to be on this course … today is the day they're going to kick me off.

Two weeks later, at completion, I was ranked number three out of the sixty participants. The outcome surprised me and made me consider the possibility that limitations are the result of *outlook* rather than circumstance.

As 3RAR had recently been designated Australia's parachute battalion, my platoon was ordered to RAAF Williamtown to take the Basic Parachute Course. After nearly two weeks of ground training, which involved us repeating each procedure until it was second nature, we were taken up in a C130 Hercules. I wondered if it was one of those I'd cycled past at RAAF East Sale.

It was our first jump. The worst part, the sick-with-fear part, was waiting for the aircraft to get over the Drop Zone. Naturally though, we were all too tough to admit that we were scared and did our best to act unconcerned. Once over the DZ and we were ordered to stand, the training took over. Like robots we hooked up to the overhead cable and began shuffling forward, chanting, *'Centre pack tie! Static-line stowage! Static-line clear-to-the-cable, hooked on and pin secure!'* A tightly packed line of men burdened by main rigs and safety chutes, like a conga-line of automatons inside the noisy, juddering, dimly lit aircraft.

After bellowing the final chant of *'Green on Go!'* I found myself at the open door and suddenly I was out; a second later an almighty WHUMP as my chute opened and I decelerated from 120kph to something a lot more moderate. I watched the ground drifting casually up towards me and when the time came flexed my legs, bending at the knees ready for the landing — and found myself executing a roll exactly as I'd been trained.

I did seven more static-line jumps at twelve hundred feet, including one at night, before I was awarded my wings and given a small increase in pay. A few weeks later I was back in Williamtown, one of eight volunteer 'stooges' who, with only static-line jump experience, were going to freefall from ten thousand feet.

Usually the training for freefall involves a whole series of jumps, cautiously graduating in altitude and 'delay' — i.e. the amount of time you fall through the air 'free' before manually deploying the chute: starting with a second's delay, then three seconds, five seconds and upwards until eventually reaching the forty-five seconds it takes to fall seven and a half thousand feet. But the battalion had in mind to halve the training period, having recently qualified paratroopers go immediately to ten thousand feet and freefall to two and a half thousand feet before pulling the ripcord.

During a week of ground and simulation training I listened to many of the stooges talk about how they were going to ace the freefall, but after five days the only drop most of them had made was out of the program. When it came to delivering, the majority of stooges were walking out of the door as soon as they discovered how dangerous military freefall could be.

Only three of us walked to the chopper in the cold half-light of pre-dawn; only two got in and only one jumped, the other stooge shaking his head and shucking off his parachute as I stood on the ramp of the Chinook surveying the entire, sphincter-clenching, palely lit panorama of country New South Wales from ten thousand feet.

On a yell from my instructor, I jumped — and immediately began tumbling out of control. All the way down I tried to roll myself into the right position but no matter what I did, the best I could manage was the 'Delta': falling head first with my arms by my side, the worst, most dangerous position for deploying a chute out of freefall. At twenty-four hundred feet my Automatic Opening Device, which they'd assured me on the ground was absolutely infallible, failed to deploy.

I was in serious trouble. I was travelling towards solid earth at one hundred and seventy feet a second; eighteen hundred feet was the minimum height my freefall chute needed to open. I had four seconds to make a decision. I pulled the D-ring while in the Delta position. The chute opened. I landed safely.

My instructor, who was supposed to evaluate my descent, had been unable to match my erratic flight path. He went completely out of his tree, screaming, yelling and bellowing obscenities about my useless and unstable exit position.

I didn't get it — I was the only stooge out of the eight to have gone the distance; I had put my arse on the line for an experiment — and now I was getting a bollocking.

After that I went back to static-line jumps, which became commonplace over the months and years I was a member of the battalion.

On one, the start of a two-week bush exercise, I speared in hard and felt something go in my knee. It was a windy day, too blustery in my opinion to be jumping out of aircraft, though it had been okay in the opinion of the officers on the ground. Now the results of the stupid Ruperts' decision were racking up as men speared into the ground like artillery shells. Before the exercise even got underway, half a dozen men had been injured and were out of it, one poor sod having broken both his legs. Tentatively, I tested my knee as I gathered in my chute and decided it wasn't too bad. I limped through the next two weeks.

I hoped the knee would heal itself, but it became progressively worse.

A few weeks prior to that bad landing I'd won the battalion 5000m championship for the second year in a row and was keen to keep my training up with Grimesy, Macca and Rick — Sall had dropped out to do his own thing in Sydney. I took myself to the battalion medical officer who arranged for me to have a minor arthroscopy. The surgeons took a look around inside my knee and chipped off a small piece of cartilage.

Returning to the barracks I had an order to see the Commanding Officer. Limping in, I saluted and was ordered to stand at ease. With my knee heavily bandaged and throbbing like hell there wasn't really any other way I could stand.

I decided not to point that out.

'You're being recommended for officer training,' the CO announced.

'Me?' I staggered slightly, which the CO presumably put down to the injured knee. 'Why me, sir?'

'You're one of the best cross-country runners we've got. The Officer Selection Board reckons you're officer material. You'll be going to the Royal Military College at Duntroon for training. You will receive your orders in the next few days. That's all. Dismissed.'

I limped out, astonished. I didn't get it. Why would the army make me an officer, just because I could run? Did they think I'd run fast into a battle? That would only make sense if my men were as fast as I was. Otherwise, I'd find myself up shit alley all on my own.

Being recognised as 'officer material' appealed to my ego, and guessing more rank would mean more pay a part of me was attracted to the idea, but there was something about the proposal that went against my grain.

I went to find Rick to talk it over.

'Makes sense,' he said. 'Sports carnivals, cross-country competitions, unarmed combat displays — this is peacetime, Red, and that stuff is important. What else can the army do but concentrate on the competitive crap? And, peace or war, winning medals and trophies and cups is what a battalion is all about. You win a few prizes and you get noticed. And if you get noticed, the army thinks you have to be an officer. The army doesn't notice grunts.'

'But why would I want to be an officer? All they care about is their pensions and promotion and how to cover their arses.'

'So? Be better than them. Be different.'

I shook my head. 'I don't know.'

I sat under a straggle of white gums on the edge of the parade ground and thought about it. After a while I made up my mind.

I would go for it. I was intrigued as to whether I could actually get through the process; Duntroon was reckoned to be the equivalent of a top-flight university, not the kind of place a kid who left school at fifteen would usually get a crack at.

The selection panels and psychological evaluations went on for months and the main thing I learnt was that psychologists and psychiatrists were generally far madder than the people they interviewed.

They were often young guys; intense, with pinched faces and thinning hair, wearing glasses and white lab coats over hunched and narrow shoulders. I couldn't understand why they wore the coats to interview me; did they think I was going to vomit on them, cry on their shoulders? I decided they wore the coats to prove they were medical men, which meant they had bigger hang-ups than I did. Their questions were always about violence and sex. Did I *like* guns? *Like* the idea of killing people? *Like* spiders? I didn't get the spiders thing at first, only later learning that if I said no it meant I was violent and if I said yes it suggested I went both ways in the sack. It was all bullshit and I answered whatever came into my head.

I passed.

Halfway through the process I got a major break, a top posting. For nearly two years I'd been angling for one of the most highly prized postings in the army — in Malaysia as an Army Training Team Instructor. It wasn't active service — it couldn't be compared to Vietnam or anything like that — but it was overseas and there were communist insurgents operating there. Sometimes people got shot, and even though the team wasn't in a peacekeeping role, there was always an outside chance of some real action.

Opportunities as good as that were as rare as hen's teeth and I was lying on my cot in the barracks happily re-reading my orders for the Malaysian posting when one of the platoon strolled in and said, 'You heard about Sall?'

'No, what about him?'

'He's been arrested. He was one of the blokes on that payroll robbery.'

'What?'

'You know he'd got into coke?'

I sat up on the edge of my bed. 'No, I didn't know that.'

'Ran up a tab with some dealers in The Cross. Owed them big time.'

'Jesus.'

I'd heard rumours about drugs, knew some grunts were into them. But not Sall, surely not him. It was hard to get my head around the news. Though I hadn't seen him since we'd stopped running together, the notion of Sall involved in a payroll robbery was barely credible. Sall was a good bloke, a fit bloke; down to earth, a mate.

Later, in Malaysia, I heard that Sall's take from the robbery was to have been $7000 and that he'd been sentenced to seven years in Long Bay Prison. Squatting still and silent in deep jungle, I pondered the impact of choice.

Not that I found it was always easy making the right choices; within a few weeks I was in danger of going to jail myself.

A bunch of us on the instructors' team had crossed the border into Thailand for a few days leave in Hatyai, spending most of our time getting legless on cobra blood and wood alcohol, watching the slithering cobras we'd selected being butchered, their blood mixed with Mekong whisky and ice. After a few days of hard drinking and virtually no sleep, I staggered out of a nightclub, hailed a tuk tuk taxi and promptly fell asleep. Waking, I found myself miles from my hotel and apparently in the process of being abducted.

In the action that followed, I damaged both the tuk tuk and its driver, and was confronted minutes later by three cops pointing pistols at me. In the police station a belligerent cop with a pair of knuckledusters on the desk of his dimly lit office informed me I was charged with damage to a motor vehicle, kidnapping a Thai citizen and assault.

Unless I was prepared to surrender my passport and sign a confession in Thai, I was going to the lock-up for as long as it took.

I knew enough not to sign a confession in a language I didn't understand. I was in deep trouble; I could be in prison for a month or more before a magistrate got around to me.

My only resort was to come on strong and tell the cop in graphic detail what fate awaited him if he was dumb enough to imprison an Australian Training Team Instructor. Having figured him for a bully I reckoned that, like most bullies, he was susceptible to being bullied. Shouting, 'Look, look,' I opened my passport, jabbing my finger at the stamp on the front page. 'See there, see what it says? It says I'm a member of the Australian Defence Force on Official Duty. You see that?' I glared at the cop, omitting to mention the duty was actually in Malaysia.

Loudly and in vivid detail I catalogued the god-awful international repercussions awaiting any crazy cop who might stupidly throw me in jail. It worked. In the end he relented, gave me an obsequious smile and arranged for two of his lackies to drive me back to my hotel where, as a parting gift, they gave me two bottles of Mekong whisky.

I left them in my room.

Although not in the same ballpark as armed robbery, I could see parallels between what had happened to me and to Sall. I'd chosen to get drunk out of my brain, which had resulted in a minor stoush with a cab driver; not a big deal back in Oz, maybe, but for a foreigner in Thailand it carried significant implications.

If I'd ended up in a Thai prison and been posted AWOL in Malaysia, no matter whose fault, I would have been personally accountable.

Back in the jungle I thought about that a lot.

CHAPTER 7

Langkawi

A MONTH later we were ordered to set up a light camp on the east coast of Langkawi Island. Our main job was to facilitate a series of survival courses for Australian soldiers training on the island, but we were also there to act as a discreet observation post, monitoring locals in the area and keeping an eye on fishing boats harboured nearby. One night I was told to report to the Captain in his tent.

'Sir?'

'Ah, Redenbach. Some civvies have gone missing, two tourists. The brass is worried they may have been taken hostage by some commies with the goal of holding them for ransom. Intelligence suggests a band of insurgents are operating out of a village in the hills about eight clicks west. I want you to take a two-man patrol through the jungle, recon the village and, if the tourists are being held there, extract them. Do what you have to do but bring them back in one piece. And yourselves. You understand?'

I thought the Captain's last words were a tad on the vague side, though I wasn't about to say so. 'Yes sir.'

'Weapons and live ammo will be issued by the armourer. Who do you want to go with you?'

I thought a moment. 'Jocko, sir.'

The Captain's eyes widened in surprise and there was a beat before he said, 'Good choice. Be ready to move out in ten minutes.'

I doubled away, looking for Jocko. I had never considered Jocko McKenzie to be one of nature's most appealing creations; not with his tombstone face, crooked teeth and skin so pitted it looked like it had taken a blast of shrapnel. The man had also been way back in the queue when they'd been handing out warmth, compassion and the milk of human kindness. There was nothing remotely attractive about him and I wouldn't have sought out his company in a pub. But when it came to moving through jungle against armed communist guerrillas there was no one I would rather have as my offsider. Jocko's ancestors had fought in almost every war waged by the British Empire, going back way before the time of Napoleon. He was a natural soldier; war and combat were embedded in his DNA no less than his blue, Celtic eyes and pug-ugly face.

The armourer issued us each an SLR plus, for me, a Browning automatic. The pistol was practically useless at anything over ten metres. I sincerely hoped I wasn't going to get that close to any insurgents. 'Why the Browning?' I asked.

The armourer shrugged. 'Orders.'

Jocko laughed harshly. 'Cause this is a two-man extraction and you're the fookin' Rupert.'

We loaded the ammunition into the magazines; three mags of twenty rounds for each SLR, two mags of thirteen rounds for the Browning. I holstered the pistol and snapped a magazine into the SLR before hefting the weapon. It was subtly but noticeably heavier than I was used to. I caught Jocko's eye and knew what he was thinking.

In the hit-and-run exercises on Levers Plateau we had always carried real weapons — but loaded with plastic ammunition. This had enabled me and the others to grow accustomed to the *crack-crack-crack* of rounds firing, yet the rifle itself had been artificially light. My SLR had *felt* non-lethal.

Not now.

Now it was loaded with the brass, metal and the lead of real ammunition. The difference between my weapon then and now was the difference between handling a koala and a king brown. Now my weapon had weight, purpose.

And out there, I reflected, somewhere in the jungle, men with similar killing machines were potentially waiting in the darkness. For me.

We smeared our faces with black greasepaint and moved off into a sultry, moonless night lit by a panoply of stars. Within yards I was struggling through the scrub, sweat pouring down my back and into my eyes. Everywhere there were mosquitoes and we were bitten mercilessly. For the first couple of kilometres all I could hear from behind me was a long, low, litany of blasphemies. When we began climbing into the hills, I turned. 'Shut the hell up,' I whispered.

From then on I heard nothing; twice I turned to see if he was still there. Behind me was a noiseless shadow; Jocko, like me, stealth walking and counting paces through the thickening jungle. Where we could we used tracks, avoiding the well-trodden pathways; the insurgents had been known to lay mines.

We were navigating mainly by the stars, which were sometimes difficult to see and occasionally we stopped to check the compass, preserving our night-vision by covering one eye as we stared at the back-lit compass. Every time I stopped I felt my knees shaking, a deep twanging vibration starting up in my gut.

I was scared.

This was a different kind of fear to the one I knew when standing in the doorway of a plane ready to leap out. That was quick; a sudden surge of panic and then it was over. Here I was locked in, with a hammering heart and plasticine knees, a bone-dry mouth and damp, clammy palms.

What I was feeling was a hair's breadth away from terror; sustained, inescapable, debilitating. My life had turned to the stuff of nightmares; it was the middle of the night and I was deep in a jungle infested by snakes and poisonous spiders and God knows what else. Jocko and I were moving almost blindly through a hostile environment in a foreign country, miles from cities and roads and, more importantly, hospitals. And somewhere in the blackness were men who meant to kill us.

Glancing at the dark shadow beside me, I wondered if Jocko was as scared as I was. No, Jocko wasn't scared. To be scared you needed an imagination and the Scots bastard was far too stupid to have an imagination. Too stupid to feel anything. He was probably enjoying all this. I wanted to punch him in the mouth.

We smelt the village at almost a click away; the glutinous odour of boiling rice, the tang of spices, the musk of oil lamps and animals and excrement from open latrines. We closed in cautiously.

This was the moment of maximum danger.

I felt my heart pumping. With so much adrenalin in my blood everything in the world was in sharp relief; every noise, every sensation, every sight was clear, crisp and as brightly magnified as a movie screen. I had never felt so scared, yet had never felt so *alive*.

Jocko and I leap-frogged through the trees fringing the village, Jocko moving forward as I covered him, to be followed by me moving forward as Jocko covered. There was an open space stretching from the edge of the tree-line to a thick clump of bushes about a hundred metres outside the village. We slithered leopard-like on our bellies to the bushes and delicately moved into them. We had a perfect view, the village and its inhabitants illuminated by the light of cooking fires and oil lamps. We heard the buzz of talk interspersed by bursts of laughter and, though it was late, watched a number of the villagers preparing food.

Suddenly dogs began barking.

Instantly there was a flickering of oil lamps inside the grass huts and dark shadows began flitting between dwellings.

We were discovered.

I felt a taste in my mouth. It was bitter and rancid and with a shock I realised I was tasting my own fear. No one had ever told me that in an action I might taste my own fear. I waited, finger outside the trigger guard of the SLR, waiting for the insurgents to come looking for us.

Nothing happened.

There were a couple of angry shouts from one of the huts followed by the yelp of chastised dogs and then nothing. Everything went back to normal. I glanced at Jocko, wondering if he too had been tasting his own terror. Beneath the greasepaint I couldn't make out his expression. We stayed in the bushes until an hour before dawn, by which time we were convinced that the village harboured neither communist insurgents nor any hostage-held tourists. I sighed. All my sweat and fear, the taste of terror and the sting of countless mosquitoes, it had all been for nothing. I'd nearly shit myself over a wild goose chase.

In the darkness we leopard-crawled to the edge of the jungle and then set off back towards camp, making far better time than we had going in.

The sun was pinking the sky when we came in sight of the camp. 'So what do you think then?' I asked.

'Fookin' waste of time, if you ask me,' Jocko growled. 'Sweating our balls off crashing aboot in the fookin' jungle and we never even got to shoot any fookin' terrorists.'

I stared at him. Was it bravado? Was he just too proud and macho to admit fear? Or did he mean what he'd just said? If he did then the guy had ice in his veins, concrete in his head. The stupid bastard was at the opposite end of the spectrum from me. All I could feel was utter and absolute relief that no terrorist had shot me.

I considered my offsider, aware of my own hypocrisy. There was no point in being critical of Jocko. After all, I'd chosen him. We had made a good team and the very thing that appalled me about him was what I would have relied on to save my life if there had been a fire-fight.

I said, 'Yeah,' and gave Jocko a friendly punch on the shoulder. 'Maybe next time.'

I reported to the Captain who said okay and well done and go and get some breakfast in that insouciant, pretentious kind of drawl some officers affect.

Two days later we received a radio report that the tourists, a German couple, had been found, hungry and thirsty but otherwise unscathed on the other side of the island.

I went looking for Jocko to tell him the news. 'Shite,' Jocko growled, 'if I'd have known we was lookin' for a coupla Krauts, I woodna have gone on the fookin' mission.' The guy was unbelievable.

Not long afterwards I received fresh orders. I groaned the moment I opened them.

I was being ordered back early from the best posting in the army to go to school: the army wanted me to attend the combined services special military education centre in Brisbane. I needed my Higher School Certificate, the minimum educational standard for entry into Duntroon. Having left school in Year Ten, I was expected to cram two years of schooling into six months.

'Bloody hell,' I moaned, 'why now?'

I was so thoroughly cheesed off that when some of the guys from the Quick Response Force invited me to go on the grog in Penang I accepted without a moment's hesitation. I was in the mood to get out of camp and drink a few beers.

We started off in the Hong Kong Bar, the place noisy and crowded and thick with cigarette smoke, the walls plastered floor to ceiling with years of photographs and memorabilia from practically every Aussie Rifle Company ever based at Butterworth. After a couple of beers the others headed off; they'd heard of a sex show in another bar. I stayed at the Hong Kong, nodding and saying g'day to guys I knew while making it fairly obvious I was happy to drink alone.

Ordering another beer I glanced through the nicotine fog to the other end of the packed, clamorous bar and caught the eye of a grunt I recognised from Holsworthy, though I couldn't remember his name. I held his eye for a moment then turned away to take possession of my beer. Taking a sip I looked up to see the guy staring at me with narrowed eyes.

I looked away and groaned, despondency settling on me like a muggy mist. All I wanted was a quiet drink. The last thing I was looking for was aggro.

I'd seen the guy in action before. His technique was to target someone smaller than himself, which wasn't difficult as he was a big, ugly gorilla, and eye-ball them for as long as it took for his blood-alcohol level to rise sufficiently to detonate his basic, innate sadism, whereupon he would slyly slip his false teeth into his pocket, storm over to his target, scream abuse at the poor, totally cowed bugger for about ten seconds and then punch him in the head. It was his party trick and I had the sneaking certainty that tonight I was Neanderthal man's object of desire.

Part of me, the sensible, cautious part, said to leave; avoid confrontation. But the other part, the part that tonight was fed up with the army's crap timing and decision-making, the part that wanted to sit at a bar and drink quietly, was not in the mood to be pushed around. The internal battle lasted a couple of seconds before Obstinate Red triumphed and Sensible Red went down in flames.

Bugger it, what did I care? Bring it on.

It occurred to me as I watched out of the corner of my eye that at least I'd have some warning. If the big mongrel was true to form he would make a move before he made his move. He would put his teeth in his pocket. I watched surreptitiously; saw the guy turn his head to one side, his hand covering his mouth. Yes, there it was. The early-warning signal.

He eased himself off his stool ... and the two guys he was drinking with did likewise. The trio moved towards me.

Shit, that wasn't in the script. I'd never seen the mongrel go for anyone mob-handed before.

Inside, Sensible Red was crying from the flames, 'See ... I told you ... I told you.'

Then and there Obstinate Red promised Sensible Red that, if he would only shut the hell up, he would never ... never ... ever ... ignore him again. But right now I needed to devise a strategy not predicated on screaming like a schoolgirl and running out of the bar.

In the few seconds it took for the three gorillas to shuffle up to me I'd worked out what to do. It was all a question of mathematics really.

The bar had gone quiet, the air electric with expectation as every eye in the deathly hush was fixed on me, the victim. I rose from my stool as the toothless wonder took a deep breath.

'You think you're fucking great,' he bellowed. 'Just cause you think you gonna make an officer ...' His voice, though loud and ferocious, was made strangely sibilant by the lack of teeth. He sounded like a roaring drain. 'You're just a fuckin ...'

Bang.

I hit him.

I'd had a couple of heartbeats to work it out and it was just right. King Kong crashed on to his arse, a look of total shock on his face. I noticed both offsiders step back, their eyes wide with surprise. Seeing their fearless leader dropped like a sack of spuds clearly wasn't in their game plan.

I took a deep breath before yelling at the top of my lungs, 'You piece of worthless shit. You useless wanker, you're not worth pissing on, you're not worth ...'

I went on for about half a minute, only stopping when I realised I was repeating myself.

The jackass was staring up at me with a look of injured innocence. No one had ever done to him what he did to other people. 'Hey, I wasn't gonna do nothing,' he whined, his voice filled with moral indignation. 'Why'd ya do that?'

'Just getting my retaliation in first.' The silent bar erupted into laughter. I watched the offsiders lift the bastard shakily to his feet before turning back to the bar and my beer. It was over. Even in the unlikely event that King Kong and his cronies might have jumped me after the decking, the laughter had sealed it. I had made the trio look like idiots and the bar had laughed at them. I took a sip of my beer. No, in fact I hadn't made them look like idiots. They had made themselves look like idiots.

I was aware of someone taking the stool next to me. It was Jocko.

'Why'd ya hit that bloke? He wasnee doin' nothin'. He was only lettin' off a bit o' steam.' Jocko was drunk, his words slurring.

'Rack off, Jocko, I'm not in the mood.'

'But why'd ya hit him?'

I sighed. 'Because he was going to hit me. You've seen his act.'

Jocko stared at me blearily. 'You think you're fookin' clever, don't ya? Being selected for a Rupert.'

I grunted. 'What is all this about me being an officer? What's it to any of you? It's typical. Someone actually dares to do better and you blokes are pissed about it.'

Jocko shook his head. 'You're never goin' to do it. You're never goin' to make an officer *and* a gentleman.'

'I like to think I'm already a gentleman. Except around arseholes. And blokes who won't let me drink my beer in peace.' I gave Jocko the hard eye — for all the effect it had.

'Yeah, but not *their* kind o' gentleman. What they want is an officer and a *snob*.'

I frowned. Jocko, drunk, had a nasty habit of slicing straight to what I suspected might be the truth.

'They're never goin' to accept you. Not even if you make fookin' Field Marshal. The Cap'n said so.'

'What?'

'The Cap'n told the Adjutant who told Sergeant Emery. He said you might make an okay NCO but you're completely the wrong type to hold a commission; said you dropped out o' school at fifteen and that before joinin' up, you was diggin' ditches. Said you come from some arsehole of a town and that you don't like football. Reckons you might be scared of physical contact.'

'Yeah? You were here a couple of minutes ago. What do you think?'

Jocko frowned again.

'That true? You don't like football?'

'How do you know all this, Jocko?'

'Sergeant Emery told me the same time he told me how we'd been set up for that mission.'

'Set up? Whaddaya mean, set up?'

Jocko laughed, his crooked teeth like ancient ruins. He slurped his beer. 'The Cap'n was s'posed to have led that mission. Only he couldn't be bothered. He di'nee think those tourists had been taken by commies; di'nee reckon there were any commies out there. So why should he spend all night sweatin' his balls off pushing through the jungle on a useless mission? So he chose you. He thinks you're weird 'cause you do all that trainin' in your own time. But he thought if there *were* commies out there and we got in a fire-fight, better you and me get brassed up than him. On the other hand, if we blew a couple of *them* away, then who do you think would have been gettin' all the praise and medals. The fookin' field commanding officer. Right?' He shook his head, swaying slightly on his stool. 'Shit, and you want to be one of them.' He cackled. 'Not much of an ambition, is it?'

'Piss off, Jocko.'

'Anyway, why'd ya choose me to go with you?'

I gazed at the flushed, baleful face. 'Because you're so bloody beautiful. I reckoned if there were bandits out there and they saw you they'd take off without firing a shot.'

The little Scotsman looked offended. 'Stuff you.'

'And stuff you, too,' I said amiably. I downed the last of my beer and got up from my stool. 'And now I'm going to find a bar where I can have a few beers in peace.' I gazed at Jocko. I didn't like the little ferret but I felt a curious affinity with him. We'd been on a mission together and somehow that formed a bond. 'See ya, Jocko. Stay safe.'

Outside, I took a long, deep breath of humid air, wishing I'd gone with the others to the sex show. It would have been a lot less disturbing.

I returned to Australia in a dour, reflective mood. I was not looking forward to going back to school.

CHAPTER 8

Brisbane

IN FACT the six months at Brisbane were much easier than I'd expected. There were a dozen of us, entrants not only from the army, but the navy and air force too.

Life was the most comfortable I'd ever experienced in the army. All that was expected of me was to listen closely to what my teachers said — especially the words used to say it — and then to remember the facts and the preferred terminology for as long as it took to regurgitate them in a set paper or examination. After that I could forget I ever knew them. Once I understood that, reiterating facts about arctic glaciers and Shakespeare's *Macbeth* was not a problem. Even Keynesian economics was relatively easy.

Coming back from a run after the end of the day's lessons, I bumped into one of the navy guys in the corridor.

'Red, some bloke called Grimesy phoned while you were out. Left a message.'

'Yeah?' I was pleased. Ronnie had been transferred; I hadn't seen or heard from him in over a year.

'He says to tell you he's been short-listed for Sergeant. And to watch the six o'clock news. I didn't know making Sergeant in the army got national media coverage.' The guy chuckled and walked away.

At six I gathered with the others in a clump of tattered easy chairs in front of the television. It was the fourth or fifth item: a heroin addict had been shot dead in a drugs deal gone wrong in Kings Cross. The man had been identified as a PTI attached to the brigade that 3RAR was part of. A picture of a guy in uniform flashed up on the screen. It was Rick. I stared bug-eyed at the box.

'You knew him?' someone asked.

'Yeah, I knew him.' I heard my tone, low; croaky.

I went for another run, pounding the pavements despite a knifing pain in my knee, trying to come to terms with the news. Sall had been bad enough but he'd been a mate and, anyway, was still alive. Rick had been more than a mate. He'd been something of a mentor, the man who'd most influenced me in my early days in the battalion. I'd known this guy … at least, I *thought* I'd known him.

The facts emerging over the next few days were sordid and sleazy. It had been a stupid way to die. As time and the miles of hard running assuaged the shock, I began to consider the choices Rick had made to transmute from the great guy he had been to Rick the heroin junkie, finally coming to the melancholy conclusion that, whatever those choices had been, they had just as surely ripped apart his body as the bullets that took his life.

Rick's choices had killed him as inevitably as the guy who had pulled the trigger.

A week later, on a sultry, tropical, Queensland morning, we were bussed to the local high school where we sat our HSC.

I passed.

I was quietly elated. A fifteen-year-old school dropout from a small town in Gippsland had passed through the process and was about to become an officer and, despite Jocko McKenzie's opinion, a gentleman.

There was one final hurdle, my medical examination.

It didn't go well.

'You're in great shape in all respects except your knee,' the medical examiner told me.

'Yes, but that's my problem,' I said. The ME shook his head.

'It's the army's problem too.'

I went back to the battalion at Holsworthy, waiting for an entire committee of medical specialists to convene and debate over my knee. It was typical of the army, I thought, to take a sledgehammer to crack a nut. Finally, the committee's judgement came down. It was puzzling, almost comical. The committee had decided that, as nothing could be done about my knee, nothing needed to be done about my knee.

Years later, when I came to know and understand management theory, I found a corollary to the maxim: 'A committee comprised of people who can do nothing frequently decides that nothing needs to be done.'

I was admitted to Duntroon.

Issued with a business class air ticket to Canberra, a day later I marched through the classically curved, white stone entrance of the Royal Military College of Australia, past immaculate gardens and heritage-listed buildings into a place redolent with history and tradition.

I was about to become an officer.

The following morning I was ordered to undergo a medical examination. I wondered what I could possibly have contracted since my last army medical but was sharply told it was standard procedure.

Standing at ease before the medical specialist I waited for the rubber stamp passing me A1 fit. The specialist flipped through my file, glanced up, surveyed me briefly and said, 'You're below medical standards.'

I couldn't believe what I was hearing. 'What? … Sir.'

'You're BMS. You've had an operation on your knee. You could be a liability.'

I marched out in a daze. Marching in I was on my way to being an officer; marching out I was facing the possibility of discharge. No one who was BMS stayed around for long; it was the kiss of death.

I appealed the decision.

It was the beginning of a bad dream: I was in Duntroon, at the epicentre of the Australian military machine yet under imminent threat of being cast out into the civilian wilderness. Feeling like the eleven-year-old I once was, waiting in line at St Patrick's for the compulsory weekly confessional, I went through innumerable interviews and medical examinations. I tried to get the committee that had said my knee didn't matter to talk to the specialist who had branded me BMS. It was like trying to screw a light bulb into a wall socket.

It was a frustrating few weeks, in the course of which I came to an important discovery.

I didn't care any more.

I remembered the day I'd been made redundant from the hardware store, when I found that my certainty about the future had been hijacked by someone else. The same thing was happening again; I was placing my future in other people's hands — people who couldn't get their act together sufficiently to communicate with each other over the simple matter of my knee.

I saw parallels with Rick, who had put his destiny in the hands of a bunch of drug dealers. All right, the army medical board couldn't be compared to heroin dealers, but the principle was the same; I was abrogating the responsibility of controlling my own destiny to outsiders.

And outsiders I didn't respect. Almost all of them treated me with disdain; in my presence, they often talked about me as if I wasn't there. Maybe Jocko had been right, maybe my ambition *was* too limited. Maybe I could do better in my life than become an army officer. After all, I'd only agreed to go into officer selection because I'd nothing better to do; because I'd wanted to see if I could cut it. And I had. I'd sailed through the whole psychiatric, army educational assessment bullshit to arrive in Duntroon, where the only thing in doubt was the thing I was most sure of. My physical ability.

Except now there was another doubt. I was no longer sure I wanted the future that, up to then, I'd felt so certain about.

Finally the decision came down. I could continue my officer training only if I elected to serve in a non-arms corps. Because of my knee I could never be a front-line officer.

It was a slap in the face — an insult. As a twenty-three-year old paratrooper, a champion battalion runner, I was being dumped in the dustbin of administration — in the Pay Corps ... the Ordnance Corps ... maybe the Catering Corps, for Christ's sake. I decided to take my discharge, along with a Veterans Affairs pension for the knee that had been the cause of all the trouble.

In the final Kafkaesque episode of the whole affair I discovered that, in order to exit the army, I needed yet another medical examination.

Marching into another ME's office I was told to strip to my jocks, whereupon the ME, with no more than a cursory look, pronounced I was in prime physical condition.

Half joking I said, 'You couldn't tell the rest of the medical board that, could you? You know I'm getting out because they say I'm BMS.'

'Yes, I could tell them.'

'Well, you're a doctor, wouldn't they listen to you?'

The doctor looked up at me from his desk like I was talking a foreign language. 'Don't be stupid, this is the army.'

I left the following week, my future already decided.

Close to twenty years after I left the army, a young 3RAR soldier became an unwitting example of how comprehensively incompetent military bureaucracy can be: tragically killed while serving in Iraq, the soldier's body was mistakenly left in a morgue in Kuwait as a different body was repatriated to his family in Australia.

To add even more pain to the soldier's widow and family, highly sensitive information about the bungled repatriation was left in a public computer at an airport in Melbourne by the Brigadier investigating the case. As the media and federal politicians screamed for a full review of Defence Department management, a senior representative of the Defence Association voiced his scepticism of the value of such investigations by saying: 'Let's face it, there have been eight or nine reviews since 1981.'

SEARCHING

1988–1991

I LIVED LIKE A MONK,
BREATHING AND LIVING NOTHING BUT
MARTIAL ARTS; GRAPPLING, STRIKING,
BLOCKING AND THROWING,
I GASPED AND PANTED AND SWEATED.

CHAPTER 9

Melbourne

DURING MY latter years in the army I'd toyed with the idea of pursuing martial arts professionally, reckoning that, as it was something I enjoyed, if I undertook it with genuine commitment my pursuit would eventually lead somewhere. Where exactly, I didn't know, though I believed wherever it was would be a good place to be.

I moved to Melbourne and found a small, neat, one-bedroom flat, which, after the barracks in Holsworthy was luxuriously private. It was in the heart of St Kilda, just metres from where the sidewalk hookers plied their trade. After a while, when they'd come to recognise me, they stopped offering me a fabulous time and instead greeted me as a neighbour. Which, in a manner of speaking, I was.

I lived like a monk, breathing and living nothing but martial arts; grappling, striking, blocking and throwing, I gasped and panted and sweated sometimes ten hours a day, seven days a week. I spent thousands of dollars on gym memberships and training fees and grading costs while feeding myself only the best fruit and vegetables and the prime cuts of the most expensive meats, enhancing my diet with costly protein powders and mineral supplements from abroad.

I fed my mind too, with innumerable books, buying everything available on the martial arts before extending to biographies, from Chuck Norris to Muhammad Ali, as well as war diaries, accounts of combat, and military classics such as Sun Tzu's *The Art of War*, Morihei Uyeshiba's *Art of Peace*, and Miyamoto Musashi's *The Book of Five Rings*.

Though I focused on Hapkido, a Korean martial art blending Tae Kwon Do and Aikido, I never allowed myself to focus exclusively on one style and made a point of seeking out experts in different styles.

After about five months I took a short break to have a second operation on my knee. During my recovery period, just as I was slowly easing back into my ascetic life, I made a horrendous discovery.

I had gone through my savings like a chainsaw on a chocolate log.

It was a new experience, one not common to a soldier living in a barrack square but known to every civilian: rent and good food and the pursuit of a life cost money; much more money than I'd thought credible.

It was a shock.

It looked as if my quest for martial excellence was going to cost me time away from training; I needed to earn the money to pay for it.

I thought about it. My training was mainly in the day and early evening — therefore I should get a night job. But exactly what? And how? In my lonely, Spartan life I scarcely knew anybody in Melbourne.

I was lucky; one of the regulars at the dojo worked as a bouncer. He got me a job at his club. Being a bouncer was not what I'd intended or planned, and the pay to be abused and cursed and threatened was abysmal at $8.50 an hour. I could see the irony: once upon a time in Sydney, I'd been a poacher; now I was the gamekeeper.

I had a strong sensation of *déjà vu* — only it was in a mirror.

Two weeks into the job a guy was bug-eyed, screaming abuse and threats, prodding me with his finger, sucking everything around him into the vortex of his chemically induced rage. He was creating a major disturbance and I needed to suppress him. For $8.50 an hour that was my job, neutralising idiots like this.

'I could take you with one hand tied behind me fuckin' back,' the guy screamed. I tried to keep the look of irritation off my face. Why did none of these wankers ever come up with anything original?

'Yes?'

'Fuckin' oath. I'll rip yer head off.'

Last week it had been kick yer head in.

'Okay mate, let's see how good you really are.'

The frenzied face changed imperceptibly. 'What?'

'Let's go outside and see if you can fight as well as you can shout.'

'Right, right.' The guy turned.

'Not that way, dickhead. There's an alley out the back.'

I led the way. Remembering my own experience I was pretty sure I knew what the guy was feeling. I pushed the bar of the fire exit door, relishing the blast of cool night air. 'Go on.' I nodded the guy through the door. Rambo charged out into the dimly lit alley and turned. 'Come on then, let's go.'

I stared at him, feeling a mixture of pity and contempt. It was like a bad movie; every word of dialogue painfully predictable. It was embarrassing to think that I had been as singularly unoriginal as the guy posturing in the middle of the alley. It was almost sad to watch. 'Get a life, tosser.'

I slammed the fire door and turned back into the club. I could almost sense the guy's relief at not having to fight, and laughed quietly when I heard the door being kicked and pounded, the muffled bellowing, 'Gutless prick ... outside, arsehole ...'

This, I reflected, had been the practice of the martial arts as much as anything I undertook in the dojo. I thought of Lao Tsu — *'The best soldier does not attack. The superior fighter succeeds without violence. The greatest conqueror wins without a struggle. This is called intelligent non-aggressiveness. This is called mastery of men.'*

Each night, after my shift at the club, I'd go home and read until dawn. Sitting in a small pool of light in the darkness, my reading gradually broadening into history and philosophy and classical fiction. I'd sleep until midday and then train every afternoon and into the early evenings, all the while devising new ways to improve; in one enlightened moment it occurred to me that dancing might help develop my balance and agility, and I signed up for an introductory lesson. My instructor's name was Lisa and she was slim and pretty, with long blonde hair and blue eyes. She smiled warmly and told me she'd take me through the steps of the waltz.

By the end of the lesson I'd decided the only thing I had going for me as a dancer was the right number of feet. Dancing was clearly not for me; there was little point pursuing it. There was, though, a lot of point in pursuing my dancing instructor.

I suggested we go for coffee — even though I couldn't stand the stuff. She gave me another of her sunny smiles and said that she'd like that. I liked her, and told her a little about myself, about my training, where I lived, and how I earned my living.

She was intrigued to learn that I had a flat in St Kilda. In those days, St Kilda was a long way from fashionable and still carried an air of red-light exotica. I invited her back to see the place. She said yes.

After that I saw her again, and then again, and then regularly until after a while I was worryingly unsettled.

I was out of my league, and I knew it. I found myself thinking about her almost as much as I thought about my training.

I hadn't planned on this — it wasn't part of my tactical blueprint to fall in love. But on the other hand ... I loved being with her. The sex was great and ... maybe ... she was the one.

Our relationship blossomed and we became, in the vernacular of the eighties, an item.

If there was one blot on our love affair it was Lisa's friends.

I didn't like them; didn't like their preoccupation with appearances; didn't like the influence they exerted over her; didn't like the fact that, when she introduced me, she felt constrained to tell them I worked in the 'security industry' rather then saying I was studying martial arts and worked as a bouncer.

And, more than any of that — they were all into drugs. Even Lisa.

'Yes, I smoke a joint now and then,' she told me. 'It relaxes me, makes me feel good. But I'm not addicted.'

'But it's dope. It does things to your brain.'

'So does alcohol. You never been drunk, Red? Lost control? Been out of it?'

'That's different.'

'How is it different?'

'Dope is addictive. With alcohol most people can take it or leave it alone.'

'Yeah? Try telling that to an alcoholic.'

The trouble with being in love with an intelligent woman was that she was ... well ... intelligent.

In all other respects our relationship flourished and we began to talk of permanency — maybe marriage — though neither of us mentioned it to anyone on the periphery of our lives.

I was becoming seriously short of money — my take-home pay was approximately half of what I'd been earning in the army — and reluctantly I began looking for a part-time job.

It was just after the 1987 stockmarket crash and jobs weren't easy to find, and the moment I started looking I found myself on a steep learning curve. Though at twenty-four I'd had different experiences, none of them were what people were looking for. Being a marksman with an M60 machine gun didn't count for much when no one interviewing me was looking for machine gunners.

Finally I found a job selling furniture twenty hours a week for one of the big department stores. I absolutely hated it, but I needed the money.

Not long afterwards I got a small break.

A guy at the dojo recommended me for a job at the Grand Hyatt as a bouncer in the bar and nightclub. The money was better, not by much but at least a little.

'But you can't work there,' Lisa cried when I told her.

I was shocked. 'Why not? It's a lot better than the last place.'

'But my friends go there,' she said, with more force than I wanted to hear.

I stared at her, bewildered and angry and in love.

'I can believe that,' I growled. 'Place is full of yuppie clones.'

'Supposing you have to throw one of them out?'

'Great,' I grinned, 'bring it on.'

She shook her head. 'I don't like it.'

Lisa's attitude perplexed me. She was an intelligent woman; why would she care what a bunch of superficial dope-heads thought? For me, taking the job was a no-brainer. It paid more money and there would have to be less aggro.

I was wrong about the aggro.

I was inside the bar, negotiating with a bunch of yuppies who, drunk and noisy, were being a recalcitrant pain in the butt, bunching up and blocking the entrance, reluctant to move. I was deliberately quiet and non-confrontational.

'What did you say?' one of the girls shouted above the noise. The rest of the group were laughing.

'I said you were all gettin' in the way.'

'*Getting*, you retard, *getting*,' she yelled. 'We were *getting* in the way. Why are you people always such morons? Is that part of the job?'

It happened a lot. It got to me; curiously I found it more intimidating than the promise of a bashing from some stoned-out-of-his-skull punter.

I decided to check out my diction for myself. I borrowed a hand-held tape recorder from a friend. Listening to myself recite into the machine told me nothing, so, without telling her, I left it on for half an hour when Lisa was in the flat and we were talking over a drink.

When she'd gone I listened to the tape. We sounded like we came from different countries. I was stunned. I could hear the drag in my voice, the badly mauled vowels, the slurring and loitering quality of the accent, the high-rising terminal, as if everything was a question.

This was something I needed to improve. I wasn't sure why. But I knew it was important; it frustrated me beyond description that people pigeonholed me based on how I spoke. The fact that I now knew my verbal skills where poor made my frustration even more acute.

I called a few drama and speech trainers to enquire about lessons, which I discovered were expensive. One teacher, more helpful than the rest, asked: 'Do you read?'

'Yes, I read a lot.'

'Then read aloud. That will improve your grammar and delivery more than anything. Listen to yourself on a recorder now and again; if you keep it up, after a few months you'll be amazed at the difference.'

I started that night, returning in the early hours of the morning to sit under the standard lamp to read aloud from Machiavelli's *The Prince,* thereafter reading aloud every night. By articulating every word I began to improve my pronunciation; rounding the vowels, sounding my tees, not dropping the g from participles. Almost by a process of osmosis, I learnt to construct grammatically correct sentences, conjugating verbs and tenses and cases with ease. Within a few months I had improved my vocabulary and my command of syntax, and after reading aloud the whole trilogy of *Lord of the Rings* I could hear and even feel a difference in my speech.

And the brats stopped sneering at me.

Inevitably some of Lisa's friends saw me at work at the Hyatt and soon it got around I worked as a bouncer. She didn't say much, though I could tell she wasn't pleased.

I realised we were moving apart, that Lisa was slipping away, that our love affair was on the downward slopes. I was amazed at how passion could so quickly fade; how easily what I'd thought of as secure and permanent was disintegrating.

Lisa was not all that was slipping away from me.

My intense single-minded pursuit of the martial arts was also getting swept over the horizon. I realised it with a shock one wet

Thursday afternoon standing alone in a sea of three-piece suits at the Hyatt and devising a new training program; trying to figure out how I could fit it into my working week. Suddenly I was back on sentry duty on Levers Plateau, calculating how to squeeze in fitness programs between ambushes and route marches.

I had come full circle.

Earning a living selling furniture and bouncing outside nightclubs had crept up on me, had taken precedence over my quest to pursue the martial arts. That night I read one of my favourite philosophers, Gichen Funakoshi, the founder of modern karate.

'You may train for a long, long time, but if you merely move your hands and feet and jump up and down like a puppet, learning karate is not very different from learning how to dance. You will never have reached the heart of the matter; you will have failed to grasp the quintessence of karate-do.'

I'd been doing a lot more than jumping up and down over the past eighteen months, but the reference to dancing struck a chord. For all my sweat and hard work, maybe I hadn't yet reached the heart of the matter. I'd allowed myself to become distracted. There was more to grasping the quintessence than I'd first imagined, maybe than I'd *ever* imagined.

In the decade since I'd taken up the martial arts I'd learnt how to perform a multitude of *katas* and patterns and choreographed movements. I'd learnt technique, form, ritual and history; had come to know how to bow, when to bow and when not to bow; even how to fold, store, iron and wear a uniform. I'd watched countless spectator events and prepared myself to take part in those same events; had paid thousands of dollars in training and grading fees. I'd studied Confucianism, Taoism and Buddhism.

And yet … maybe there was more.

CHAPTER 10

Seoul

SOMETIMES EVENTS fall into place with a weird, mystical synchronicity.

Happenstance occurred less than a week later.

Breathing hard and dripping sweat I bowed and moved to the side of the dojo after another workout. Mr Jung shuffled after me. 'You getting good,' he said.

Mr Jung was an Eighth Dan Grandmaster and I trained with him six days a week. I still couldn't quite beat the guy but I noticed Mr Jung was breathing as hard as I was, was even showing a few beads of sweat. It gave me some satisfaction to know it was getting harder for the little Korean to beat *me*.

'Maybe time for you to go.'

'What do you mean?'

'You go Korea. Train there.'

'Yeah?'

'I know Ninth Dan there. He good. He train you even more.'

'He a Grandmaster too?'

Mr Jung nodded. 'But he more than that. He World President. He phenomenal.'

I suppressed a smile. It was the longest word I'd ever heard Mr Jung mispronounce. 'You mean it? You could introduce me to this guy?'

'Yes.'

'That's great Mr Jung. Thanks. Thanks a lot. But what about the dojo? Who's going to take care of it for you?'

85

Mr Jung shook his head. 'Don't worry. I write all Korea master and say for him to take you.'

The letter from Seoul arrived a few weeks later telling me I was accepted as a pupil of the World President. I was rapt, though I gulped heavily when I saw the cost of the training fees.

But, what the hell. I was on a quest; money couldn't be a consideration. It was time for me to move on, to shake the dust of Melbourne off my feet and seek improvement and experience elsewhere. I would sell what little I owned; max out my credit cards, borrow as much as I could. It was worth it to train with a real guru, to journey to the beating heart of the Budo spirit.

I took the bus east along the Princes Highway to tell my family and catch up with a few friends I'd known before I joined the army. When I told them I was going to train in Asia, they were mildly amused yet faintly puzzled. To me they seemed like Hobbits, afraid and unwilling to step outside the Shire.

Within days I'd sold all I owned, raising enough money for the flight with some over in reserve.

My hardest task was to part with my collection of second-hand books; in terms of money they were pretty valueless, and they meant a lot to me. Sadly, I took them back to where I'd bought them: to the small, musty, sepia-lit bookshop in Prahran with the stooped, elderly owner in his half-frame spectacles and daggy cardigan. I told the old guy I was off to Asia.

The man said it wasn't policy to exchange books for cash and that I'd have to exchange the books for … 'Hang on a minute,' he wheezed and shuffled into the back of the shop, reappearing a moment later with a leather-bound edition of the complete works of Banjo Paterson.

'Here, you can exchange them for this. Take it with you. Then, wherever you go, you'll be taking Australia too.'

I examined it. The leather, though abraded, was thick and full-grained, the edition dated nineteen thirty-eight. 'You sure?' I murmured. 'This looks expensive.'

'Son, you're a reader. Not many of us left. We have to stick together. Enjoy it.'

I looked up. I was touched. No one had ever called me a reader before. I shook the old boy's hand. 'I appreciate this. I won't forget it. Thanks.'

The parting with Lisa was more painful than I'd anticipated. We both knew the affair had run its course, but I'd never loved anyone the way I'd loved Lisa. We didn't go back to my place; there was no point. It was over; I was moving on and Lisa ... well, I didn't know what Lisa was going to do but, whatever it was, I wished her well. We kissed goodbye, promising to keep in touch, both knowing the promise would last no longer than the fleeting recollection of that final kiss.

* * *

Seoul was a shock.

Apart from a few trips to the bars in Penang and Hatyai, most of my experience of Asia had been the jungles of the Malaysian peninsula, populated by smiling, brown-skinned people and luxuriant with exotic plants. Craning my neck from the deck of the crowded airport bus on the morning of my arrival I couldn't see a single exotic plant and scarcely any trees. Instead, I stared at the ultimate urban nightmare: a thunderous, congested city much bigger than Melbourne, in fact a mega-metropolis crammed into an area the size of Gippsland yet more populous than all of Australia. And here no one was smiling. The Koreans stared at me unashamedly, as if I were Frankenstein's Monster or the Abominable Snowman.

The bus deposited me in the centre of the city where I was surrounded by the roar of traffic, my brain punctured by the sound of snatched clutches and the hellish, demented, wasp-like dissonance of unsilenced 100cc mopeds. I'd learnt a few words of Korean and those, along with the instructions I'd been sent, enabled me, after traversing a maze of narrow streets and sinister-looking alleyways, to find the dojo. The guru was the next surprise. I'd been expecting to meet an older, bulkier, Bruce Lee, with short, greying hair and the brown weather-beaten face of a seeker after truth. Instead, Seung was squat, and had a gut. His face was grey from spending too much time inside and his dark hair was long and greasy and coloured unnatural ink black — I could see dye stains on his temples.

His eyes were bleary and he smoked. This was not what I'd been imagining. I could hardly conceal my amazement as the guy welcomed me into his office at the back of the dojo and settled me into an armchair before leaning back behind a big teak desk and lighting up. 'You travel a long way,' he said. 'You like a drink?'

'Yes, thanks,' I said, anticipating a glass of water or tea ... perhaps juice.

Seung motioned towards a young woman — presumably his secretary — who moved to a cabinet and poured two measures of rice spirit. It wasn't yet noon. Maybe the booze explained the bleary eyes.

I gazed around as I sipped the drink. The walls were plastered with certificates; in a showcase a couple of dozen trophies gleamed in the dull light. 'So when do we start?' I asked.

'Soon, soon. First we drink, then I show you where you live.'

After another shot Seung led me through the city's thick, poisonous haze and another warren of narrow streets to what looked like a warehouse. It was an apartment block unlike any apartment block I'd ever encountered. Inside were crowded rows of wooden cells, hardly more than boxes, each eight by ten feet with a bare floor and a small rush mat. Seung pushed open a plywood door. In my box was a worn blanket, a small cabinet and a bowl and bucket in the corner.

'Toilet at end of corridor,' Seung told me. 'Not good. You use bucket. Bowl for washing. Water from well outside.'

'Where's the bed?'

'You sleep on floor. You in training now. Okay, I leave you settle. You start tomorrow.'

Settling took me slightly under a minute. I'd brought almost nothing with me, and what little I had brought was going to be too much for this place.

I scarcely slept at all and found my way to the dojo early. Seung didn't arrive for over an hour, by which time I'd made the acquaintance of his assistant instructor, Chin.

Chin was in his mid-thirties, about ten years older than me, and even with the difference in culture and difficulty with language, I could tell he wasn't over the moon at my presence. He surveyed me in the same manner as had the less-than-pleasant people on the bus.

'You do forward rolls,' he ordered.

'Sure, why not.'

I'd been doing forward rolls for an hour and was beginning to feel sick when Seung arrived. I straightened up. 'No, no, you go on,' Seung commanded and disappeared into his office. I kept at it for another twenty minutes before the urge to vomit overcame me and I staggered into the alley outside the dojo. Returning, I noticed the look of satisfaction on Chin's face.

I trained with Seung that afternoon. Despite the drinking and smoking, I had to admit the guy was talented. Apart from his Ninth Dan in Karate, Seung had developed his own school, a combination of Tae Kwon Do, Taek Kyon, Hapkido and Soo Bahk Do. It was of this new school that he was World President. The training was hard but there were some good moves and I felt I could learn something.

After a couple of hours Seung called a halt. 'You come back tomorrow,' he said. I returned to my box, stopping to eat a plate of *juk* (rice porridge) on the way. For want of something better to do I began reading aloud Banjo's poems. I settled quickly into a pattern, in the mornings training sometimes with Seung but more often with Chin, who made me do forward and backwards rolls until I vomited. In the afternoon I trained with Seung or Chin. Sometimes there were classes, mixed ranks occasionally but usually just brown and black belts. Chin was a Sixth Dan and had been practising martial arts since he was four. Technically he was very skilled, especially in kicking and punching, but I thought his practice had weaknesses. And he was lazy. As was Seung, who often turned up late for morning training. And, though I was okay with Seung insisting that I call him *Sah Bum Nim* or Number One Master, I wasn't so happy when Chin insisted on the same when Seung wasn't around. The guy had attitude and went out of his way to give me a hard time in sparring. Within days I was a mass of bruises.

One particular move I was made to rehearse repeatedly was a pivoting and leaping kick. It was a good move but no matter how high I kicked, Chin insisted I kick higher. One day I performed the leap against the dojo wall, found a tape measure and measured the height my foot was striking. It was three metres.

At just over 1.8 metres, I was for the first time in my life living in a place where I was considered tall. I couldn't understand why the much shorter Koreans would wish to deliver such a high kick. I raised it with Seung. Barefoot in the middle of the mat I bowed as Seung strutted into the dojo. 'Master, why am I practising this high kick? Surely it can only be effective if my opponent is a man standing on another man's shoulders.' I grinned, to show I was joking.

Seung didn't smile. 'It is necessary. Supposing you meet a bear or some other large beast.'

'Then I'd run the other way.'

Seung shook his head. 'That is not a good answer.' Behind me I heard Chin mutter something about *meguks* — which literally, I'd learnt, meant American man, but was a derogatory label applied to all white-skinned foreigners — and it occurred to me that these particular Koreans had no sense of humour.

Not that I had much to laugh about. My money was running out and all I could afford to eat was *kimchee* (pickled cabbage) and boiled rice with, occasionally, a little cheap meat. Every day I walked the overcrowded pavements from my box to the dojo through a choking, murky miasma of pollution, the noise of the city beating down into my brain. When it rained, which was often, even the rain was dirty.

With such a poor diet I was unable to train for more than a couple of hours before I was exhausted and I noticed Chin making no effort to hide his deepening look of contempt. But adjusting to my Spartan life was proving difficult; I was unused to washing in cold water from a well and sleeping on a floor without benefit of a mattress — even the dirt at Levers Plateau had been more comfortable. I began to wonder what the hell I was doing.

I'd come to think of my cell as a hutch, a packing case, no more than a slightly enlarged tea-chest, and wondered what would happen if I met a girl. 'You wanna come back and see my tea-chest?' Sure. That would work. As far as I could tell, none of the Koreans, all of whom were decidedly unfriendly, brought women back. I would have known if they had. With the cell's plywood walls I could hear the guy next door farting. He farted often.

My time in the hutch was spent poring over a Korean phrase book or reading Banjo Paterson. I came to learn *The Man from Snowy River* by heart, reciting it aloud, playing with the cadence of the rhythm and metre, enjoying the feel and spirit of the words. The old man had been right; reading it did take me back to Australia.

I was permanently hungry and tired; black and blue and broke. I needed a boost, and though my funds were rapidly diminishing decided to hunt down a couple of beers. I headed off to the nightclub district of Itaewon in search of a pub and found a bar filled with off-duty American service personnel. Though they were friendly and talkative, after a while I began to understand why the Koreans disliked me so much. On the presumption that anyone Caucasian was American, they assumed *I* was American — and despised me accordingly.

Of course, with forty-five thousand military personnel on the peninsula, it wasn't too surprising the American presence was resented, but it seemed to me that several Yanks in this particular bar weren't helping to improve their image. They were like blind giants. Within minutes they were telling me how America had saved South Korea's 'ass' from the North in fifty-one and, when they discovered I was Australian, began telling me how America had saved Australia in World War II. 'Without us, you guys would all be talking Japanese,' one loudmouth told me, 'We saved your ass.'

He was probably right, but I didn't know whether to thank him or kick him in the nuts. Instead I took my leave, found a different pub and joined a different group of *meguks* who didn't consider themselves members of the master race. They were a welcoming bunch of Texans and Californians and with them was another Australian, a guy from Sydney called Alan who turned out to be a good bloke who didn't like football, liked cricket but talked mainly about books. I wondered if he was gay; but, as I too was talking about books, it was possible the guy was wondering the same about me. What the hell. I didn't give a stuff what side of the wicket he batted so long as he didn't make any moves on me.

Alan was in Korea teaching English as a second language. When I told him what I was doing in Seoul and how broke I was, he said, 'Why don't you do what I do? Teach ESL. They're crying out for teachers.'

'Don't you need to be qualified?'

'You speak English, that's the most important qualification. I can get you a job at my place tomorrow.' I started the following week. Once I got into it I found the work easy enough. My pupils were in their late teens and eager to learn.

I discovered I was a good teacher, mainly by remembering what Mrs Gannon had done and doing the exact opposite, though I was careful not to work too many hours and fall into the old trap of eating into my training time. The money wasn't great, but it kept the wolf a little further from the door.

Even so, it was a bloody thin door.

The school had a small first-aid room with a set of scales. One evening I slipped in and weighed myself. I stared at the figure on the scales in disbelief. I'd dropped from eighty-seven kilos down to seventy-eight. I had been in Korea eight weeks and lost nine kilos — not one gram of which had been fat. I'd been in peak physical condition when I left Melbourne. It had taken me eighteen months of expensive eating and hard training to get there.

And I'd lost it in eight weeks. At that moment I was ready to jack it in and go back to Oz. If that's what could happen in two months, what would my body be like in six months? My quest was impossible and I was stupid to have even imagined I could study martial arts in Korea.

All I was heading for was a black belt in anorexia.

CHAPTER 11

Itaewon

I WALKED back to my hutch deep in thought. How had Uyeshiba and the others managed? Their diet must have been much like mine. And if they could handle it why couldn't I? No, I wasn't going to jack it in. In Melbourne I'd reached a peak of physical fitness in part by eating well. But Melbourne wasn't the end of my advancement. I had a long way to go yet.

No, I would stick with it. Three months later, although still subsisting in my packing case on *kimchee* and boiled rice and washing from a bowl of cold water, I was training six hours a day without exhaustion. Though I still dreamt nightly of a mattress, I'd adjusted to my ascetic lifestyle. I was learning new moves — and giving Chin a hard time in sparring.

One day after training, Seung called me into his office as I was towelling off following a sparring session with a couple of Second Dans.

'You doing good,' Seung said. 'I been thinking. Why not you get your black belt and then go back to Australia and sell my style. You set up dojos and run whole operation there. Under franchise from me. You could be a big man and make much money. We both make a lot of money.'

The mention of Australia and money in the same breath caught my attention. I stopped wiping the sweat from my chest. 'Yeah? You mean it? That sounds great. But how long before I get my black belt?'

'I put you on fast track. Make you black belt quick. You have plenty experience from other place. We use that.' I was elated, even though Seung's scheme didn't sound entirely on the level. Fast-tracking wasn't exactly in the Budo spirit, especially to make money. But I didn't care. I'd never felt so alienated in my life. I was sick of Korea, sick of the loneliness and hostility and racism. Chin was open in his displays of superiority and Seung, too, in his demeanour and body language showed what he felt about the *meguk* among them.

To celebrate I went to Itaewon — the nightlife hub of Seoul. I'd been only twice since my first visit. Drinking in pubs was definitely outside the orbit of my subsistence living. Alan was there. Though we worked in the same place I hardly saw anything of him; he was friendly but detached and I guessed the guy was probably on a quest of his own. He introduced me to a woman; a short, dark-haired, gorgeously proportioned, good-looking girl who spoke English with a Korean intonation and an American accent. Her name was Ann See and she was American-Korean; her father, she told me, had been a member of the occupation forces in the late 1960s.

She was hard to read, but seemed to offer a hint of promise in her almond eyes, and after Alan had made it clear that he and Ann See weren't an item I asked her if she wanted to go for a meal. I knew it was crazy; I didn't have money to spend on women but, then again, this particular woman was particularly attractive.

She suggested a popular restaurant. It was busy, full of noise and light and the kind of life I hadn't lived for months. Inside, she bumped into some people she knew and introduced me. To impress her I said, in Korean, 'I'm pleased to meet you.' The people, a man and two women looked startled.

When they'd gone, Ann See rounded on me. 'Why did you say that?' she demanded. She was obviously upset.

'What? All I said was, I'm pleased to meet you.'

'No you didn't. You said, I'm happy to see you go. These are my friends and you insulted them.'

I stared at her, panicking as I watched images of a night of sweaty passion evaporating before my eyes. 'Oh, hell, I'm sorry.'

It took more beers than my budget could stand to get her back on track, that look back in her eyes, but by the time we sat down at the table a lustful glow had returned. She was telling me about her apartment.

Things were definitely looking rosy. Though I had every intention of shagging her like a rabbit on crack, no way could I take her back to my hutch to do it. The way events were working out I might, if I was very lucky, get to spend the night on the unbelievable luxury of a mattress.

'I have to go to the bathroom,' she announced. 'It's all that beer. Order for me will you. I always have number 68, the beef. It's good here. So is the pork. You should try it.'

The waiter arrived with the menu as she left the table. I looked up at the impassive face and detected the thinly veiled dislike of yet another *meguk*. I waved away the English menu, demanding the one in Korean, noting with satisfaction the change on the waiter's face. In Korean I ordered the beef for Ann See, then found the pork and ordered that too. The waiter's face shifted from slight surprise to total astonishment and I felt good.

Ann See returned and the food arrived shortly after. Things were going well as she talked and swigged her beer and tucked lustily into her plate of beef. I did likewise; it was the first meat I'd eaten in over a month. But after a few mouthfuls I stopped.

'What's wrong?' she asked.

'This pork. I think it's off.'

'I don't believe it. Not here. It's always good here.'

'Well, it doesn't taste good to me. It doesn't smell all that great either.' I was loath to make a fuss; I didn't want to do anything else to cool her mood, but this was meat I was talking about and I didn't get to eat it that often. 'It sure doesn't taste like pork.'

'Let me try.' She leaned across and forked a lump of meat, popping it into her mouth and chewing avidly. I watched her face change. 'What is this?' she demanded.

'It's supposed to be pork.'

'This isn't pork.'

'Well, it says pork on the menu. And that's what I ordered.'

'Show me.'

I grabbed the Korean menu, jabbing at the line of characters. 'There. See. Pork.'

'Jesus,' she screeched, 'that isn't pork.' She spat a gob full of meat on to her plate. 'That's *dog. You ordered dog.* I'm eating *fucking dog.*'

I stared into her eyes … and watched the lust turn to stone-cold malevolence. No way was I going to get anywhere near her mattress. Not tonight. Not ever. I'd only spoken Korean to show off, and look what it had got me. I'd stuffed up on the pork … and the porking.

I watched her shove her plate aside, readying to leave. *Bloody hell, this is so unfair*, I wailed inside. *So what if I ordered dog? That's no reason not to root me stupid. It's not like I ate the dog's balls.* I stopped. *Oh, — supposing …*

It took weeks for my finances to recover from the fiasco in the restaurant.

Seung's fast track meant frequent gradings — and grading fees were expensive. And though I'd paid my fees up-front, Seung was charging me for the extra training. It was clear that in his book martial arts meant material affluence. The guy had all the shallow characteristics of a flamboyant showman, making his style as commercially popular as he could.

At the English school I ran into Alan who said, 'I've come to say goodbye.'

I was surprised. 'Goodbye?'

'I'm going to Japan, next week. I've had it with Korea.'

I was disappointed. He was scarcely a friend but he was the only other Aussie I knew in Seoul. 'Well, good luck.'

'I'll stay in touch. I'll write to you when I get there.'

Six weeks later I got a letter in my post-office box. Alan was enjoying Japan. In the same post was a letter from Brian, the guy from the dojo in Melbourne who had got me the job bouncing at the

Hyatt. Coincidentally, he too was in Japan, studying under a 'great Grandmaster' — if I ever wanted an introduction he could fix it. In the meantime he was off to India to study under the greatest martial arts teacher and guru of them all ... Aaryan Ravi.

I'd heard Seung talk of Ravi; it was the only time I'd ever seen the Korean show any kind of humility. Whoever this Indian was, he had to be a living legend to get that kind of reaction.

I was working hard, moving up through the ranks at an accelerated pace while accumulating resentment from the other grades like a magnet attracting tacks. I could see their point; when it came to the mechanical moves of the World President's style, I was less than ordinary. Where I did do better was in the fighting, in hitting targets and gaining control of opponents. In those quarters I held my own.

My black belt grading was a major event, with hundreds of Seung's disciples and devotees gathered to witness it. In keeping with his showmanship, Seung had also invited the media and a bunch of local politicians. The grading was in two parts; the first, an orchestrated sequence of fixed techniques against compliant opponents. Since my days in the army I'd hated the stylised and choreographed ballet inherent in so many martial arts and unarmed combat styles and, though I wasn't bad at it, I knew I wasn't all that good either. I caught sight of Chin's sneer as I was going through the sequences.

The second part of the grading was free-motion sparring, which I loved. Grappling, kicking, punching and elbowing, I felt less constrained and, subsequently, performed with greater fluidity. At the end of the grading, World President Seung, in the manner of a Roman Emperor, ceremoniously awarded me my black belt and presented me with a certificate and, curiously, a decorative tie pin. I stepped down from the small, red-silk covered podium, aware of the scowls of Seung's subordinates.

At training the next day, Chin insisted on repeating the robotic, ritualised steps I so obviously disliked, using me as an example of how not to perform them; singling me out and announcing to the class, 'See the *meguk*. Do *not* do it like that. That is how you must not do it.' After a couple of hours I'd had enough of dancing to the capricious dictates of the malignant pygmy and gave up trying. Chin halted the session. 'Why you stop? Why you so bad, so shameful in this practice?'

I spoke in broken Korean. 'Because I think it's garbage. Total crap. Fit only for wankers.' I used the English word for wanker, and when Chin demanded a translation, I used body language that was truly international.

Chin's face turned ugly. 'You think. You come out here and I show you they not garbage. I show you wrong.'

My heart surged as it had in the clubs in Sydney. Stepping into the middle of the mat I wondered if I'd bitten off more than I could chew. Chin was a better long-range fighter than I was; the guy could probably out-kick and out-punch me. It was time to go back to basics.

Chin made a move. I ducked, charged and with a body slam took him to the ground where, after a short struggle, Chin tapped out in submission. Leaping up, he sidestepped away and I went after him, invading his space, denying him room to manoeuvre, taking him down with a leg sweep and forcing him to tap out again.

And so it went, constantly closing the gap, taking Chin to the ground with body slams and leg sweeps. Theoretically this shouldn't have been a problem for Chin, as his style incorporated numerous techniques for dealing with an opponent when grounded, but they were just that — theoretical — and in my opinion were useless against a non-cooperating opponent. Like me.

The 'demonstration' turned menacing, the other grades watching wide-eyed as Chin became more and more frustrated, his face turning grey with rage and breathlessness. He was suffering aerobically, his breath coming in rasping gasps. It wasn't a surprise, the guy, good at the set-piece moves, didn't train sufficiently hard for honest fighting. Finally, after a very long thirty minutes of what was close to becoming an ugly brawl, Chin gave up. He shuffled to the side of the mat, bowed perfunctorily and stalked out of the dojo.

Seung called me into his office that afternoon. Sitting behind his desk and chain smoking, he gave me a lecture on showing respect. Clearly Chin had complained. To finish, Seung said, 'Now you have black belt, you go back to Australia and send me $20,000.'

'What?'

'That's what you pay for my franchise. For first year.'

'I don't know,' I said doubtfully, 'I'll have to think about that.'

It took me a week. Seven days later I walked into Seung's office in my street clothes. Seung was startled. 'Why you not training?'

'I've come to say goodbye.'

Seung looked pleased. 'You go back to Australia? You send me money?'

I shook my head. 'It's not going to happen, Seung. Here.' I dug into my pocket, took out the decorative tiepin and dropped it onto the desk.

The look of happy avarice slipped off Seung's face. He frowned. 'Why you not want pin?'

'Because it's shit. All of this.' My gesture took in the walls covered in certificates and the cabinet filled with awards, the whole dojo. 'It's all shit. And I'm outta here.' I turned and picked up my bag. 'See ya.'

I bought a train ticket to Pusan, where I caught the second-class ferry to Japan. I'd faxed Alan in Tokyo who had faxed back saying he could get me a job teaching English. I'd also faxed the Grandmaster under whom Brian had been studying. I had yet to hear from him.

On the second morning of my journey, as the dawn was blushing the Sea of Japan to a glowing pink, I stood on the deck of the ferry holding not only my recently won black belt certificate but all my previous certificates — my lifetime's collection of awards from every different style in which I had ever been involved.

I dumped the lot into the ocean.

CHAPTER 12

Tokyo

I STAYED with Alan, sleeping on the floor of his tiny flat. He found me an airbed but after a night or so I went back to sleeping on the floor. It was more comfortable. I still couldn't make up my mind if the guy was gay or not, but after a few days I began to relax. It occurred to me that Alan was on his own personal journey and deeply committed to finding himself. And, I thought, probably making a much better job of it than I was.

It seemed I'd spent the past eleven months of my own Odyssey living in discomfort to little end. What useful techniques Seung had to teach me I could have learnt in a couple of months. For the rest of the time he had been happy to take my money, merely for the 'honour' of training with him. I'd been manipulated; not just by Seung, but also, I now realised, by Jung.

Training with Jung in Melbourne I'd not only worked harder than anyone else, I'd cleaned and painted the dojo; even washed Jung's car and mowed his lawn — all for free. And when it looked like I was getting good enough to possibly beat him in sparring, the guy ships me out to Korea to save face.

It wasn't only widows and orphans who needed protection from the predators of this world. Pilgrims were vulnerable too. I wouldn't make that mistake again.

Alan arranged an interview for me and I secured a job teaching English before travelling to see the Grandmaster. The subway was complicated and I knew no Japanese, so finding my way about the city was a challenge. Tokyo was overwhelming, the air as filled with combustion emissions as Seoul; the city, if anything, was even noisier. But there was a difference. This was a world city, a capital with cachet, and Seoul, for all its size and hubris was, in comparison, in a minor league. Here, no one stared at me, even though I was a *gaijin* — a foreigner.

Haruki Tezuka was an Eighth Dan with hard, oriental eyes and a face like a fall of rock. Thankfully he spoke good English. The dojo was pristine, run almost on military lines. Tezuka quizzed me about my background.

'I didn't bring any certificates,' I told him.

Tezuka waved dismissively. 'What matters is how you perform on the *tatami*. Get changed.'

I sparred with Tezuka for forty minutes. The guy had a compact physique; his body was tough as teak and he was exceptionally skilful, though a couple of times I saw the hard eyes spark with surprise as I managed to get a few reasonable moves in. At the end of the bout Tezuka nodded. 'Yes, I will train you.'

I was pleased. 'Brian, a mate of mine, trained here under you.'

'Ah, yes. He has gone to India to train with Aaryan Ravi.' There was something in the way he said the name, almost with reverence, that made me glance at him.

'Is he good?'

'He is said to be the best.'

'Have you met him?'

'No. Come into the office and we will talk about your training schedule.'

Tezuka's fees were even higher than Seung's but I believed the guy had something to teach me. To supplement my teaching income I took casual work cleaning offices and washing dishes. After about ten days I thanked Alan and moved out of the flat, finding a cheap hostel where the room was a minor step up from my Korean hutch — a slightly bigger packing case with a thin futon — though probably not as good as Sall had enjoyed in Long Bay; perhaps rating two stars in the world directory of live-in tea-chests. I bought a phrase book and began studying Japanese in between reciting Banjo Paterson. I trained daily, sparring with a young guy called Katsuhiro, who I renamed Kat, and with a guy about my own age named Hayao, who I called stupid wanker … under my breath.

I liked Kat; he was reasonably talented and made up for whatever he lacked in athleticism through sheer hard work and a lot of heart. Hayao, on the other hand, appeared totally up himself. There was a strong whiff of entitlement about the guy, like the world owed him just for being alive.

'What is it with that guy?' I asked Kat.

'Ahh, he is Master Tezuka's prostective son-in-law.'

'What?' Kat's English was good, certainly better than my Japanese, but some words were beyond him. 'Do you mean prospective? He's engaged to Tezuka's daughter?'

'Yes. For him it is a good marriage. Master Tezuka is a rich man. He is connected to the Yakuza.'

This was news to me. 'The Japanese mafia? Are you telling me I'm training under a godfather?'

'He has trained many of them. He is very powerful. It is wise to show him respect. You must be careful not to provoke him.' Kat made a face. 'That would be very dangerous.'

'So Hayao slides along in the slipstream of daddy-in-law's connections, right?'

'Pardon me?'

'Forget it, Kat. But thanks for putting me in the picture. I'll give the wanker a wide berth from now on.'

It didn't work out that way.

A few days later I found myself sparring with Hayao. In the middle of the bout I spun around to my right, my left leg shooting out for a crescent kick. It was higher than I intended but, even so, Hayao should have anticipated it and countered. As it was, the edge of my foot smashed into something hard and bony.

'Ow, fuck.' I staggered around the mat, the edge of my foot feeling as if it were on fire. I bent and tested it gingerly. It was badly bruised but there were no broken bones. I looked up. On the other side of the mat Hayao hadn't fared so well. He was on his back and moaning. I limped across to him. One glance was enough. I'd broken the guy's jaw.

Tezuka emerged from his office and, followed by Kat, crossed the dojo to stare down at his future son-in-law. I watched him anxiously, not knowing whether to beg for mercy or ship out quick for the other side of the world. Tezuka looked up and gave me a stony look, difficult to interpret … but then every look from the guy was that way; not once had I seen him smile.

Staring at me he growled something in Japanese and stalked back into his office to make a phone call. I imagined Tezuka telling his mafia mates to hurry over to measure me up for a pair of concrete boots.

'Bloody hell, Kat, what did he say?' I stammered. 'What did he say?' Already I saw myself taking up residence at the bottom of Tokyo Bay.

'He say Hayao should have blocked the strike. It is his own fault.'

'Really?' I felt my system surge with relief. 'You sure? He said that? Really?'

'Yes, of course.'

A couple of paramedics arrived with a stretcher. They examined the semi-comatose Hayao, gave me a suspicious look and carted the poor sod away. Somehow all the pleasure had gone out of training and, figuring I'd done enough damage for the day, I changed.

Walking back into the dojo the following morning I almost collided with a young woman. She was petite, Japanese and stunningly beautiful; I caught my breath and stared at her. 'I'm sorry.'

She smiled at me. 'That's okay. I wasn't looking where I was going.' Her English was perfect with just a trace of Aussie.

Kat padded across the dojo. 'Red, this is Yumiko, Master Tezuka's daughter.'

I did my best to keep my face composed as she held out her hand.

It was a bit embarrassing being introduced to the fiancée of a guy I'd just put in hospital. Just then Tezuka appeared, gave me one of his sinister looks and said something to his daughter. Her face changed. 'Excuse me.' She followed her father into his office.

I turned to Kat. '*She's* engaged to Hayao. What in hell does she see in him?'

Kat shrugged. 'His family is rich. They have many businesses. I think maybe the marriage is arranged.'

Yumiko appeared at the dojo every day at mid-morning and stayed until late afternoon. With Hayao in hospital she was taking over the administrative work he had been doing for his future father-in-law. She was keen to practise her English and made a point of seeking me out. Most early afternoons we were the only people in the place.

I didn't mean it to happen. At least that's what I told myself, though I knew it was bullshit. Men mean it to happen all the time. It's the way the world works … own a dick — get in trouble.

Of course I was drawn to her, yet I was genuinely surprised when I found myself suddenly locked in a passionate embrace with her; even more surprised at her ardent response. After a moment she pulled away. 'Look, I'm sorry,' I told her, 'I didn't plan to do that.'

'That's all right.' She was flustered as she gathered up her things. 'I have to go.' She hurried out of the office. For the rest of the day and all night I worried whether I was about to receive a visit from some friends of her father's. Tezuka appeared next morning and was his normal dour, focused, tough-as-teak self. Relieved, I sparred with him for an hour before he left to attend to business. Tentatively I stood in the doorway of the office. Yumiko looked up, her beautiful face impassive. 'I live with my father and mother,' she told me. 'But a friend has an apartment. She is away for a while. This is the address,' she pushed a slip of paper across the desk. 'If you want, I will meet you there this afternoon.'

I was craving the passion I'd known with Lisa, and if nothing else Yumiko was passionate, but being with her was like drinking sea water when you are dying of thirst. There was nothing quenching about Yumiko. I was crazy and I knew it. I should have had her once and left it at that, but my brain wasn't working.

I began seeing her regularly; twice, sometimes three times a week.

This wasn't walking on the wild side — this was running on the edge of suicide. I was screwing Yakuza-connected Tezuka's daughter while her rich, powerful fiancé was in hospital with his face wired up and wedged in a web of scaffolding. What on God's earth was I thinking? Yumiko was forbidden fruit, especially to a *gaijin* like me.

But I couldn't stop, not even when Hayao got out of hospital and finally showed up at the dojo. She was a drug and I needed to keep seeing her. I wondered if some fatalistic death wish had germinated in me.

She talked a little about herself; how she had spent a year learning English in Sydney when she was a teenager. Her mother had accompanied her, but she'd managed to escape a few times to experience the wilder side of life.

I asked her about Hayao. She didn't love him she said, and didn't wish to be his wife, but she was a dutiful daughter and marrying Hayao would make her father happy. I wondered how happy it would make her father if he knew his *gaijin* pupil was pronging his only daughter. No, I didn't even want to think about that.

It all blew apart, as deep down I knew it would, six months into the affair. I was walking to the dojo when I heard someone rush up behind me. I spun around. It was a sick-looking Kat. 'Red, Red, do not go to the dojo.'

'Why not?'

'They know about you and Yumiko.'

'What? How?'

'Hayao was suspicious. He had her followed. They know she's been seeing you. I heard Hayao telling Tezuka last night. Tezuka was very angry.'

'Bloody hell.'

With a leer Kat moved closer. 'So … what was she like?'

'Not *now*, Kat.'

Kat's face changed.

'You must not go in the dojo. You must leave Tokyo immediately. It is very dangerous for you.'

'Yeah.' I turned towards the subway. 'Look Kat, I appreciate this. Thanks.'

I hurried back to the hostel to retrieve my stuff, packed and was out in three minutes. I called Alan from a pay phone at the station, told him what had happened and asked him to do what he could to square my sudden departure with the school. Alan told me of a friend in Osaka who was a Buddhist monk and could maybe help me for a few days. I caught the train to Osaka.

The monastery was on the outskirts of the city; it took me hours to find it and when I did I was surprised to discover the monk was an Australian from Perth, a tall, lanky, gentle guy whose name was Paul. Paul said I could sleep on the floor and I was grateful. A floor in a monastery was infinitely preferable to a bed in a hospital or, worse, a hole in the ground.

The monks put me to work sweeping and generally helping out. I was content to do it; the monastery was a serene and placid place, an island of tranquillity in an ocean of menace, and the easy motion of sweeping helped me to think.

My initial intention had been to get a flight from Osaka to Sydney, however I didn't have the money and, when I thought about it, I wasn't so sure I wanted to do that. To run from Tokyo had been sensible; to exit Japan felt somehow craven. Of course it was more dangerous remaining in the country if Tezuka decided to come after me but, curiously, the monastery infused me with a sense of safety.

Something prompted me to write to Tezuka. Perhaps it was the spiritual nature of the place I was in. I felt constrained to apologise, to acknowledge responsibility for what must have seemed like a betrayal, and tell Tezuka it wasn't Yumiko's fault.

Within a week Paul had found me a job on a local golf course as a part-time caddy and member of the ground crew. A few days later, with no sign of Tezuka or any of his heavies, I thanked Paul and the monks and took my leave, finding myself yet another hutch before going in search of a martial arts Grandmaster I'd heard of when I was in Tokyo. The guy was an Eighth Dan and I signed on to train with him. It was a risk; Tezuka might hear where I was, but I'd come to Japan to study martial arts and I intended to do so.

After a while I began to relax. There was no sign of retribution from Tezuka and on the golf course I was enjoying the work, happy to be out in the open and breathing fresh air. Only twelve per cent of land in Japan is flat, and, away from the cities, it's a beautiful country. I felt privileged to be able to labour in the hills and rugged terrain around the golf course.

One morning I was lopping some trees with the rest of the maintenance crew when after about an hour I heard a blood-chilling scream. One of the men had misjudged the angle of the chainsaw and sent the blade ripping deep into his upper thigh and femur. I ran to where the guy huddled at the side of the fairway, crying with the pain and shock and gushing blood. Pushing my way through the gang I took one look and bent to apply pressure to the femoral artery. The guy screamed as the blood spurted through my fingers.

'Breathe,' I ordered, 'breathe slowly.' I tried to remember the Japanese. 'Kisoku, kisoku.' I didn't know if it was the right word and I had no time to worry about it. I placed my free hand on the guy's chest to force him to control his breath.

I looked up at the faces of the gang clustered around. 'Tell him to focus on his breathing,' I bawled, 'it'll help take his mind off the pain. Tell him to con-cen-trate.' Someone translated and gradually the man's respiratory system slowed, reducing the flow of blood, and by the time the ambulance arrived I was pretty sure the guy was going to live.

A day later I heard the doctors had saved the leg and from then on, though still a *gaijin*, I was a little more accepted.

Like Jung and Seung and Tezuka, the new guru charged big

bucks for the privilege of training with him and once more I found myself living hand-to-mouth on a subsistence diet of boiled rice and cabbage; though I tried to get work teaching English, without references and Alan's help I had no success.

My past caught up with me almost two months later. Stepping out of the dojo one night I saw a shadow detach itself from the wall and move quickly towards me.

I tensed, readying.

CHAPTER 13

Shanghai

THE SHADOW was Kat.

'Kat? What are you doing here?'

'Master Tezuka sent me.'

I scanned around behind Kat to see if he was in company with a couple of Tezuka's thugs.

'I am alone,' Kat said.

'How did you know I was here?'

'Tezuka knew after just a few days where you were.'

'And he's waited all this time to come after me?'

'He no longer wishes you injury. He sent me to tell you. He was very angry at first but you sent him a letter and he says you stay out of Tokyo and away from Yumiko and no harm will come to you.'

'How is Yumiko?'

'She has gone to America with her mother. She is no longer going to marry Hayao.'

'No?' I was surprised.

'No. Master Tezuka said he is not worthy of her. Hayao let you beat him in the dojo and then he let you sex Yumiko. Tezuka said if Hayao were a man Yumiko would not want sex someone else. He give Hayao the big flick.'

Sometimes, I was as thick as two short planks. The penny didn't drop for over a week, and, when it did, I was in the worst possible place: sparring in the middle of the tatami.

I froze as I got it … the truth … the revelation. I dropped my guard and my opponent caught me with a reverse back fist to the side of my jaw. 'Ow … shit.' I clutched my jaw and moved to the edge of the mat.

Well, I thought, a crack on the jaw was no more than I deserved. How could I have been so dumb? Once more I'd been manipulated. I'd thought at the time that it was all too easy, but I'd wanted to believe that Yumiko had been stricken by my fabulous good looks and manly charm.

Bullshit.

She had set me up.

She'd expected her father to find out and had known he would despise Hayao for letting himself be cuckolded, especially by a foreigner. She had used me, had been prepared to see me badly beaten up — or worse — so she could slip her arranged marriage. I'd been played for a sucker from the start.

I lasted another five months in Osaka, by which time I'd had enough. The Grandmaster was as heavily into hyping his particular martial arts school — which was little more than an amalgam of several other styles — as Seung had been. It was disappointing. I'd come to the head of the river only to find the waters just as muddy here as in the West.

I'd been in Japan for thirteen months, Korea for eleven. The 1980s had closed and the '90s had begun. Yet I still wasn't ready to call it a day. I reasoned there had to be at least one Grandmaster guru who was worth the oxygen he breathed. So far I'd heard of two; the living legend Aaryan Ravi in India and a guy in Shanghai, Kuan-Ti, said to be the greatest martial arts exponent alive. I'd try Shanghai; it was nearer and anyway China was communist. There should be no sordid commercial exploitation of the martial arts there.

I wrote to Kuan-Ti, hoping someone in his dojo could read English, and called Alan, who told me of an English school in the city. Four weeks later, after a lot of hassle obtaining a three-month visa, I bought a ticket for a second-class ferry ploughing east across the China Sea to the great port of Shanghai.

China was the toughest three months of them all. Two days after arriving I was scammed by a moneychanger on the street who, though I watched him like a hawk, finessed in an incredible sleight-of-hand a few large denomination notes into small ones. It was a portent of things to come.

Kuan-Ti was another guru who had built an awesome reputation on choreographed moves and not much else. What's more, the guy was militantly commercial. I saw no sign of equality and the brotherhood of the proletariat in Kuan-Ti's little corner of the communist paradise. His fees were sky-high, while the wages at the English language school were abysmal, and for three months my diet was even worse than it had been in Korea; twice I ate dog and was glad of it.

Towards the end of my sojourn in China I decided it was time for a reckoning.

After close to two and a half years in Asia I was in a mineshaft of debt so deep it would take me years to pay it off. And on top of the debt and discomfort, the bruising and bad diets, the constant antipathy and alienation, I hadn't found what I was looking for. Not one master who inspired me, not one training ethic that made pragmatic sense.

I had one last throw of the dice.

I would go to India and train under the great Aaryan Ravi.

Everywhere I'd been, people had mentioned Ravi's name in whispers. The guy was a living legend. He had been everywhere, Korea, the Philippines, China, Japan, to master all the advanced secrets of the world's most lethal fighting systems. It was said he could render a man unconscious with the lightest tap on a pressure point. Yet he was also said to be a master of the healing arts, a philosopher and a philanthropist. If there was one man who could be my mentor and my teacher, it had to be Ravi. I raised another loan and faxed New Delhi. The return fax arrived two days before my visa ran out.

I took a flight to Bombay, via Taiwan, before taking the bus across the city to the great Victorian, neo-gothic railway station — the Gateway to India — where I stood in line for two hours to buy an economy-class ticket to New Delhi. The train, arriving an hour late, was a steam locomotive with an endless string of carriages, every one jam-packed with humanity and livestock, the compartments overflowing with goats, live chickens, women in colourful saris and men in turbans. Scores of people squatted on the carriage roofs, some even on the couplings between the carriages.

Swept forward on the tide of people rushing to get on the train, only to be shoved back by the surging ebb of those getting off, I managed to scramble myself a window seat in a compartment crammed with passengers in possession of bicycles, an enormous collection of umbrellas, sacks of millet, a few chickens, a lame goat and a greenhouse door. Inches from my nose were the bare, non-too-clean feet of people sitting in the luggage racks above me; below others lay beneath the wooden bench on which I was sitting. The guy in the ticket office had said it would take fourteen hours to reach New Delhi. It was going to be an interesting ride.

In fact the journey took fifty-two hours and by its end I was so dehydrated and overpowered by the smell of sweat, tobacco, hashish, chicken shit and goat's piss, I swapped my camera for a drink of tea in a rough, red-clay cup hawked by one of the innumerable tea vendors singing 'Chai! Chai!' along the tracks. The train occasionally moved so slowly that people had gotten off and walked ahead to wait for it to catch up; it unaccountably stopped for hours in the middle of an endless, baking plain and many of the passengers had alighted to cook rice at the side of the track, only to be left behind when the train started up again.

When, finally, we limped into New Delhi station, I dragged the map I'd been faxed from my backpack and threaded my way through a labyrinth of garbage-strewn alleys and dusty side streets to the front entrance of the holy of holies — the Mecca of the martial arts — Aaryan Ravi's dojo.

My heart sank.

If the dojo was not what I'd expected, even less so was Ravi. The guy was short, podgy and wearing a pair of Ray-Ban sunglasses.

Right then I knew I'd come full circle, that the train ride from hell had brought me to the same place I had started out from over two years earlier. Ravi was an Indian version of Seung.

I struggled to maintain an open mind; it was a mistake to rush to judgement; the guy had such a fabulous reputation there *had* to be some substance in the stories about him. But deep down — I knew.

I stuck it out for a month, just to make sure I wasn't being prejudiced. I found a cheap hostel in an area populated by mutilated beggars and skinny kids hawking everything from their sisters to sham Swiss watches, and turned up for training every day. But I knew with total certainty that what Ravi had to teach me wasn't worth my time, the final straw falling when the tubby little Indian mounted a display of martial arts for a local photojournalist.

Dressed in a pair of Calvin Klein underpants, Ravi put on a tape of Madonna's *Like a Virgin* and began prancing around the dojo in front of me, the journo, and a congregation of awestruck admirers. The assembled disciples were clapping loudly and the journo's camera clicking madly as Ravi, failing to move in time to the music, smashed a few boards and performed some high-flying kicks; breathlessly stopping now and again to deliver a homily on the virtues of discipline and self-knowledge.

Years afterwards, watching an episode of *The Simpsons* on a domestic flight in Australia in which Homer is stripped to his underpants, I laughed uproariously, reminded of the ludicrous performance. The other passengers must have thought I was nuts.

Later, after the journo had gone and the admirers had dispersed, the guru produced a bottle of Black Label and, while expounding his philosophy of self-discipline and purposeful living, proceeded to get merrily pissed.

I left the next day, heading for the airport and the cheapest flight to Australia.

I had come to the end of my search for the Holy Grail of martial arts. After almost thirty thousand kilometres of hardship I had made an important discovery. There was no Holy Grail. Gurus were an illusion and all the living legends were dead. Yet my quest hadn't been a complete waste of time and money. My experiences and efforts had shown me that what I'd been searching for was not to be found at the head of the river. It was inside me.

And had probably been there all the time.

CHAPTER 14

The Red Centre

THE PLANE banked over Botany Bay, the wheels whining down for the landing at Sydney International. It was my first sight of Australia in almost two and a half years and I felt a huge sense of warmth and wellbeing, like an intergalactic spaceman coming in sight of the mother ship.

I caught the bus to Melbourne; and found my way to Brian's flat. I'd sent him a fax as soon as I knew I was leaving India and he'd offered to put me up for a few days, keen to know what I thought of Aaryan Ravi. I resolved to be diplomatic — I needed a roof over my head — but I needn't have worried. Brian was less interested in hearing what I had to say than in launching into a paean of praise for the little Indian.

Brian couldn't see past all the hype. Not that he was alone in that. Other, sharper guys who journeyed to practise with one of the living legends, though they might see through the bullshit, would be loath to admit they'd wasted their time and money. In self-justification, or as a way of bolstering their own reputations, they too would laud the guru. Either way, Ravi and the others made money out of selling the only real asset they possessed — their inflated opinion of themselves.

Back in the city I thought about calling Lisa, but decided against it. I learnt she had moved in with a new boyfriend and felt a call from me would be more of an embarrassment than a welcomed surprise. Anyway, I had more pressing concerns.

My financial situation was critical, my credit rating at meltdown.

Brian got me casual work on the doors of a couple of pubs but the work was squalid and the pay terrible. There was nothing available in Melbourne, though word was that casinos in Western Australia and the Northern Territory were looking for experienced people. I sent letters and a CV off to pubs and casinos in Darwin, Alice Springs and Perth, adding, for good measure, Cairns, which, like the others, had the advantage of being warm. I'd never liked the cold, and, since my return from Asia, I was feeling it more acutely.

I received only one reply, from the Alice, the security manager at the Casino saying he might have work in a couple of months. I couldn't wait a couple of months. I needed work now. I checked my finances. All the money I had in the world amounted to exactly the airfare to Alice Springs.

I decided that was a good omen. I could get myself there. After that … well … getting work would be down to my powers of persuasion. That, and fate.

Brian thought I was crazy, flying to the Centre in the faint hope of a maybe … perhaps … sometime. But Brian, a good bloke in his way, didn't get it. I was riding the waves; I couldn't wait for the 'right' wave to come along in my life. I needed the work; I needed the money and it was, I realised with a shock, the only thing I could do.

I caught the flight, everything I possessed in the world accompanying me in one small roll bag. I was wrong about my money. Arriving at Alice Springs I discovered I had fifty cents. Not enough for the bus. It was a twelve-kilometre hike to the casino, easy enough except it was the middle of the day and over forty Celsius. Well, if nothing else, I'd escaped from the cold.

Arriving at the big, squat building I found an outside tap, stripped to the waist, had a rinse and changed my sodden shirt for a fresh one. I was set. I marched through the glass doors into reception.

She had one of the most beautiful faces I had ever seen, a perfect oval, with high cheekbones and eyes of cobalt blue. Her hair was cut in the latest fashion and, though I was no expert, she looked like she knew what she was doing with make-up. It was the kind of face *Vogue* featured on their front cover.

'Yes? Can I help you?' The tone was haughty. I wasn't surprised. Women who looked like her saw no need to be nice to blokes who looked like me.

'I'm here to see the security manager.'

'Do you have an appointment?'

'No.'

'He doesn't see anyone without an appointment.' Her delivery was devoid of any compromise.

'He wrote to me. Said there was the chance of a job. So here I am.'

'But he doesn't know you're coming.'

'No.'

She looked contemptuous. 'Then he won't see you.'

'Look, I need a break. I've been training in Asia for two years and all the money I had in the world I spent flying here from Melbourne.'

Disdain turned to curiosity. 'You flew here on an off-chance?'

'Yes. That's why I need you to get me in to see him.'

She considered me for a moment. 'Even if you get in there,' she said doubtfully, 'he won't give you a job. Not just like that. He's a hard man.'

'Just give me the chance. That's all I'm asking.'

She shrugged, turning to the console on her desk. 'It's not much of a chance,' she murmured. She pressed an extension number, spoke quietly for a few seconds and replaced the receiver. 'He says he'll give you five minutes but you'll have to wait.'

'Sure, that's okay. Thanks.'

'You've been training in Asia?'

I nodded. 'Martial arts.'

We talked intermittently for almost an hour before I was summoned into the office of the security manager. I was there twenty minutes.

She looked up as I walked back into reception. 'Well?'

'I start tonight.'

'Really.' She was impressed.

'Yeah. And thanks for your help. I'm Red, by the way.' I held out my hand. She shook it.

'Simone.'

'I'll see you later, Simone.' I crossed the reception to retrieve my roll bag.

'Look, do you have anywhere to stay tonight?'

I turned. 'No.'

'I've got a spare room. My shift finishes in half an hour. If you stick around, I'll take you to my place. You can sleep there.'

I was there three weeks and never once slept in the spare room; never even saw it. The moment we walked through the door of her flat it was on. She was voracious.

Afterwards, languorously lying back in her bed, I smiled as I thought about what Brian would have said if he could see me now, sexually sated and already employed. No doubt he would have said it was pure, bloody luck.

I was disinclined to believe in luck, but I had to admit that this time I'd come up not just smelling of roses but smelling of the whole frigging florist shop. *This is living,* I thought. *It doesn't get better than this.*

Three weeks later the smell of the flowers had turned putrid.

The job was a shock. I'd expected it to be tough, but the frequency of confrontations surprised me. Most nights I was involved in disputes of one form or another and though they weren't all physical, they were always heated.

Simone too was something of a surprise. For someone so good-looking she was, I discovered, impenetrably stupid: swirling lazily behind that beautiful face was a mind as vacuous as an empty wheelie-bin. Her conversation consisted exclusively of the film stars and celebrities featured in the gossip magazines she devoured daily. For Simone, if it wasn't about women's fashions or the latest antics of some Hollywood cretin, then it didn't matter or it didn't exist.

A couple of weeks into our brief relationship, she told me she had never, ever, read a book. She seemed proud of it and I knew I had to get away.

By then I was chatting up a croupier called Kathy. The movie *Pretty Woman* had just been released and Kathy was a dead ringer for Julia Roberts. The thing was, Kathy didn't *know* she looked like Julia Roberts, and behind her gorgeous brown eyes I could detect both wit and intelligence. After we'd spent a couple of weeks together, she asked me to move in with her. She didn't need to ask twice.

I told Simone the truth; I reckoned I owed her that much. She was strangely sanguine about it and offered to drive me and my stuff over to Kathy's place where she dropped me with a friendly farewell peck on my cheek. After that she never spoke to me again and whenever I found myself in a room with her she acted like I wasn't there. I really didn't understand her at all.

Kathy was the only good thing about my time in the Territory.

Kathy, and the sunsets.

Most evenings I would stand at her door watching the sun go down in a blaze of glory, never before realising there could be so many shades of red and orange; watching, as the dark, desert night descended, the sky swept by a wash of pinks and purples and violets before dissolving to a lavender haze so fine and diaphanous I could almost smell it.

As indigo segued into deepest black, I would turn inside to change into my collar and tie before setting off for another night of hand-to-hand combat.

It was a depressing existence. I knew I was lucky to have the job but it wasn't much of a job to feel lucky about. I was earning the same money I'd been getting in Melbourne three years earlier. And that, even with my $42 a fortnight Veterans Affairs pension, was never going to get me out of my black hole of debt. Not ever.

My working life was spent in a place where it was impossible to tell day from night: an artificially lit aircraft hangar filled with polished jarrah tables and green baize cloth, with garishly flashing lights and the moronic sound of crashing levers and tinkling coins, the atmosphere laced with greed and expectation, the bars around the periphery of the pit noisy with drinkers banking on being winners. All of whom, before the night was out, would still be losers; some of whom would be turning ugly and rancorous.

A few punters, the rare few, came prepared to lose a couple of hundred dollars as the price of a good night out. Win or lose they would enjoy themselves and leave, probably pissed, certainly noisy, but definitely no trouble. These were the adults.

As for the rest — well — I didn't get it. Did they come to a casino expecting to make money? Had they never heard that the odds favoured the house? Or did they expect Lady Luck to shift the odds in their favour for the night? If so then they might as well believe in the Tooth Fairy.

In the university of a casino floor, one of the first things I learnt was that the banal *lingua franca* of drunken threats was the same no matter where I was. I'd heard it all before in the clubs of Melbourne, though the first time someone snarled, 'I know where you live, shithead,' this being the Alice, they probably *did* know where I lived. That worried me until I thought about it and realised that the real impact of any threat lay with me, the recipient, and not the issuer. It occurred to me that threats were issued by people who had lost control. By reverting to threats they were acknowledging their loss of influence. In a wry way, a threat was almost a compliment — proof they were struggling to deal with the situation at hand.

How I responded to, 'I'll be waiting for when you finish work, you bastard. I'll be in the car park, with six of me mates,' was my choice. I could worry about it, I could react violently — or I could give a dismissive snort and stonewall.

I preferred the latter; saying nothing, my face so impassive that the inevitable follow-up was, 'You hear what I said, dickhead?' Even then I didn't respond.

People who make threats are very, very stupid.

The loudmouthed aggressors told me what they intended to do

and thereby gave away the most crucial advantage in any combat. Surprise.

Usually, in the face of my silence and lack of reaction, the threats died and they forfeited all control of the situation.

It was a very powerful experience.

Even when a threat did translate into action and one of the loudmouths threw a punch, they would usually fall over their own feet. The people who issued threats generally lacked the technical skill to make good on what they'd threatened and when, on the odd occasion, someone did know what they were doing, they generally voiced their intentions and gave away the game before they'd even started.

It would have been laughable if it hadn't all been so stupidly pathetic.

On the other hand, the hard cases who, drunk and losing, erupted into violence without warning, were not funny at all. These were not young bucks pushing the bouncers to see how far they could go; these were men — and a few women — who *liked* violence, who came to the casino as much for a fight as for anything else.

Though rare, the genuine fights were brutal: often there was blood, sometimes broken bones. And once more I learnt that prescribed moves in a dojo against a compliant opponent bore almost no relevance in this real-world fighting. Martial art skills were definitely an asset, but only if they could be adjusted to fit the situation.

Here, when the brutality did erupt, I needed to immediately control my adrenalin dump — the sudden rush of epinephrine triggered by fear — drawing on all the useful aspects of the 'flight or fight' syndrome while revoking those that could freeze or debilitate me. I was employing skills that bore no relation to the more balletic moves of traditional martial arts. It was a mental thing almost as much as it was physical; I needed to win more than the other guy.

So I won.

But it was never pretty.

It seemed to me I was constantly in combat, whether physical or verbal, and that much of the reason for this was the high profile nature of the other bouncers. Most of them were steroid-pumping, bodybuilding goons with ponytails, pierced ears and tatts; their ethic of 'in-yer-face-so-don't-fuck-with-me,' screaming provocation.

High profile appeared to be the policy of the casino and was definitely the preferred posture of my supervisor, Safan Milovanovic, known, unsurprisingly, as Milo. He was the biggest of the steroid pumpers, standing at one hundred and ninety centimetres and weighing at least a hundred and twenty kilos. He had livid blue tats on his thick neck, a long ponytail and a face like a hog on heat.

I was not his favourite person, not only because Milo hadn't been involved in my selection but also because I adopted the low profile approach.

'There's nothing wrong in being low-key,' I said to Milo. We were in the small dingy room that served as the supervisors' office. 'The adults appreciate courtesy and quiet; some of them even comment on it.'

'Adults? They're all fuckin' adults.'

'I wish,' I sighed.

'You go around the place being polite and the punters think you're piss-weak.'

'It's a free country; they can think what they like. Makes no difference to me.'

Milo's eyes narrowed. 'Being a pretty-please wanker encourages the bastards to have a crack at you 'cos they think you're a pussy, then me and the others got to come runnin' over to bail you out.'

'It's actually the other way around,' I said.

'The other way round?' Milo had a black gift for making a statement or asking a question in such a way that everything sounded like a violent accusation. His ability to blend stupidity with arrogant superiority was extraordinary.

'Look, the bulk of the dramas in this place are caused by people so pissed with booze and pissed off at losing they just lash out at anything ... but especially the nearest symbol of authority. These guys are so out of it they'd take on a thousand pound gorilla if it were dressed in a collar and tie. They're not selecting who they have a crack at.'

'Whaddaya mean?'

'I mean we all get caught up in that from time to time. It's the others you need to focus on.'

'What fuckin' others?'

'The ones who come looking for trouble. Now admittedly, some of them think I'm an easy mark and take a crack. But they're stupid. I know they're stupid because they underestimate me. So, I have surprise on my side, and by the time they realise they're wrong, they're outside the door wondering how the hell they got there. Which means that, in the time I've been here, you and the others have only had to cross the floor twice to help me out. I, on the other hand, have had to go running across the floor more than a dozen times to pitch in for you guys.'

'Fuck off.'

'It's true, Milo. Your high profile attracts the blokes who come looking for trouble; the ones who know what they're doing, who know how to fight. They rarely bother with me; I'm too low profile, not enough of a challenge. But you and the others — hell, they can't resist it. You're a magnet for shit.'

The porcine face glowered, the little eyes hardening with malice.

I was pleased with myself; I'd made a cogent case for low profile security on the casino floor. I told Kathy about it the following day, just before she went to work.

I didn't see a lot of Kathy.

Often I'd get back only a couple of hours before she was due on her shift. I'd crawl into bed and we'd make warm, sleepy love. We were hips that passed in the night; we had fun together and beneath the beauty lay a clear perception. Like many croupiers she was intelligent and observant, though most punters never saw beyond the boobs.

Her reaction when I told her of the conversation was surprising.

She gave me a quizzical look.

'What?' I queried.

'You think that was wise? Talking to Milo like that?'

'Why not? I made a good case.'

'You may have made a good case. You may also have made a bad enemy.'

'Yeah, but I'm right, aren't I?'

'Sometimes being right is less important than being safe and happy in your work.' She kissed me. 'I have to go.'

I watched her walk down the path. The trouble with living with a perceptive woman was … well … she was perceptive.

I had an uncomfortable feeling she had just made a valid point.

CHAPTER 15

Alice Springs

'WHY DO you fight?' For once our days off had coincided and Kathy and I were lying in bed. 'I mean,' she went on, 'why do men fight?'

'Because they're still boys, they haven't grown up.'

'So, why do boys fight?'

'Testosterone, mainly. They're slaves to their hormones; can't keep their emotions under control.'

'That's it? Hormones?'

'Sure. Why are teenage girls so bitchy? Same reason. But by the time a guy reaches nineteen or twenty he's pretty well learnt to take control of his emotions. So the reasons for fighting disappear or, at least, can be handled differently.'

'So what are they? The reasons I mean?'

I thought about it.

'Ego, lust, anger, greed, revenge. Oh yeah, and some guys enjoy it. But they're probably sick.'

'So which one of those is yours?'

I laughed. 'I knew you were going to ask me that. None of them.'

'None of them?'

'No. I fight out of necessity.'

She laughed, a tinkling sound I loved to hear. 'Necessity? That's a cop-out.'

'Yeah? Why?'

'Because it means you only do it because you have to. That you'd run away if you could.'

'That's right.'

She frowned at me. 'You would?'

'Of course. What, do you think I'm stupid? If I could avoid a fight I would.'

'Even if some people thought you were a coward?'

'Yes. If, under those circumstances, I worried about what other people thought, then my ego would really be out of control. Wouldn't it? The best reaction to the threat of violence is avoidance. Run like crazy the other way.'

'But you don't run away.'

'Because I'm paid not to.'

'So you fight because you're paid to fight.'

I thought about it. 'No, not really. I fight from necessity. I'm paid to keep the peace … to stop other people fighting. To do that effectively I have to know what I'm doing.'

'Fighting fire with fire.'

'Yeah, if you like.'

'So none of the reasons like ego or revenge or whatever come into it for you?'

'Definitely not. The most important thing you learn in martial arts is to take the emotion out of combat. You let emotions like that in and you're bound to lose.'

She smiled at me. 'You know, you remind me of one of those Japanese warriors. What are they called? Sam …?'

'Samurai.'

'Yes. You're a Samurai.'

I shook my head. 'I don't think so. The Samurai had masters for whom they fought. I'm more like the Ronin.'

'What are they?'

'Ronin were Samurai who had no master. They were on their own; no masters and no permanent means of support. They wandered from place to place teaching self-defence where they could and hiring themselves out for dangerous jobs whenever they had the opportunity.'

'Ronin. Never heard of it.'

'Literally translated it means waveman. A soldier tossed about, as by the waves of the sea.'

She laughed; again that tinkling sound. 'Some wave, Red. Surfing you this far inland. Washing you up as a bouncer in a casino in Alice Springs.'

'Don't think I care for the washed-up bit,' I said, starting to feel a little sorry for myself.

She touched my arm tenderly. 'No, no, I didn't mean it like that.' She appraised me and after a moment said, 'But you do know you could do better, don't you? Much, much better.'

I grunted. Another of Kathy's painful shafts of insight.

* * *

Leaning against the main bar a couple of nights later I surveyed the room. Tonight it looked like being a quiet, easy shift.

'Red?'

I swung around to the voice behind me. There was no mistaking the squat figure and ugly face, the skin as pockmarked and welted as a waffle. 'Jocko? Bloody hell, what are you doing here?'

We shook hands vigorously, and for the moment I forgot I didn't much care for the bloke. 'How long has it been?'

The ugly face contorted in thought. 'Must be four years, or is it five? So what you doing? I heard you got out of the army.'

'Yeah. You were right. I never made officer. Had the chance but …' I shrugged, 'reckoned I could do better. So now I'm a bouncer here.' Jocko laughed at my joke. 'What about you? You still in the army?'

'Nah. I got out more'n two years ago. Got pissed off with all the bullshit. I'm in private security now. Working for one of the mining companies. Most of 'em have their own private armies,' he cackled, 'though they don't call 'em that. Security consultants, that's what we are.'

'You want a drink?' I asked.

'Aye. I'll have a whisky.'

I ordered Jocko a double and myself a ginger beer. 'So, is it a good life, then, this private security?'

'Aye, it's okay. Some bullshit, but nowhere near as much as the fookin' army. And the pay's terrific. Plenty of work too; Africa, Indonesia, PNG. You want to give it a go, Red. They'd hire you in a heartbeat. Hell, there's so much work in PNG they'd hire you even if you was in a wheelchair.' He cackled again.

'So what brings you to Alice Springs?'

'Me and a couple of lads been checking out a facility over the border in WA. Drove over here for a bit of life.' He gazed around balefully. 'Looks like we wasted our fookin' time.'

'Wait for the weekend. Then it makes the Shat at Holsworthy look like Mother Teresa's parlour.'

We talked for almost an hour. Jocko, once the whisky took effect, was into talking about old times. 'You remember that recon we did on the island?'

I nodded. 'How could I forget it?'

'I gotta tell you something about that night, something I never told anyone ...'

Over Jocko's shoulder I saw Milo gesturing at me from across the pit. 'Look, Jocko, I'm sorry, that's my boss wanting me. Don't go away. I'll see what he wants and be right back. Okay?'

Jocko nodded drunkenly. 'No worries. I'm going for a piss.'

'What the fuck you doing?' Milo demanded. 'You know it's against company policy to drink on duty. I could have you fired.'

I took a deep breath and said, levelly, 'What, for drinking ginger beer? That's all I've been having. You can check with the barmaid. Who, incidentally, has been doing good business serving the bloke with me double Black Labels.'

Milo gave me a dark look. It was one of his favourites. 'So why are you propping up the bar with a punter. You should be doing your job.'

The author (right) with his brother,
mother and sisters. Buchan 1966.

In Mrs Gannon's
class. St Patrick's
College, Sale 1975.

17 years old.
Kapooka 1981.

With a few of the lads. Penang 1985.

Back from the Dojo with Kat. Tokyo 1990.

ABC-783
Alice Springs

Lasseter's Casino became the site of a violent brawl early this morning when two bouncers turned against each other. The dispute resulted in one of the bouncers being rushed to the Emergency Department of Alice Springs Community Hospital. Police are investigating the incident.

Transcript of an ABC news bulletin, 1991.

Morning jog. Lae, Papua New Guinea 1992.

Blindfold wrestling
with an instructor
from the Special Task
Force. Pretoria,
RSA 1994.

Nelson Mandela's Presidential Protection Unit -
the author is on Mandela's right. Pretoria, RSA.

Caveat

Covering

Facsimile Transmission Cover Sheet

Transmission Details		Document Details	
Serial Number:	**Date and Time of Transmission:**	**Reference:**	
From: TPS HEREFORD	**Fax Number:** 01432 35▮	**Subject:** KONTACT TRG	
To: MR R REDENBACH	**Fax Number:** 0027 12 ▮		
		Total number of pages including this cover sheet	1

Authorizing Officer	Transmit Operators
Rank, Name and Appointment: ▮▮▮	**Rank/Grade and Name:**
Signature: ▮▮▮	**Signature:**

Message/Remarks:

HQ Hereford Garrison
Stirling Lines
Hereford HR2 6HF

Rob,

Thanks for the reports on the Kontact course students. The course was very well received by all, especially the more senior members (who can be quite cynical of new techniques – but not this time!). I am interested in running a 5 day course, similar to that just gone, before the end March or latest v. early April 96. I am not sure of number – short lead time accepted!

PS Pse note address top right.

Covering

Caveat

Classification

[Thanks for the reports on the Kontact course students. The course was very well received by all, especially the more senior members (who can be quite cynical of new techniques – but not this time!). I am interested in running a 5 day course, similar to that just gone, before the end March or latest v. early April 96. I am not sure of numbers – short lead time accepted!]

A hand-written facsimile from the Second in Command of 22 SASR after the first Kontact course at Stirling Lines.

Brecon Beacons, looking from the highest point of Pen-y-Fan (2907 feet) to Cribyn (2608 feet). Wales 1996.

Members of the Los Angeles FBI SWAT team participating in Kontact training. California 1996. (Photo courtesy: US National Tactical Officers Assoc.)

Nelson Mandela thanks the author for his contributions to Close Personal Protection. Presidential Estate 1997.

From first date to wedding in 12 days. Johannesburg 1997.

Mandela says farewell shortly before the author and his family depart for Australia, 1998.

SOCOG's one-armed
combat instructor.
1st Commando Base.
Randwick 1999.

Members of the Dutch Police in action -
after receiving Kontact training at the
Ossendrecht Academy. Netherlands 2003.

Liam, Cuan, Reilly, Brontë, Blake, Natasha and
the ex-bouncer. Gold coast 2003.

A lighter moment during a two-week personal security course for volunteers from UNICEF and World Vision. Kenya 2005.

Happy to be alive - a few hours after being ambushed en route to BIAP. Baghdad 2005.
(The hole in the top right-hand section is from one of dozens of shots fired during the attack.)

A caricature by Jeff Hook.

'I am doing my job. I'm keeping an eye on the pit while being pleasant to a customer. Anyway, it's not like we're busy tonight. There's practically more of us than there is of them.'

'Who is he anyway?'

'He's a mate from the army.'

'They let little turds like that in the army? Some fucking army. Anyway, I want you in the front bar. We're short-handed and there may be trouble.'

'Okay.' I turned to signal Jocko I'd be back. The place at the bar was empty.

'Now,' Milo snarled, 'not next fucking week.'

I shrugged. 'Okay.'

Whatever trouble was brewing in the front bar was inside Milo's head; the place was as quiet as a cathedral. I remained there until my break then went to see if Jocko was still around. He was nowhere to be seen, either at the tables or in any of the bars. I was vaguely disappointed.

In a curious way I had enjoyed bumping into him. The fact was, Jocko had gone up in my estimation. Compared to the company I was presently keeping, the little ferret had balls; he had gone out on armed patrol and had neither stuffed up nor fallen over. By contrast, Milo and most of the others were total idiots. They talked a good fight, but whether they'd have cut it in the jungle at night … well … I doubted that a lot.

I wandered upstairs to the administration corridor, past the scruffy broom cupboard that served as Milo's office and past the staff canteen that was dominated by two things I couldn't stand: the place was always thick with cigarette smoke, and a big-screen television flickered full-blast twenty-four seven. I never used the place. Two doors further on was the security-camera control room. I knocked and entered.

As usual, Tim was hunched over a video monitor. He was a thin, skinny guy in his early twenties, totally besotted with video technology. I had recently heard the term 'geek' for the first time and knew immediately it had been coined for someone like Tim. Milo and some of the others made fun of him, pushing him about and generally bullying him. All of which, I thought, was really stupid. If anyone had the power on the casino floor it was thin, weedy Tim. It was his cameras that caught Milo and the others occasionally selling pills to selected customers at the door, that detected most of the big rent-a-fists playing pocket billiards, that caught Milo picking his nose behind a pillar.

Tim had the goods on all of them.

I liked the peace of the darkened room with its bank of silently flickering, black-and-white monitors on the wall in front of Tim's desk. It was a sanctuary, an island of quiet in a sea of oafishness. Tim hardly ever spoke, leaving me to my thoughts … and to watching videotapes of past confrontations.

'How you going Tim?' I said, sitting down at a bench on the far wall behind him and slotting a videotape into a player.

From the other side of the shellback came a squeaky, 'Yeah, I'm okay.'

I turned to the monitor, my thoughts on Jocko as I watched a rerun of the previous evening come up on screen. I'd been involved in a commonplace confrontation and I wanted to see what had happened and learn from it; the fact that the casino recorded the fights on the floor was one of the few fringe benefits of my crap job.

The guy, big, drunk and convinced he was being cheated, had attacked a croupier. I had cannonballed in, needing to restrain the guy quickly, always the hardest part of the job.

In my experience restraint and control were relatively easy to practise in a dojo: although opponents would struggle to avoid being restrained, it was rare they were prepared to bite your ear off. Not so in the casino. I knew trying to restrain a prehistoric humanoid who was bigger, stronger, and far thicker — and therefore far more impervious to pain — than me, would always involve me in a degree of hurt; my only recourse was to control where and how much I got hurt.

In this instance I had grabbed the guy's hair and pulled him off the croupier. The guy had turned and I'd let go. For a moment it looked like he would go quietly — then he'd started swinging. I had flinched away from the blow, so that most of its force glanced high off my head, before stepping in to wrap my fingers behind his collarbone as I dropped my centre of gravity and wrenched downwards before driving a knee into the peroneal nerve of his thigh. As he went down I grabbed the belt of his trousers and dragged the bastard out of the casino.

I watched the video dispassionately, looking for where or how I could have done better. I watched it again, half my mind on the last time Jocko and I had met. I grinned as I remembered — the Hong Kong Bar in Penang ... the night I had decked the toothless mongrel. That had been a nice strike. The guy had given me some warning, had made that move I could count on before he made his move.

Something resonated in my brain. I reran the video footage I had just watched. Yes, there it was. The punter had also made a move before he made his move. It was a slight one, dropping his left shoulder before swinging at me.

I rifled through the tapes and played other recordings of confrontations. And when I looked for them, there they were — in every case the other guy had made a move before he made a move — a shift of the head, a blink of the eyes, a twitch of the shoulders.

When my shift finished I returned to the control room and spent an hour watching not only my own fights and scuffles but some of the other guys' too. It was always the same: a person about to escalate from verbal to physical made a move before they made a move.

I left at dawn, deep in thought. In all my years in martial arts training, no one had ever told me that; no one ever said to look out for my opponent signalling his intention. Of course many instructors had spoken of being aware of telegraphed strikes during a bout, but this was different; this was about the transition from possible force to actual violence. I wondered what else I'd never been taught or missed along the way.

I stopped halfway across the car park to gaze up at the vision of a sky streaked with pink, stationary in those few moments when the light was pale and tranquil before the hammer of ~~the~~ sun beat the land to a living hell.

Years before I had overheard my sister summarising our father's life ... piece by piece she dissected his failures and measured his worth by what he *hadn't* done. My sister then critiqued our mother and declared that she too had failed to do anything of note. At the time her evaluation had seemed off-handed, but a seed was sown: I was going to protect against the day when *I* would look back and pass judgment on my own journey.

Back at Kathy's place, instead of crawling into bed beside her I sat in an armchair in the lounge staring out of the window. Kathy got up a couple of hours later and sleepily wandered in. 'You okay?' she murmured.

'Yes, I'm fine. I've finally got it.'

'Got it? Got what?'

'The way out.'

'Way out of what?'

'This place; this crap job. I can't stay here for ever, Kath, I'll go nuts.'

She smiled as she sat down. 'I could have told you that. So what are you going to do?'

'I'm going to write my own unarmed combat program and travel the world teaching it.'

Her eyes widened. 'Wow. Sounds impressive. When did you decide this?'

'I think it's been kicking around in my subconscious for ages, but things happened last night that suddenly made me realise I've got all I need to teach something really different. Special.'

'But aren't there lots of people teaching that kind of combat thing already?'

'Not what I have in mind. The program I want to teach will be for the sole benefit of the participants — not the spectators. And definitely not as an ego-boost for the trainer.'

'So what's different about that?'

'Are you kidding? I spent too many years and more money than I could afford in shonky, shallow, vanity-driven, martial arts programs whose point was purely to make the participants *look* good — and the trainers rich.

They were all, basically, about showing off. Hell, with all the choreographed moves and techniques, we could have been on *Dancing with the Stars*. From my experience, most martial arts are no more than show business.

My program will be different. My program will be for people who train to improve — not to impress.'

'But show biz sells, Red. People buy into all that glitz and glamour. They buy the sizzle, not the sausage.'

'Yeah I know that. But I'm not going to be pitching it at trendy fitness centres or to get written up in fashion magazines. I'm going to sell it to the people who really understand and value unarmed combat: elite law enforcement agencies, special forces in the military.'

'So how can you sell to people like that?'

'Only one way: make my program world-class. Genuinely world-class. The people I'm selling to would see through garbage in an instant.'

She stood up and smiled down at me. 'It sounds great, Red. So when do you start?'

'I've started already.' I stood up. 'But I have a way to go yet.'

'Yeah?'

I nodded. 'If I'm going to sell to elite special forces, first I'll have to devise the program and then I'll have to gain their trust. And to get their trust I need their respect. And to get their respect I have to have experience — lots and lots of experience. I need to be in a position where I can put my program into regular use; in a place where I can teach it to other people.'

'Sounds like you're going to be moving on.'

I caught the note of regret in her voice and kissed her on her cheek. 'Yeah, but not for a while yet.'

I started carrying a small notebook around with me, jotting down ideas and key points I thought should be included in my program — and the things that should definitely be excluded.

I spent hours in the video room studying the silent, flickering images; analysing the body language and the move it preceded — a head-butt, punch, kick or even the throwing of a drink — the ubiquitous move before the move. I watched the other bouncers, noting the techniques that worked and those that didn't.

One poor bastard, a new guy, brainwashed by all the martial arts techniques he'd learnt, spent four minutes trying to quell a drunk who, taking advantage of Happy Hour's dollar drinks, had quaffed ten rum and cokes before vomiting all over the bar. After four long minutes the new guy was still struggling, his face shining with sweat, his hands and shirt smeared with the drunk's vomit. Finally, one of the old hands, grabbing the punter by the belt, dragged him from the bar. The new guy, unsure what to do with his hands, shuffled off to the staff washroom wailing that the drunk's moves had been 'artificial'.

I scribbled in my notebook that in fact the drunk's moves and responses had been real-world; it was the techniques learnt in the dojo that were artificial.

After a few weeks Milo began noticing how much time I was spending in the control room.

'It's my own time,' I said evenly.

'Are you and that little pisser Tim giving each other blow jobs in there?'

'That's right. We're getting married soon.'

Milo's piggy eyes narrowed. 'You need to watch yourself. Your six-month staff evaluation is coming up soon. You want a good one, you'd better think about getting on the right side of me.'

'Why? I do my job. Anyway, my job spec says I have to be polite to the punters; it doesn't say anything about being nice to you.'

I knew I was pulling the tiger's tale talking like this, but I didn't care.

'You'd better be, all the same.'

'Don't tell me you want a blow job?'

'Fuck off. You know what I mean. You want a good appraisal you'd better decide what it's worth — you haven't paid me a cent so far. If you want a good evaluation, I want fifty per cent of your next month's salary.'

I could hardly believe what I was hearing. 'I'm supposed to be *paying* you to keep this job? You expect *me* to pay *you* for a good evaluation?'

'You want to stay employed and out of hospital — yeah.'

'The pay is crap to begin with, and now you want me to hand half of it over to you.' If anyone deserved a smack in the head, it was Milo. 'It'll never happen.'

'Yeah? We'll see.' He turned and walked away.

That night there was a major confrontation in the main bar. I had no idea how it started, but attracted by the shouts and cursing I raced into the bar. It was ugly; four bouncers, including Milo, against seven, no, eight, drunken punters, the fighting watched by a crowd definitely on the side of the drunks. I waded in, all the while aware of the crowd turning more ugly by the moment. There were about thirty of them, shouting and shimmering with hostility. Should they decide to join in, we bouncers would be in deep shit.

After what seemed an age we managed to get the rioting drunks under control, ejecting them from the bar to gargled threats of, 'We'll be back you bastards. We'll fix you.'

'We were lucky to get away with that,' I panted, turning to Milo after we'd bundled the drunks outside the door. 'If that crowd had got involved we'd have needed to circle the wagons.'

'Bullshit. We'd have handled them.'

'In your dreams. If that lot had got stuck in it would have been Milo's last stand.'

Milo turned on me, his piggy face vicious with hostility. 'I'm fucking sick of you and your smart mouth. You don't shut the fuck up, you're gonna find yourself getting a bashing one night and no one will be bothering to help you out. You get what I'm telling you?'

I couldn't be bothered answering and instead just walked away.

The following night I was on duty in the main bar when three of the ringleaders from the fight stalked in. I felt the hairs on my neck rise. Most people who promised to come back were never seen again. This lot were something else, clearly intent on revenging last night. I recalled Sun Tzu. *Subdue the enemy without fighting.*

Walking up to the leader of the three, I stuck out my hand. 'Listen I just want to say I was really impressed with you last night. You blokes can really fight. Let me buy you all a beer.'

The trio gaped at me as I called the barmaid over and ordered the beers. I watched their eyes darting back and forth between each other, trying to figure their next move. It was obvious they were on the back foot and I guessed they probably hadn't enough intelligence between them to add up to one average IQ.

As the beers arrived, the leader murmured, 'Err, yeah, thanks.' He downed his beer then turned and walked from the bar, followed quickly by his minions.

I was pleased with myself. My satisfaction lasted about twenty minutes.

Milo stormed into the bar. 'What the fuck are you doing?'
'What?'
'Three arseholes from last night come back and you *buy them a beer?* What kind of fucking bouncer are you?'
'A bloody good one. Those clowns got bounced outta here and they didn't even know it. No fuss, no trouble ... no broken bottles or heads. What more do you want?'
'I've just about fucking had it with you, you prick. You're on your last fucking warning.'
'I haven't had my first warning yet,' I said equably.
The porky face turned crimson and for a moment I thought Milo was going to go for me. My jaw tensed as I watched for the move

before the move. It didn't come. I was glad. With a supreme effort Milo turned away.

'That's it … that's fucking it,' he snarled.

I turned to the barmaid, making a 'what's-his-problem' face. 'Now you've done it,' the woman said darkly. 'I've seen him in that mood before. Someone's going to cop it; some poor bastard will get the crap bashed out of them. You'd better watch yourself.'

An hour later I was shocked to see Kathy waving to me from her table. She never acknowledged me in the casino — I had always thought it odd that, while every other woman in the place talked to me, the woman I *had* slept with and the woman I *was* sleeping with, acted like I didn't exist. It was yet another thing about women I didn't understand. I hurried over. 'What?'

'Milo has taken little Tim out the back. He's going to bash him.'

'What for?'

'Tim showed some of the bar staff a video of Milo picking his nose.' I laughed. I couldn't help it. Kathy wasn't amused. 'It's not funny. He's only a kid. Milo will kill him. You've got to stop it.'

'You want me to fight Milo?'

'If it comes to that.' She gave me a look that, under other circumstances, would have shrivelled me to an empty husk. 'You were the one who said you fight out of necessity. Well, this is necessary.'

My heart sank. 'Where is he?'

'In the loading bay out back.'

They were thirty metres from the door, Tim pinned up against the wall and whimpering as Milo, his hand around Tim's windpipe, punched him in the midsection. For a moment I had a vision of a skinny, frightened kid caught in the headlights of a police car, being beaten by a big cop in a paddock in Tassie.

'Leave him alone, you piece of shit.'

Milo turned, letting Tim slump to the ground. 'Oh, come to save your little girlfriend, eh?'

'Just leave him Milo. What the hell's he ever done to you?'

The big bouncer swivelled and kicked the moaning figure viciously. 'Little bastard was showing videos of me to the girls, having a laugh at me scratching my nose.'

I laughed; it sounded like a sharp bark and I wondered where it had come from. 'Scratching your nose, be fucked. You were picking it you dickhead — that's how you jerk off.'

It worked. Milo turned from the crushed figure and marched towards me.

'You fucking bastard. I told you what would happen if you didn't shut that fucking mouth ...'

I watched him in the gloom. I'd seen countless videos of Milo fighting; knew his technique intimately; knew the move he'd make before he made his move.

And there it was, a shift to his left leg before feinting with his left elbow and then striking with his right fist. I came up on my toes and, as Milo made his feint, pivoted and lashed out with my foot, striking for the locked left knee.

There was a sharp crack and Milo screamed. I spun and dropped my hips as Milo staggered; I grabbed the front of his jacket with both hands and slammed him hard into the wall. I heard something crunch as I let go and seized Milo's hair, crashing his face into the unforgiving brickwork. Milo went down howling.

Leaving him on the ground, I moved to Tim and lifted him by his shirt. He was crying.

'Okay, clean yourself up,' I told him. 'Think you can finish your shift?'

He nodded and whispered, 'I think so.'

'Good man.'

I grabbed his arm and half lifted him towards the casino door, which suddenly crashed open, spilling a couple of bouncers, Milo's mates, into the gloom.

'What the fuck happened here?' one demanded.

'Milo had a go at Tim. Now he wishes he hadn't.'

'Yeah.' The man sounded threatening.

'If I were you I'd worry about him.' I nodded at Milo who was clutching his knee and grunting. 'He's going to need transport to the hospital. I don't think he'll be walking for a while.' I helped Tim inside.

Less than an hour later the security manager sent for me. 'I don't appreciate being called out of my home on account of fights between my staff,' he snapped.

'I'm sorry. Do you want to know what happened?'

'I've already been told. You attacked your supervisor and put him in hospital. His kneecap is in pieces, he's got a broken humerus and a cracked cheekbone. I hope you're fucking satisfied.'

'Actually, he was attacking me.'

'I'm not interested. He was your boss, you attacked him and now you're fired. Your money is made up to tonight. Collect it from the cashier's office and get out. You've got ten minutes.'

I shrugged. 'Have it your way.'

Kathy, when she came home, was remorselessly apologetic. 'I'm so sorry. I didn't think you'd get fired. It's all my fault.'

'Forget it, Kath. It was inevitable. You were right. He'd have killed little Tim.'

'Yes, but now the police may be involved. The security manager said you could be charged with aggravated assault.'

'I'll worry about that when it happens.'

I programmed myself to wake at dawn and shortly afterwards heard the swish of tyres outside. I was up in an instant and by the time they began banging on the door I was dressed. I hurried to the door and opened it. There were five of them, headed by a lean, grizzled Senior Sergeant. He was, to quote Banjo, ... *hard and tough and wiry — just the sort that won't say die.*

'You know why we're here?' he growled.

'Yeah.' I stepped outside and closed the door behind me.

'You coming quietly?'

'Yes. This is my girlfriend's house. I don't want any trouble here.'

'Sensible lad. Now, give me your wrists; I'm going to cuff you.'

'No need for that,' I said as evenly as I could. 'Any one of you'd be more than a match for me if I decided to get stupid.'

The Sergeant evaluated me with a seasoned eye, but accepted the challenge.

Without cuffing me they put me in the back of the police car and took me to the station where I was held for most of the day. Kathy came to see me.

'It's my fault you're in here,' she wailed. 'I'm so sorry.' I shook my head. 'Don't be Kath. You didn't do anything wrong.'

'What's going to happen to you?'

'I don't know. No one is talking to me. But the cops aren't bad blokes; it could be worse.'

Twelve hours after I'd been taken to the station I was escorted into the Senior Sergeant's office. 'You can go,' he said. I was surprised.

'What, just like that? No charges?'

'No, some runt called Tim gave us a statement. Told us what happened. Little bastard tried to bribe us.'

I was shocked. 'What, Tim?'

'Said if we let you go, he'd give us video tapes of Milovanovic and some of his mates selling drugs in the casino.' The Sergeant paused. 'Of course, the police can't do deals like that.'

I detected the hint of a sardonic smile hovering around the man's lips. 'But you're letting me go, all the same,' I said quietly.

The Sergeant laughed. 'And Milovanovic is being charged with possession and sale of drugs. He'll be in hospital for a while and when he comes out, he'll be off to court. The bloke's in a world of strife.'

Kathy collected me from the station, got me home, took me to bed and then cooked me a great meal. It was Kathy's preferred solution to most major problems; a root and a rump steak. For the life of me, I couldn't think of a better one.

A couple of days later she returned from the casino with a message from the security manager.

'He says you can have your job back if you want,' she told me.

I wasn't interested. 'He can go and screw himself. Anyway, I'm moving on.'

'When?' I heard the catch in her voice.

'Not for a couple of days yet. I've got a bus to Darwin and then I'm flying across to Papua New Guinea.'

'PNG? What the hell is up there?'

'Experience.'

'What do you mean, experience?'

'There are scores of security companies up there. I'm going to find one and teach them my combat program.'

'You don't have a job to go to?'

'No.'

'You mean you're flying up there on the off-chance?'

'I flew here on the off-chance.'

'Yes, and you never liked it here.'

'I don't know, Kath. It wasn't all bad. I met you.' Stupidly, this was the closest I'd come to telling Kathy how much she meant to me. Since my affair with Lisa in Melbourne, I hadn't said the words 'I love you' to anyone.

'Oh Christ, Red, don't tell me that. You'll have me blubbing like a baby.'

'Come here.' I took her in my arms and held her close. 'It's not for a couple of days,' I said softly. 'Take some time off.'

After a moment she pulled back and gazed into my face. Tears were rolling down her cheeks. 'This is just another wave, right? Taking you up there.'

'I suppose.'

She laughed, despite the tears. 'I think maybe you're just a crazy waveman.'

'Yeah, probably.'

GOING FOR BROKE

1992–1998

THIS WAS MY RISKIEST VENTURE SO FAR.
WHEREAS I'D AT LEAST TRAVELLED TO
KOREA WITH AN INTRODUCTION,
AND TO ALICE SPRINGS WITH THE
HALF-PROMISE OF A JOB,
HERE I'D LANDED KNOWING NO ONE.

CHAPTER 16

Port Moresby

MORE THAN two-thirds of Papua New Guinea is mountainous rainforest, yet what surprised me was how unlike South East Asia it was. I'd been expecting thick green jungle and sharply forbidding mountain ranges; what I saw from the aircraft window was an uninspiring series of drab, brown, treeless hills. Though descending the steps from the plane at Port Moresby was like dropping into a hot swamp; the place was simmering with the equatorial heat I'd known in Malaysia. By the time I crossed the tarmac to the immigration building I was drenched in sweat.

It occurred to me as I rode the bus into Port Moresby that this was my riskiest venture so far. Whereas I'd at least travelled to Korea with an introduction, and to Alice Springs with the half-promise of a job, here I'd landed knowing no one and nothing about the place; the sole prompt to coming a throwaway remark by a half-tanked Jocko at the bar.

I checked in to a hostel, found a local directory and looked up security companies. Hell, Jocko had been right, there were scores of them. I photocopied the list before pondering which ones to go for first — not that it really mattered. It was early afternoon. I bought a street map and set off on foot around the city.

The first two I found were hole-in-the-wall affairs and I gave them a miss. The third had a couple of Land Rovers bearing the company's logo sitting behind a fenced-in compound. I walked in and asked for the owner.

Fifteen minutes later I'd persuaded Bine Menai to hire me as his

149

Operations and Training Manager. Good old Jocko had been right; the security industry in PNG was crying out for expats with a military background. But, I discovered, when it came to the pay, Jocko, that useless, drunken bastard, had been totally wrong. The pay wasn't terrific; indeed, at this firm the pay was non-existent.

Menai told me he had no money to pay me and suggested I work for nothing, at least for the first month or so. After some horse trading, we settled on a deal in which I'd work for no more than I needed to buy groceries and pay my rent. When the deal was finally struck I was working for about fifteen Australian dollars a day.

I started early the following morning, introducing myself to some of the men, checking the vehicles and radios, familiarising myself with the duty rosters, and accompanying a couple of the guards on their rounds. In the afternoon I received a report over the vehicle's radio that one of the men had been attacked. We sped to the spot where an ambulance was already in attendance. The guy was in a bad way, his arm fractured, and a deep, ugly gash in his forehead that was pouring blood and needing at least a dozen stitches.

Though in pain the guard reported how he had been attacked by three men; the one who had opened his forehead was wielding a stone axe, the other two armed with a homemade shotgun and an M16 assault rifle. The guy was shaking with fear and shock.

I saw him off in the ambulance before returning to the Land Rover. Three men, with the last ten thousand years' evolution in weaponry between them, had, without warning, attacked one of my guards who, with no training, had no idea what to do under the circumstance.

Back at base I wasn't impressed by Menai's nonchalant reaction to the attack. 'Happens all the time,' he said blithely.

'Then I need to make sure these men are properly trained.'

I worked every day of the week, creating a training routine based on my experience and the ideas I'd formulated in Alice Springs. It was trial and error; some of my ideas were impractical, some were too advanced for the guys I was training, some were easily understood by one lot of guards but not another. Within weeks I'd mapped out a rough prototype of a program that seemed to work; already I'd started to see improvements. It was a satisfying process.

Bine Menai was satisfied too. I heard from one of the clients that, as the men were now better trained, Menai was putting up his prices. I went to see him. 'I've been here more than a month,' I said. 'I haven't had a day off getting these blokes organised. It's about time I was paid a decent wage.'

'Yes, but I have many debts,' Menai whined.

That makes two of us, I thought.

After about ten minutes I'd managed to raise my salary to the kina equivalent of thirty dollars a day. Menai had outmanoeuvred me. Ordinarily I would have told the tight-arse to stuff it — except that I was getting an opportunity to teach and develop my program.

Menai told me everything would be resolved when he had paid his 'debts'. I doubted it. He was one of those people who lived on the premise, 'You scratch my back and I'll ride on yours.'

I said as much to Chris the next time I saw him in the dojo.

Though it was a bit of a struggle to get there, I'd joined a local dojo to keep in practice, and had met Chris on my third visit. The guy was Canadian, and a competent all-round mixed fighter. He made a living as a pilot, flying supplies in a light aircraft into inaccessible areas of PNG.

He was also a useful contact.

I told him what I was being paid.

'How much?' he yelped. 'What are you, a charity? Listen buddy, if Menai won't pay you a living wage you wanna tell the guy to stick his job where the sun don't shine.'

'Yeah, but at least I'm field-testing my program. And anyway, I don't know if I'll get another job. Someone told me they were crying out for expat security people here and that the money was really good. Well, I haven't seen any sign of it.'

'The money *is* good. Listen, leave it with me. I know a few people in this Godforsaken country. I'll fix you up, buddy. Don't worry about it.'

The next time I saw Chris at the dojo it was about a month later. 'Come and have a drink,' he said.

'I don't have a lot of money on me,' I said, slightly embarrassed.

The big Canuck laughed. 'Don't worry about it. You will have. Soon.' We went to a nearby bar where Chris bought a couple of beers and we found a quiet corner. 'There's this security company,' he began, 'either the biggest or the second biggest in the country. It employs hundreds of guards. The guy running it is an Australian. Tough old dog, but he knows his stuff. He's looking for someone just like you as his Training and Operations Manager.'

'Yeah?'

'He wants to talk to you.'

'That sounds great. But did he talk about money?'

'Sure.' Chris dug into a pocket of his bush shirt, dragged out a scrap of paper and pushed it across the table. 'He says if you're the right guy for the job he'll pay you top dollar. Australian dollars. There.' He pointed.

I stared at the figure. 'A thousand a week?' For the first time in my life I was staring at a good salary. I looked up, suddenly seeing some light at the end of the tunnel.

The job was across the ranges, in Lae.

Chris offered to fly me up the following week.

CHAPTER 17

Lae

LAE WAS a sprawling provincial capital, with maybe 80,000 inhabitants: a tropical mix of mist-covered mountains, coconut plantations, urban town-houses, tin shanties, bare-footed pedestrians and ceasless humidity.

We met in the lounge of the Lae International Hotel. Sandy Warnock was a big, taciturn man who'd been in PNG decades. He told me he had a lot of business interests in the region and wanted someone to manage his security company which, he admitted, would be a hell of a job. The last two candidates had left within weeks. Ten minutes into the meeting he offered me the job at a thousand a week.

'When can you start?' he asked.

'Well, I don't have a contract where I am but I don't want to just walk out on my men. Say a week?'

'Be here in a five days,' Warnock told me. I wasn't sure if I liked the guy, but I was pretty sure I could work with him. His rules were simple: do good work and you kept your job; stuff up and you were out. That was fine by me.

Five days later Chris flew me into the airport where we said goodbye on the tarmac, shaking hands in the bright, sweltering humidity. 'I fly here often,' Chris said, 'so I'll be seeing you.'

'You bet you will. I owe you a few beers for fixing this, Chris. Thanks.'

'No problem. Oh, I almost forgot. I've got something for you.' He moved closer and pressed something cold and heavy into my hand.

'What the hell is this?'

153

'What's it look like? Chopped salami?'

'But what do I want a pistol for?' The barrel of the Smith and Wesson thirty-eight gleamed dully in the bright light.

'Sleep with it under your pillow.'

'You're kidding.'

'No, I mean it, man. You could need it. And here's half a box of ammo.'

I laughed. 'Come on, mate, you make it sound like I'm going into a war zone.'

'Maybe not a war zone, but close enough.'

I began to think that, perhaps, Chris wasn't exaggerating when I saw the two ex-British army Saracen armoured personnel carriers emblazoned with the red, black and white of the company's livery sitting like squat, metal bugs in the company compound, itself surrounded by six-metre chain-link fencing topped by rolls of razor wire. I wondered what kind of security company needed armoured personnel carriers.

I started work immediately, doing what I'd done before, inspecting vehicles and equipment, liaising with clients and accompanying the men on their rounds. Inside twenty-four hours I'd come to the stark realisation that of the three hundred men and one hundred dogs I'd inherited, most of the dogs were the better trained.

Certainly at first glance the men looked the part — self-assured in their uniforms, confident, physically arrogant — but I'd been a bouncer too long to be taken in by hollow crap. Though they appeared competent, as security guards they were pathetic, one of their most alarming features being their penchant for starting fights: not, to my mind, the ideal attribute of a security guard. Even more alarming, having started the fights — the men almost invariably lost them. From day one I started teaching them my program. Over time, their performance got better. My program, which I called for want of anything better, 'full contact partner-resistant body drill and combat strategies', was getting results; the ideas and concepts I'd been developing since my army time were proving themselves in practice. Things were going well. After a session in the storeroom that doubled as my lecture room I collected up the papers on which the supervisors had been making notes. Almost without exception the dozen guys had spelled the word 'contact' with a 'k' — kontact. That was all right; they weren't being employed for their literary skills. But then the penny dropped. There was something about the misspelling — the 'k' gave the word muscularity, a robustness it lacked when spelt properly. I liked it. That would be the name of my program. Instead of my current longwinded title it would be simply that — Kontact.

Not long after coming upon my program's new name there was a commotion in the outer office and the door burst open. It was big Tommy, his dark face glistening with alcohol and rage. He stormed across the floor towards my desk, behind him, framed in the doorway, a startled, open-mouthed Melanie — my secretary — and a couple of other supervisors. 'You bastard,' he yelled, 'you can't fire me, you white prick.'

'Watch your mouth, Tommy. Melanie's in the room.'

'I don't give a fuck. You can't fire me.'

'I can and I did. You were a supervisor. You were supposed to lead by example. I gave you warnings but you didn't listen. I told you, if you were late for your shift any more, or if I caught you sleeping on duty, or drunk — I'd fire you.'

'Everyone sleeps on duty.'

'Not any more they don't. And not everyone was chiselling a percentage of the younger guards' wages out of them.'

'Well, I wanna fight.'

'What?'

'You heard. We fight. You fire me — you fight me.'

I stared at him. *Shit, why now?* I didn't feel all that great; I was getting a cold or the flu or something and now this big bastard had to challenge me to single combat. I was tempted to tell him to piss off. Where did he think he was — the Wild West? The Middle Ages? Then it occurred to me that this was PNG and it was both. And I realised I *had* to fight the guy. It wasn't my ego I was seeking to protect; in PNG there were dozens of Tommies simmering in the ranks; waiting, watching. They were all right under strong leadership, but — like most cowards — if they detected vulnerability they'd attack. This fight was necessary: it was better to fight one Tommy now than a pack of them over the months ahead. The problem was, I wasn't sure I could win.

Tommy, with his big reputation and massive ego, had a lot of reason to want to win this fight, and though he was a lazy shithead he was, nevertheless, a competent kickboxer. And, as with any challenge fight, with the gauntlet already thrown down I had no chance of surprise. We were going to square up, and, all things being equal, that usually meant the stronger, more athletic fighter would win. Which, in this case, was definitely Tommy, at close to ten years my junior. And right now I felt like crap.

'Okay, but outside. And just you and me. No one else there.'

'You don't want anyone to see me beat you, eh?' The tone was scornful.

It was exactly the reason. I reckoned I could maybe get away with being beaten, but I'd never get away with being *seen* to be beaten. It was a risk all the same. Without witnesses, if Tommy decked me, which was likely, there was nothing to stop him kicking my head to pulp.

'I don't want to embarrass you,' I said mildly.

I took my pistol from its holster and dropped it on the desk. 'I don't need this,' I announced. It looked like a show of bravado. What it really meant was that if Tommy kicked my head in, I didn't want him getting his hands on the weapon.

We marched past the stunned supervisors. I caught Melanie's eye as we passed and gave her a wink. I don't think I was fooling anyone — especially myself; I was seriously worried.

We stopped behind the administration building, Tommy swinging around and shaping up.

The fight lasted less than ten seconds.

Tommy opened with a few jabs and a cross towards my head, but his distance was off and he fell short. I was watching for his move before his real move, aware that Tommy, trained in Kontact, would be watching for the same from me. Tommy was in the perfect position for kicking through after his punches and I saw his lead leg leave the ground for a low roundhouse kick to my calf. I accepted the strike, registering its lack of power. It was a feint — this was his move before his move. The real danger was in the next strike, a full roundhouse with maximum force to my head. In the second before Tommy delivered the strike I leapt forward, grabbing the initiative and instantly changing the kicking competition Tommy had in mind into a grappling, elbowing brawl. I yelled loudly an inch from his ear. He reflexively reared back, allowing me to deliver a palm strike to his groin, followed immediately by an elbow strike to the eye and a leg sweep. Suddenly, big Tommy was down in the dust, curled up in a ball.

Straightening up I tried to compose myself; apart from being relieved, I was bloody surprised. 'Tommy's back there crying,' I told the supervisors as I strolled back into the office.

'Pick him up, dust him down and then throw him off the property.'

They hurried away.

Melanie was staring at me saucer-eyed. 'You okay?' I asked. She nodded dumbly. She looked like I felt; sick.

My cold or flu got worse and I finally hauled myself off to the doctor, a gruff, grizzled Tasmanian and an old PNG hand who, after about thirty seconds, said, 'You've got malaria.'

'I can't have malaria; I take my antimalarial tablets every day.' Even as the words came out I knew it was a stupid thing to say.

'You always wear long-sleeved shirts? Sleep under mosquito netting?'

'Yeah, well, most of the time.' Now I was really sounding like an idiot.

'Most of the time doesn't do it, son. Do it *all* the time. You hear?

Now this isn't a bad attack but the next one will be and the one after that could be very serious. I'll give you some medication and you need to rest.'

'I'll be right,' I murmured.

I collapsed and was sick for three days, sweating it out in the tin sauna I called home. Melanie offered to nurse me. I thanked her kindly, but refused: watching me sweat and puke in the fetid air of the shack would have put the girl off men for life. I did, though, get her to go shopping and cook for me; with money in my pocket I could afford to buy good food and that plus a little rest saw me on the mend, though I was still pretty crook when I returned to work.

That afternoon one of the supervisors came into the office. 'Boss, there's a mob of local boys out there, wanting work.'

'It's too close to Christmas. I'm not taking anyone on now. Tell 'em to come back in the New Year. I'll be recruiting then.'

The man went away. He was back in a couple of minutes. 'They won't listen boss. They getting sparked.' I sighed and stood up. The malaria had left me feeling weak and a little shaky and I needed this like I needed another attack.

Outside, just beyond the compound gates, was a substantial crowd; a central core of young men, mostly drunk, surrounded by a mob of flotsam and jetsam from the streets. More were joining every moment. I hardly recognised my own voice as I said, 'Listen, I don't have any jobs right now.' The crowd was restless, I reckoned they hadn't heard me. I raised my voice. 'Look, I'm not recruiting now but there'll be jobs in the New Year.' Somebody yelled something about promises no bloody good, the tone aggressive.

'I understand that and I promise…' I addressed them for a couple of minutes, trying to placate them; massaging the mob. I reckoned I was doing a good job until a rock the size of a golf ball whizzed past my head. So much for that theory. Another crashed into the fibro-cement wall of the building, followed by one whanging off the bodywork of a car parked in front. One of the supervisors standing next to me screeched in pain as he clutched a spurting wound on his forehead. Suddenly, the sultry air was filled with flying projectiles and the sound of windows smashing and rocks crunching into vehicle bodywork. Crouching under the hail I yelled at my men to help me shut the compound gates. When that was done, I ordered one of the armoured personnel carriers up to block them. Afterwards everyone retreated to the offices where we watched the mob throwing stones at the armoured carrier until they got bored and shuffled off.

I stayed late to supervise boarding up the windows and to take account of the damage to vehicles before dragging myself back to my shack. The power was off and I lit a few candles, puzzling over why a mob of rascals would turn up pissed and expect me to give them a job, especially so close to Christmas. And then to start chucking rocks; hell, what did they think …

I stopped, scrabbled around for my diary and checked the date.

It was my thirtieth birthday.

I slumped onto my cot and allowed myself a smile. Just like a lot of people on their thirtieth birthday — I had got stoned. In my case, literally. It would be something to tell my kids. If I ever had any. Right now there wasn't much prospect of it. I was thirty and living in a tin shack, celibate, deeply in debt, suffering the after-effects of malaria; my most valued possession a leather-bound edition of Banjo Paterson; my most necessary possession the Smith and Wesson under my pillow.

It wasn't much to show for thirty years.

But then, I reflected, being a waveman maybe that was all I could expect.

Chris turned up shortly after New Year with some good news. 'Word's getting around about your program,' he told me. 'The PNG police task force and the military want you to train some of their people and the security team that protects the Prime Minister's residence wants you to train them too.'

'Great. I'll talk to Sandy about it.'

Within weeks I was training all three groups.

In view of the increased business I was pulling in Warnock gave me a small raise. It wasn't much but I reckoned it would help pay my debts off that much quicker. Having fully recovered from the malaria, I was enjoying the training and getting to know some of the officers and NCOs from the army. They had their problems, some of which they shared over a few beers. Apart from not being able to recruit enough good men, they had difficulty feeding the men they did have. There simply wasn't enough high-protein food to go around. I thought I might have a solution for that.

I went to see a client I'd undertaken some payroll escorts for. The guy owned a big property north of Lae that was plagued by feral buffalo. I suggested that some officers and I might hunt the buffalo; we'd supply meat to the army and, by way of acknowledgement, a proportion to the nearby villages. The guy accepted happily.

We set off at dawn; six pairs of two, my partner an army captain called Mark Kinnisopa who carried a German Anschutz. I was impressed … a real hunter's weapon. I was armed with an army-issue SLR.

Four hours into the bush and the energy-sapping humidity was as crushing as a ton of wet cement. I felt exhausted; breathing was like sucking air through a wet towel and I had long ago ceased to sweat. Yet my heart was hammering crazily. For four hours I'd been checking every bush, reacting to every movement of the wind in the long grass, acutely aware that feral buffalo were fast and potentially deadly. What the hell was I doing stalking them in their own territory with a guy I didn't know; who might be carrying that good-looking rifle solely for show; who might never have hit anything he'd aimed at in his life.

And all to feed a few soldiers and villagers.

I was beginning to lose the battle to convince myself that I wasn't mad or wasting my time when three big buffalo burst from the scrub eighty metres away and charged. I didn't think it possible, but instantly my mouth turned even drier, my palms and armpits suddenly sweaty. Six years as an infantry soldier paid off; I aimed and fired two shots into the chest of the closest animal. It stumbled and went down. I pivoted, aimed again and squeezed the trigger. *Click*. The rifle had jammed.

Wrapped inside a weird, misty euphoria I watched the lead buffalo swerve, pick up speed and charge straight for me. Everything in my world slowed down — then sped up — then slowed again. I knew I was scared but I couldn't feel it; I was anaesthetised, somewhere on the other side of fear. As my body mechanically performed the stoppage drill — *weapon fires-weapon stops; cock-lock, tilt-left, look-in* — I also watched the beast closing in on me; could see the hot breath from its nostrils, the plumes of dust erupting from its hide as it thundered towards me.

Suddenly, a shot rang out. The beast stumbled, almost went down, righted itself and, with all the tenacity of an enraged big male buffalo, kept coming at me. A second shot boomed, and the heavy-calibre bullet tore into the animal's heart. It died as it was running, crashing into the dirt ten metres from me.

As the third animal veered away Kinnisopa dropped it with a single shot. Turning to me and grinning from ear to ear he hollered, 'You owe me a beer for that one.'

Just before I doubled over and spewed my guts, I murmured, 'Mate, I owe you the bloody brewery.'

It took me days to dismiss the technicolour images of what would have happened to me if that big buffalo had actually connected.

Chris flew in a few weeks later and we went for a beer.

'I hear you're feeding a whole lot of villagers and half the army,' he chuckled.

'It was easy enough to arrange. The army gets fed and my client gets the buffalo culled. It's one of those win-win situations. So long as nobody gets hurt,' I added.

'You're in deep with the army, eh?'

'Thanks to you. They like the program. Kontact works for them.'

'Listen, buddy, how'd you like to sell it to your own people?'

'What have you got in mind?'

'I know a few Australian army instructors up here advising the locals. I told them about you. They say they'd be interested in some kind of presentation.'

'Yeah?' I was excited.

'You'd have to give it in Australia. Duntroon. You know the place?'

'Yeah, I know it.'

Chris gave me a name and I got in touch. It took me less than a month to arrange a presentation at Duntroon to instructors from both the army and the federal police. Sandy Warnock was delighted; the security company would be invoicing my training business, though I had to pay for my own airfare. It was another case of 'you scratch my back and I'll ride on yours' but, at that point, all I cared about was making the most of the opportunity, and devoted all my spare time to thinking about and planning the demonstration.

I left nothing to chance, writing out my presentation word for word before memorising it verbatim; making sure I was word perfect.

Flying into Canberra I felt the same sense of coming home I'd felt returning from India, though it was a curious feeling to be back in Duntroon as a civilian. The place looked pretty much the same; there were even a few faces I thought I recognised. I was assigned a large room though I had only a small audience. There were five of them, but they were all highly influential.

I was hyped and ready; trembling with nervous anticipation like a racehorse.

My first major presentation. My first big chance.

CHAPTER 18

Manila

IT WAS a disaster: an unmitigated, total, consummate cock-up.

A morning presentation, I started with 'Um, arr, good afternoon. I mean, no, good afternoon, no, um, good morning.' From there it went down hill. Fast.

Four minutes in I forgot my lines, made a guess at what I wanted to say, said something I recognised from the end of the presentation, carried on wrapping up the event before I'd started it, stopped, said something that wasn't in the script at all and then began mumbling incomprehensibly as my mind went blank and my palms turned clammy.

Nine minutes in one of the audience, a tall, arrogant-looking major, sighed loudly, stood up and strode from the room, passing directly in front of me on his way out of the door. From the look on their faces I could see the remaining members of my audience were staying out of pure, heartfelt sympathy for another human being committing the public-presentation equivalent of *hara kiri* before their eyes.

I wanted to die; wished the floor would open up and swallow me; deeply regretted that Mark Kinnisopa had bagged that buffalo. If only he had let the thing kill me.

The presentation dragged to its sorry end like a dying animal and I flew out the following day thankful to be escaping Australia, wanting nothing more than to lose myself in the steamy heat of deepest PNG. When Sandy Warnock and Chris asked how it had gone I mumbled something about it going as well as could be expected and maybe hearing from Duntroon sometime. I never heard a word of course.

I got another dose of malaria. Soon after I'd recovered I travelled to meet with a client, the organiser of a big agricultural show. The event was the highlight of Lae's calendar, and in view of the fact that it would feature two big beer tents, I recommended the client hire at least sixty guards and twenty dogs. The cheapskate, more concerned about maximising his beer sales, opted for twenty guards and ten dogs. It wasn't enough.

The tents were packed and by mid-afternoon almost all the men were drunk. A fight broke out between two rival groups and my men, though vastly outnumbered, waded in with the dogs to break it up. In the ensuing melee two of my guards were badly injured and had to be transported to the hospital. One of them was a dog handler and his dog Zeus, a big, aggressive German shepherd, now minus its master, was uncontrollable. Zeus had been shoved into a wire-fenced kennel where it was being taunted by a bunch of drunks. The racket of the dog leaping at the wire and barking maniacally, along with the drunks laughing and bellowing, was unbelievable. The client demanded I get the dog out of there.

I eyed the snarling animal, its hackles raised and eyes bulging, its big yellow teeth bared. Was that blood on its muzzle? This animal was a carnivore. In the absence of its master it hated all human beings with a vengeance. And to get to it, I had to crawl down a long, tunnel-like flue into the kennel. I would be going into the animal's personal space, on all fours.

I considered Kontact and what possible scenarios I could draw from. What could I look for in body cues? It was a stupid question. The dog was giving me all the cues I could possibly want. It wanted to rip my throat out.

One of my guards reckoned it was impossible to get to the dog and that we should shoot it. I wasn't keen on that idea; the German shepherd was a valuable asset and anyway it wasn't the dog's fault it was out of control. If I had my way I'd rather shoot the bastards taunting it.

I made a decision: I chose to believe it was *possible* to restrain and control the dog. I thought about Alice Springs where I'd restrained and controlled a lot of humanoid animals pretty successfully. The principles had to be the same. I would have to take a hit — in this case a bite — my only choice being where the bite would be. I pulled off my shirt and wrapped it around my left forearm, dragged open the door of the tunnel, crouched, and set off at a crawl.

The crowd outside the wire went mad, screaming at the dog to attack me. As far as they were concerned this was the ultimate spectator sport. The dog backed up, its barking reaching a new level of frenzy. As I crawled I told myself repeatedly that the dog was more frightened of me than I of it and that it was *possible* for me to come out of this in one piece. I could do this, I assured myself, and hoped it was true.

I closed in on the barking animal. Just at the moment I judged the dog was about to attack I proffered my forearm. Zeus hurled himself at me and bit down. Even with the protection of the shirt it hurt like hell, but at least he didn't draw blood. I slammed my elbow into the side of the dog's head. The dog yelped and staggered sideways … but didn't go down. The crowd was instantly silent, waiting with bated breath for the next attack.

It never came. The German shepherd whimpered, sank to its haunches and flattened its ears. In the power structure of the animal's social hierarchy Zeus had just promoted me to top dog. I backed down the tunnel, the dog following peacefully. I emerged to uproarious clapping and cheering. Handing the dog over to one of my guards I looked at the crowd. The same people who had been baying for my blood now cheered me. Wankers.

Shortly afterwards, with the adrenalin cooling and the precise nature of what I'd done crystallising in my head, I couldn't decide if what I'd done was gutsy or overwhelmingly stupid.

I had a similar dilemma a few weeks later when yet another disgruntled ex-employee came looking to revenge a sacking. I heard my name being called and looked out of the office window to see the man bellowing in the middle of the compound. He was wielding a short-handled skinning knife. In the time it took me to walk through the outer office and into the compound my heart rate had shot to over two hundred beats a minute.

'I'm going to *kill* you,' the guy screamed. I walked tight-lipped but purposefully towards him. At just outside his stabbing range I leapt forward and to the side, striking out with a lead hook punch to the back of the hand holding the knife. As the blow landed I spun away from the blade, grabbing my assailant's weapon arm and delivering an elbow strike to the radial motor point in his forearm, followed immediately by a low knee to the peroneal nerve of his thigh. Cradling the man's head in my hand, I head-butted his temple. The guy went down. I stamped on his knife hand and booted the blade across the dusty compound. It was over in seconds, though when I thought about what could have happened I started shaking and found myself desperately needing a shit.

I told Chris about the fight the next time he flew in. 'You know, they have some really good knife-fighting styles in the Philippines,' Chris said. 'I'm due up there soon. Why don't you fly up and we can go to a good dojo? Practise with some of the professionals.'

The idea was appealing. Apart from my disastrous visit to Duntroon, plus a couple of bouts of malaria, I hadn't had a day off since arriving in the country. I was due for some leave.

'Yeah, sounds good.'

'We can take in some cage fighting, too.'

'No thanks, I've seen cage fights. In Sydney; when I was in the army.'

Basically, they were bare-knuckle boxing bouts between a pair of tattooed slobs in a cellar bar with outrageous cover prices. If you didn't choke on the cigarette smoke, you choked on the warm beer. Or at the sight of the topless waitresses.

'Yeah, but these are different. Absolutely no holds barred. The real deal.'

'That's what they told me in Thailand. But apart from some good kickboxing they were just the same. Even cage fights are not totally no-holds-barred: you can't bite; can't eye gouge, there are rules. And whatever they are … they're not real. Two blokes get in a cage together they know they're going to fight. It's a contest. No surprises. Not really. I mean, they're not going to be suddenly running a marathon, are they? But in the real world there *are* surprises. You're walking down the street minding your own business and thinking about whether you should buy that pair of shoes when suddenly you're dealing with physical aggression. Suddenly you're in a fight and there *really* aren't any rules. *That's* the real deal. Everything else is just wallpaper.'

Chris was staring at me. 'Red, gimme a break. Lighten up, why don'tcha. You definitely need a vacation. And while we're there, I think we gotta see about getting you laid.' I laughed with him.

By the time I came to fly out I wasn't laughing any more. I felt awful, felt like I was getting another dose of malaria. I tried to cancel my ticket but the airline wouldn't allow it, so, between bouts of sweating and shivering and trying to eat without puking, I flew to Manila.

Chris met me at Ninoy Aquino International. 'Hell, you look like shit,' he said.

'I feel it. No way I can go to a dojo, mate. Sorry.'

'Don't worry about it. There's a cage fight just out of town. We'll go there.'

The event was an hour's cab drive away; twice we had to stop to allow me to throw up. The fights, short, brutal and very bloody, were punctuated by long drinking sessions for the patrons, many of whom were more interested in the under-age girls and boys being offered for sale by the club.

I was too sick to drink, though Chris more than made up for me, knocking back San Miguel beer like it was lolly water and whooping drunkenly every time he won a bet on a fight — which he did with unbelievable consistency.

By the end of the night he was yelling like a banshee with a pocket-full of pesos having the time of his life. I on the other hand was so overwhelmingly shattered that Chris had to physically load me into a cab.

I woke up in a cheap hotel room with Chris leaning over me. 'Listen, buddy, I have to get back to PNG. You're too sick to travel. You gotta stay here and sweat it out. I've paid for the room for a week and fixed for the Mammasan to take care of you. Okay?'

I nodded. Talking was too much effort.

The Mammasan was hopeless and after a day I paid her to leave me to suffer alone. I ached from my jaw to my ankles and the slightest movement was agony. I shivered and shook like a heroin junkie going cold turkey. Most of the time I was vomiting and shitting, my stench so bad it would make me vomit again.

At some point during the ordeal my head cleared briefly and I was overcome by a sense of certainty of purpose. It was a fleeting, but powerful sensation. As terrible as things were — and they really were terrible — I knew that somewhere in my future there was a life waiting for me that was as good as my current situation was bad.

After what seemed a month, but was only a few days, I'd recovered sufficiently to fly back to PNG. As weak as a baby I went to see the Tassie doctor who took some blood, returning when the test results were in. The doc looked serious. 'You've had falciparum malaria, the worst possible kind. You could have died.'

'Oh.' I didn't know what to say.

'Oh isn't good enough, son. Move out of that damn tin shack you call a home. It's a magnet for mosquitoes. And for god's sake, take precautions. Falciparum usually doesn't come back, but if it does, it could kill you.'

I found a furnished bungalow about a kilometre from the compound. After the shack it felt like five-star living, and though I had to pay rent I was happy. I had just finished paying off all I owed and for the first time since leaving the army six years before I was totally debt-free. I felt liberated.

The bungalow boasted a television, something I had neither seen nor missed since being in PNG. For a novelty I turned on CNN and watched the news. It was full of South Africa.

After twenty-seven years as a prisoner on Robben Island, Nelson Mandela had been released and was about to lead South Africa into its first truly democratic election, with Mandela certain to become the country's first democratically elected president. It was an inspiring story and I couldn't get it out of my head.

I wasn't inclined to hero-worship; I'd had that knocked out of me travelling over half of Asia in search of a 'guru' worthy of the title. I knew there were no gurus; I doubted there were many real heroes. But if there were, then Mandela had to be counted in the front rank.

I watched the news as often as I could while reading everything I could get my hands on about South Africa, gradually realising that I wanted to be a part of all that was happening out there. Slowly, it came to me.

I had something to offer. Kontact. I would travel to South Africa and teach my program to the police and the security services ... hell, to Nelson Mandela's bodyguards, if I could. Teach them to be better bodyguards and in so doing gain a whole new degree of respect for my program.

It was a great plan. At least, I thought so.

CHAPTER 19

Pretoria

'YOU WANT to what?' Chris's tone held that special mix of sympathy and condescension people reserve for half-wits. I told him again. He laughed. 'Man, you're nuts. Mandela is one of the most famous people in the world. His security will be in the hands of pros, a crack squad of highly trained guys. What the hell is an Australian civilian going to teach them?'

'I'll teach them Kontact.'

'Look, Kontact is great for platoons of goons like you've got here. But what could you teach professionals they don't already know? Why go to South Africa if you don't have a job waiting? You don't know anyone there. So how on earth are you going to sell your program?'

The latter questions had been preoccupying me for weeks. I'd called the South African consulate asking for a list of the country's police stations and been told, none too politely, to shove off. After a bit of thought I decided if I could get my foot in the door at one station maybe I could leverage what I wanted. I dialled the international operator, asked for and received the number of the Soweto police station.

I needed a story and after a day or so came up with one. I called Soweto, asking for the commander of the station, telling him I was an Australian journalist doing a story on how tough the South African front-line cops had it in comparison to their soft Australian counterparts. After a few minutes the commander warmed to the story and a day later faxed me the complete classified list of every

171

police station, prison and military outfit in South Africa. I put together a mailing campaign outlining the benefits of Kontact and sent brochures and covering letters off to more than seven hundred addresses.

Eight weeks later I'd received the grand total of two replies, both informing me with thinly veiled hostility that South African instructors were the best in the world, and anyway, no foreigner could ever be involved in the security of South Africa's politicians.

It was all the encouragement I needed. Two contacts had turned me down — which meant that seven hundred and ten hadn't. The fact that they didn't immediately grasp the value of Kontact wasn't enough to put me off. I *knew* it worked.

I gave notice to Sandy Warnock, who wasn't happy. I did nothing to soften his mood; I didn't want to feel that if things didn't work out I could come back to the job in PNG. This, I decided, was a time for burning my bridges.

I flew back to Australia, to Bairnsdale, to tell my family my plans. They weren't encouraging: having just got myself out of debt, why would I risk everything going to South Africa? I admitted I had enough to keep me going for a couple of months, maybe three. My brother laughed and said he'd see me back inside a month, in a tone of voice exactly like Chris's.

I landed at Johannesburg International and hitchhiked the fifty kilometres to Pretoria, immediately noticing from the cab of the truck how much I liked the look and feel of the country; it was more than the cloudless blue sky that appealed to me, there was a vibrancy, an expectation that something exciting was just a few heartbeats away.

With my list of addresses I walked into one of Pretoria's police stations and asked to see the commander. The man who emerged was a big Afrikaner: irritated and scowling, the archetypal apartheid cop. I offered my hand to shake his. He looked at me as if I had leprosy. Folding his arms tightly across his chest, he grumbled something in a language I'd never heard before. It sounded a bit like German, maybe Dutch.

'G'day,' I said. 'I've travelled from Australia to teach a new unarmed combat program to South African security specialists.' The cop grunted. The action seemed to cause him pain.

'Actually, I've really been inspired by the example of Nelson Mandela. The guy spends twenty-seven years in prison, comes out, becomes the most powerful man in the country and he's got the courage *not* to seek revenge. Isn't that incredible?'

The cop, starting to turn an intriguing shade of purple, seemed disinclined to agree with me.

'Anyway, what I'd really like to do is train the bodyguards of Nelson Mandela and in the process make them better bodyguards. I've spent years developing my program and for anyone who isn't arrogant or complacent it really will improve their skill level.'

I waited for a response from the cop. There was none — apart from a complete cessation of breathing on his part.

After what seemed an age, the cop exploded into life. In heavily accented English he raged, 'You can't teach us anything. We're the best in the world. What would some Australian know about our country? We are the best in the world. And we don't have any money to pay you for training and even if we did we wouldn't pay you because we are the best in the world.' In among the ranting I kept catching the word *voetsek*. I had no idea what it meant except that clearly it wasn't complimentary. The commander told me to get out.

It wasn't a promising start, though it turned out to be typical of my next two months in South Africa. I crisscrossed the country, visiting police, prison and military units at which my reception was almost invariably the same; it was as if someone had written the script. I heard the word *rooinek* often and learnt it meant foreigner. It made me smile. In Korea they'd called me *meguk* and in Japan *gaijin*. I didn't know what they'd called me in PNG; with several hundred languages it could have been a lot of things. But there were worse things than being called a foreigner, and anyway, I was a foreigner.

But it wasn't helping. My experience so far had been one of fierce

173

resistance, xenophobia and raw racism: white, black and brown. And I was running out of money. After nine weeks of nothing I reckoned I had funds for about one more week, ten days at most. And I hadn't had a sniff of interest. Though I'd left my number everywhere, the mobile phone I'd purchased when I arrived in the country had only rung once — and that was when I'd called myself from a payphone to make sure the thing was actually working.

I was staying in a sleazy motel in Cape Town when it rang a second time. I was so shocked I fumbled it, nearly dropped it and was flustered when I answered, 'Hello.'

The voice at the other end was anything but flustered. 'This is Warrant Officer Albertus Wessels here. I've heard about your unarmed combat training program. I want to set up a demonstration.'

Again, I almost dropped the phone. Trying to sound cool and businesslike I said, 'Okay, where?'

'Soweto. The commander there will listen to you and if he likes what you have to say, he'll arrange a demo. That okay with you?'

'Sure. When?'

'Day after tomorrow. If they like it in Soweto we'll maybe try it elsewhere. But no promises, mind. It'll have to be good.'

I wrote down the details. 'Will you be there?'

'No, but I'll get a report.' The line went dead.

I gazed at the phone. I liked the sound of Albertus Wessels. No bureaucratic bumbling with this guy. He was prepared to give Kontact a shot. Now it was down to me. I was a little worried about returning to Soweto after being practically thrown out the first time. I didn't recognise the name Wessels had told me and hoped the guy was the boss instead of some minion. I also hoped it wasn't the officer out of whom I'd conned the list of stations.

The guy I saw was the District Commander, the highest rank I'd so far managed to see. He listened quietly to my presentation before asking for a demo, which he set up with two of his instructors. They were both big, and good kickboxers, but their practice was inhibited by their training in the dojo; they followed set moves which made them predictable and relatively easy to handle. Wessels called me the following day.

'Soweto liked your demo,' he said. 'You'd better come up here so we can talk face to face.' Wessels was at a station in the far north of the Transvaal. By that stage I'd been living on oranges and biltong for a week; I spent the last of my money on the bus fare.

I took to Wessels from the outset. He was genuinely friendly and from his questions showed he was keen to learn about Kontact. But the main thing I liked about him was his quiet air of confidence; this guy had seen a lot of combat in Angola; he was a veteran with extensive operational experience who didn't feel the need to impress anyone. He spoke quietly and acted modestly. And from the way the District Commander in Soweto had talked about him, I had a notion Wessels' reputation was respected throughout the force.

The guy was also a miracle worker. After a day together and a lot of phone calls he managed to get funding for a trial course of Kontact. He also gave me my first introduction to South African hospitality, inviting me to stay with his family for the duration of the course.

Twenty guys stood before me on the first morning. By mid-morning three had dropped out — Kontact was too tough for them. Two more dropped out in the afternoon and the following day I dismissed another three who were little more than oxygen thieves. Twelve people finished the course, out of which I intended awarding certificates to three — one of whom was Albertus Wessels.

Sitting behind his desk in his office Wessels chuckled. 'You know, here in South Africa everyone who finishes a police course gets a certificate. You're going to have nine very unhappy policemen out there.'

'I expect I will, but I want this certificate to have real value. I don't want it in the hands of a bunch of slugs. If that happens, Kontact will be considered second-rate. I want to create *quality* ambassadors for this course, not quantity.'

'Show me the list,' Wessels said.

I pushed it across the desk. Wessels pointed to a name. 'Why didn't he pass?'

'He didn't come up to the appropriate standard.'

'And what about him?' Wessels jabbed another name.

'He's very fit and very fast but he's also very closed-minded; doesn't want to try anything new.'

Wessels laughed. 'Well, he's a national martial arts champion. And the other one is a Brigadier's son. Both these guys are legends in their own lunchtimes. I'm going to enjoy seeing their reactions when you tell them they didn't make it.'

Both men were visibly shocked and plain bloody angry. After the awards ceremony they cornered me and told me I was a bastard and that I'd never teach in South Africa again. I repeated what they'd said to Wessels who smiled.

'Well, I don't know about the first part, but they're wrong about the second. I'm setting up another course for two weeks time.'

'That's great. By the way, what does *bliksem rooinek* mean?'

Wessels laughed. 'It means a foreigner who's in need of a good thrashing.'

My policy of encouraging perceived value, of creating an elite coterie of Kontact certificate holders, paid off almost immediately. Those who received certificates returned to their units to talk up the program with pride and enthusiasm. Some of those who failed asked to return for a subsequent course. The certificate and what it symbolised became valuable, its value enhanced by its scarcity, its scarcity a function of the enormous effort required to obtain it. Word spread quickly that only the very best possessed a Kontact certificate, and even I was amazed at the exponential growth of my program.

Six months later, living in a small, pleasant apartment in Pretoria, I had delivered training to instructors from the South African Army, Navy, Police, Prison Service, Special Task Force, Drug Unit, Internal Stability Unit, SWAT teams VIP Protection Unit and, best of all, to instructors of the Presidential Protection Unit of Nelson Mandela.

Along the way I'd made some good friends; Albertus Wessels was now Wessie, a close friend as well as supporter. We had become neighbours after Wessie had been promoted to Captain in the Police National Training HQ in Pretoria. Another supporter was Wessie's boss, Senior Superintendent Fred Blaaue, along with Sergeant Fryk Strydom of the Special Task Force. All of them had skill and they each had insights to offer about Kontact, which I took on board and applied. And, as always, feedback from the front line also helped refine the program, making it even better.

A couple of months after moving to Pretoria I travelled down to the Free State to run a two-week course for about sixty police instructors. The course was to be run in a soccer stadium in the heart of the local township. The stadium, built at the height of apartheid, was enormous, rising like an ocean liner out of a sea of tin shanties. It was redolent of the communist era of Eastern Europe, when dictators would build huge and enormously expensive cultural centres in the midst of squalor.

Consulting with the local superintendent, I learnt that by seven in the morning the temperature would be in the mid-thirties and by nine, 43°C. I decided we should escape the worst of the heat by starting training at three forty-five am.

At five-fifteen on the first morning, just as dawn was breaking, a group of men and women shuffled into the stadium and positioned themselves on one of the terraces. After ninety minutes of hard training I wondered if we were to have an audience. One of the guys told me this was the local gospel choir come to practice.

They began as the men and I turned back to our training. It was heart-lifting. It went beyond words and was as much a feeling as it was a sound, a low rumble of African harmonies. When they sang their own traditional songs their voices were deep and hauntingly beautiful, and when they launched into some classic hymns they sang with a joyous sense of celebration and exuberance. It was a privilege to listen to them.

One song stayed with me for the rest of the day. It began with a mournful cry from a lone baritone, calling something that seemed as timeless as Africa itself. The cry went on for many heartbeats and then, suddenly, it stopped. What felt like an age passed and the silence seemed filled with expectation rather than nothingness. Another sound began, but so soft it was hard to tell if it really was a sound. Slowly a beat grew, one voice ... then another. At some point, it was difficult to tell just when, there were many voices ... a great many. Each was strong and proud and independent, yet each one was so obviously an indivisible part of those around it. Together the voices radiated power and dignity and purpose. I felt the skin on the back of my neck prickle and a sensation of unity echo around the shadows of the empty stands as the African sun blossomed over the horizon.

They came again on the following dawn but on the third morning failed to show. I was disappointed and mentioned it to one of the senior officers on the course. The guy was surprised. 'I thought you wouldn't like all that bloody noise and monkey chatter — I told the *kaffirs* to bugger off.'

That afternoon I went into the township looking for members of the choir and was pointed in the direction of a mountain of a man who was one of the singers. I told him it had been a mistake to send the choir away and that I wanted them to come back the following morning.

Which they did, and every day thereafter, and the amazing thing I noticed was how positively everyone on the course responded to the singing and to the atmosphere it generated. So much so that when the course finished, there was a real bond among men who, themselves a microcosm of South Africa, Afrikaners, English-speaking white South Africans, Indians, Coloureds, Zulus and Xhosas, had all been deeply connected by Kontact and the haunting singing of the choir.

Back in Pretoria there was more good news. For months I'd been mainly training the trainers, who had gone out into the field as ambassadors of Kontact. They were good guys and I was confident they had the professionalism not to cut corners when they trained their people. But, with the best will in the world, with the training at one remove I knew subtleties could be lost. It seemed someone else knew that too as, immediately on my return, I was told I'd be training Nelson Mandela's bodyguards directly.

I had realised my dream.

For security reasons, the training had to be conducted within the bounds of the Presidential Estate, which made finding the right venue something of a problem. I finally selected the lawn of the President's gardens as my training site. Sometimes, in the middle of training, I would see the glossily polished Presidential Mercedes sweeping past in the sunshine on its way in or out of the estate.

One morning it stopped and out of the corner of my eye I saw the rear window glide down; Nelson Mandela, Nobel Laureate and President of the Republic of South Africa, was watching me training his bodyguards. I couldn't help myself; as opposed as I was to show and exhibition I turned on the juice, putting the guys through their paces with a vengeance. Mandela watched for at least ten minutes, and I was hoping all the while that he was impressed.

When I glanced covertly at the limo I was shocked to see Mandela beckoning me over. I straightened up. 'Excuse me, guys,' I said nonchalantly, 'the President wants to talk to me.' I moved towards the car and was about three metres away when Mandela jabbed a bony finger through the open window.

'You, Australian,' he said in that instantly recognisable voice, 'be careful of my flower beds.'

The Mercedes whispered away.

CHAPTER 20

Hereford

THE VISION I'd had in the dawn of an Alice Springs' car park had been realised to an extent far greater than I could possibly have hoped. Within two years of landing in Johannesburg, Kontact had become an officially accredited training program of the South African Police Service. People were booking months in advance to take part.

I had my small group of close friends, a nice place to live, even the occasional girlfriend. I was also on respectful nodding terms with Nelson Mandela. I knew of course that in certain circles there was jealousy; by South African standards I was being paid a small fortune to deliver my training, and a few disaffected people still thought I was a *rooinek*. But with people like Wessie and Fred and Fryk endorsing Kontact, the jealousy was no more than an irritation.

I had attained the sunny uplands of success and it felt good. It was a sign of how far my life had progressed that whereas in PNG I'd slept with a Smith and Wesson under my pillow, in Pretoria it was a notepad and pencil. Often I woke in the night to jot down a thought related to how I could improve Kontact. There was still further I wanted to take it.

Having invested so much time and effort into the program, I had to know if it could be accepted at the highest possible level; if what it delivered was as good as I thought it was. I didn't want praise; I wanted satisfaction. And to get that I'd have to wash up on some new shore and start all over again. Sitting in my flat I made a list of the world's top ten Special Forces units. The one I selected had to have years of operational experience, be internationally recognised, and be a trusted leader in the world of Special Forces. One stood out above the others, Britain's 22 Special Air Service Regiment, the men who had so dramatically stormed the Iranian Embassy in London in 1980. I wanted *them* to adopt my program and endorse it.

I had an information pack printed which I posted to Hereford in England. After a couple of months with no reply I mailed another. With still no response I was tempted to forget it. Life was good, very good in fact, but something wouldn't let me rest. In hindsight, it's possible my motivation stemmed in part from my relationship with Lisa in Melbourne – her friend's lack of respect for my ambitions fuelled my drive to advance.

After a struggle I obtained the regiment's phone number and dialled the number from my office. I was eventually put through to the unit's Second in Command. I introduced myself, saying I had an unarmed combat program in which I was sure the 2IC would see merit. I'd scarcely launched into the benefits when the cold and chiselled voice at the other end told me it wasn't interested in anything I had to sell.

I responded by saying I appreciated his position but I really believed he would see merit in the program if he saw how it worked. 'What about I call by your office, introduce myself, outline the program and perhaps we can arrange a demonstration date,' I said.

The voice, increasingly clipped and icy, informed me that the regiment had an excellent unarmed combat program, one with which it was perfectly happy and, even if it hadn't, no one in their right mind would consider taking one from some foreigner cold-canvassing over the phone.

I repeated my offer of a meeting.

The voice was as cutting as the Arctic wind.

'Are you deaf? Or do I have a speech impediment?' The phone slammed down.

Opening my laptop, I tapped out a letter thanking the man for his time and saying, yet again, that I believed the regiment would see merit in my program. I finished by stating the date and time I'd call at his office. I faxed the letter, then went out and did something I'd never done before. I bought myself a business suit and an Italian silk tie. Back in my office I booked a ticket on the next available flight to London, grabbed my passport and international driver's licence and caught a cab to the airport.

Less than twenty-four hours later, carrying a smart-looking buffalo-skin briefcase, I was marching through the main gate of Stirling Lines in Hereford. Doing my best to look like an officer and a gentleman I nodded curtly at the Ministry of Defence policeman at the gate. The policeman returned my nod and called me sir. I followed the path leading towards the barracks, reached a closed gate, and found my way blocked by another MoD cop. This one held a machine-gun across his chest and instead of nodding demanded to know what I wanted. I told him. The man jerked his head at a booth off to one side. I noticed the glass had the green sheen of bullet-proofing. The policeman behind the glass looked like an American cop, complete with a pistol at his hip. When he asked for my ID, I slipped my business card under the glass. The man read it … aloud and very slowly before asking, his tone oozing condescension, 'And what do you want to know, son?'

'Nothing from you. I'm here to see the Second in Command.'

The cop gave me the hard eye, grunted and pressed a buzzer and a wire-mesh security gate swung open. Walking through and around the side of the booth, I found myself across the counter from the man, now murmuring into the phone. 'Yes sir. Certainly, sir.' The cop put down the phone and, without a word, left the booth.

Afterwards, I was never sure if I waited an hour or just ten minutes. I know stress and pressure can distort time, just as it can distort shape and size and colour, and standing in that holding bay I felt the stress of a hammering heart. At last a fit-looking trooper wearing the unit's coveted beige beret and 'winged-dagger' badge marched in and motioned me to follow him. Even at the double it took a while through a succession of corridors, walkways and across frost-covered playing fields to reach the Second in Command's office.

The first thing I noticed was my fax on the desk. The second thing was the man's face, as welcoming as a gun turret. He waved me peremptorily to a seat and told me to get on with it. I was ten minutes into my presentation before the face behind the desk showed the slightest sign of animation, but after fifteen minutes he was energetically asking questions and inside half an hour he'd agreed to a full demonstration.

I walked out of the barracks as if I was walking on air.

A week later I was back; I was in the barracks' gymnasium and facing twenty of the regiment's finest, their body language screaming at me, 'We are the best in the world and who the hell are you?'

After a few minutes of technical explanations I knew I wasn't getting through. To hit the mark with this mob I had to do something different. And quickly. I went for broke. Turning to the Second in Command I said, 'I need a volunteer. The best you've got.'

After some murmuring among the squad a big bloke strolled out to the front. I looked at him. 'I'm going to give you thirty seconds to take me to the ground and make me submit. If you can get a wristlock on me, do it. If you can dislocate my shoulder, go for it. If you can apply some type of secret, ninja, Special Forces choke hold and knock me out, don't hold back. Whatever you do, do it with *absolute commitment*. Okay?'

The big trooper dropped his eyes and shifted his shoulders in that universal nuance of body language that states, unequivocally, 'Yeah, not a problem. You're a moron and this is a piece of piss.'

Then I put on the blindfold.

I heard the low unified gasp from the squad; a few quiet chuckles. I raised my hand to tell the trooper when to attack. I felt confident, yet I knew how easy it was for something to go wrong.

I dropped my hand.

The big trooper charged in like a bull. After fifteen seconds, both the blindfold and a large chunk of my hair had been ripped off. But the trooper hadn't forced me to submit. Keeping my eyes closed I knelt down and waited for the trooper to attack again. He came in even harder. Fifteen seconds later the timekeeper called time and I opened my eyes. The big trooper, breathing hard, gave me a lopsided grin and ruffled what was left of my hair. I'd won, but there was nothing magical about what had taken place. All I'd done was employ one of the most uncomplicated forms of defence that exists: non-compliance. When the trooper pushed, I pulled. When he grabbed high, I grabbed low. When he used linear force, I used circular evasion. My counters were not 'techniques', just spontaneous movement intended to frustrate and neutralise the trooper's efforts. And it worked.

The 2IC marched across the gymnasium floor. 'I want the course for my men. I'll pay the price you quoted. Now give me a date.'

To show my gratitude for all he'd done for me, I flew Albertus Wessels in from South Africa to help run the course. Wessie had become an instructor in the program and the South African Police, delighted that one of their own would be training the famous 22 SAS, sent him to Hereford on paid leave. Afterwards, when it was all over, Wessie moaned, 'Don't ever say thanks to me again. If this is your idea of a big thank you, I think I'd prefer you were an ungrateful *rooinek*.' He was only half joking.

The course was the toughest I'd ever conducted; six days of anaerobically intense, free-motion drills with such a massive build-up of lactic acid that, by the end of the first day, my body was screaming. I staggered back to the mess, fell on to my bed and stayed there, too exhausted to eat, until the following morning. At the end of day three, I seriously wondered if I'd have the strength to continue and, on the evening of the final day, I was so exhausted I couldn't lift my soup spoon.

Now I understood. Not for nothing were these guys considered the best by every other tribe in the jungle of Special Forces. Their fitness and attitude were almost unbelievable. On the first day, having introduced a basic knife defence exercise — a dynamic, free-flowing activity using a marker pen — one of the troopers had his eyelid ripped open. Holding his eye socket the guy casually jogged over to the base's medical centre, had it stitched — and then rejoined the class. But in the end the injuries and the pain and exhaustion were all worth it. The course feedback was better than I could have dreamt; even the senior participants agreed it was the best unarmed combat training they'd ever taken part in. The Second in Command booked another course.

I spent four months with the regiment, providing training for the officers and men and being trained with them. Despite being an antipodean, I gained clearance to be signed into the books of 22's reserve unit as a potential recruit which meant I could live on base, eat in the mess and wear a British uniform, except for the coveted beret. I even had an army serial number: 24961786.

I marched, shot, ate and drank with these men who, I realised, were as different to the Hollywood stereotype of special forces as Hereford rain is different to Pretorian sunshine, although with them I came to understand the full import of the expression 'swears like a trooper'. Almost their every other word was 'fucking'.

I used the word a few times myself when all my toenails turned black and fell off. I'd travelled west with the regiment's 'L' Detachment to Wales, to their training ground in the stark, dark, hauntingly beautiful Brecon Beacons. It was spring, it never stopped raining, and the ground was suitably soggy for the regiment's special form of orienteering: hour upon hour of lugging an SLR and a sixty-kilo rucksack across sleet-swept mountain tops. After two weeks of this the starting line-up of two hundred men had been reduced to fifty. And thanks to poor-fitting boots, I had lost all my toenails.

But it was worth it; the view from the summit of Pen-y-Fan across to Cribyn was breathtaking — although considering the effort it took to get to the top, taking a camera out of my ammunition pouch was also breathtaking.

During my months with the regiment I continued to refine Kontact with a combination of chainsaw and fine tooth-comb.

The end result was startlingly simple; like a crisp, clean work of minimalist art.

186

Drawing on the advice of people like Wessie and Fred and Fryk, and analysing the wisdom inherent in such approaches as Musashi's *Five Rings* and Boyd's *OODA Loop*, I settled on a four-step cycle in which to gain victory over an aggressor:

1. Shift balance
2. Shift focus
3. Seize opportunity
4. Compel response

Shifting balance is best achieved through non-compliance, and one of the best forms of non-compliance is movement. In the animal world, the most common response prey will employ when they realise they are under attack is movement. Whether it's a bird, a fish, a reptile or a mammal, the primary action-orientated response is to move. The rationale for this is universal in its application: a moving target is harder to hit, hold, bite or throw. An additional benefit of non-compliance is that you demonstrate you will not easily submit. There is enormous value in sending this message.

Shifting focus is done by causing pain or a distraction. In some cases the pain or distraction (in the form of a strike, or a loud yell or throwing a drink into an aggressor's eyes, for instance) can be enough to end the encounter, however its purpose is not to finish but rather to create a 'window of opportunity'. For example, if an aggressor attacks with a knife, their focus will be on the blade and their target. If the defender does something such as kick the assailant's kneecap, the focus of the aggressor will momentarily shift to the smashed knee. That shift in focus provides the 'window' for the defender to follow up and take control of the situation.

Seizing opportunity is, more than anything else, a matter of choice: the choice of being a participant, not a spectator. The SAS motto — *Who Dares Wins* — says it all.

Compelling response begins with step three of the cycle. By being proactive, not reactive, the participant capitalises on the irrefutable combative fact that *action beats reaction*. Response is compelled by *not* fighting the aggressor in the way they want to fight you. If they grab; you strike. If they strike; you grab. If they go high; you go low. If they push; you pull.

To put it another way, don't box a boxer, don't wrestle a wrestler, don't kick a kicker. This seems ridiculously obvious, but go to a boxing gym and what do boxers do against other boxers? They box! The Vietcong could never have influenced the US withdrawal from Vietnam if the VC had tried fighting the Americans in the way the Americans fought the Vietnamese.

The leap from individual combat to large-scale operations is not as wild as it may at first appear. Listening to veterans during training sessions at the barracks' gymnasium or over a few pints at Saxty's Bar in Hereford, it wasn't difficult to see parallels between empty-hand strategies and irregular (guerrilla) warfare.

* * *

While taking Kontact to the regiment had improved the program, I didn't realise just how high its reputation had risen … until I got a call from Buckingham Palace.

Senior officers of the Royalty Protection Group wanted to talk to me.

I was processed into the Palace through a side entrance and cobbled courtyard and then escorted along a wide corridor stretching for what seemed a kilometre ahead of me. I had expected it to be richly ornate, with flock wallpaper and deep-pile carpet — in fact it was quite shoddy, with linoleum flooring, pale and peeling blue plaster walls in need of a paint job and lots of cubicles on either side with scuffed wooden office furniture. A smell of mould and stale cigarette smoke pervaded the air and I was forced to conclude that the monarchy was just another branch of show business: all the money was spent at the front of house.

Even so, as I marched along it occurred to me that this sure as hell beat working in a hardware store in Bairnsdale. This, I told myself, was living. I was feeling a bit full of myself, but if you can't feel a bit full of yourself while striding purposefully along a corridor in Buckingham Palace, when can you?

I had several meetings with the guys from the Protection Group. They'd heard good reports about the work I'd done with the SAS at Hereford and were interested in hiring me to train their people. As part of my orientation I accompanied some of the protection teams assigned to safeguard British Cabinet Ministers and Members of Parliament; even getting a behind the scenes security tour of the Parliament at Westminster.

I was impressed by the Protection Group's professionalism; there were no dramas and no extravagant, attention-seeking behaviour. I'd laughed at the naivety of the movie *Bodyguard* with Kevin Costner, knowing from experience that Close Personal Protection was dull; it was *meant* to be dull. It was the last line of defence and if something went wrong at that level then something had gone very badly wrong further up the line.

After six months in the UK, I had gotten used to living in England. I was single, successful, and relatively affluent. Life was especially good. I had some good friends, including Andrew Chalmers, the Second in Command; there were plenty of long, chardonnay lunches, money in my pocket and a rich choice of things to do and places to go.

I was living high on the hog and enjoying it, yet I also found myself yearning for South Africa again; for its clean, crisp air, the feel of the high veldt, even for the taste of *biltong*.

I returned to Pretoria, to the place I found myself calling home, and focused once more on developing Kontact, analysing feedback and conducting evaluation seminars. It was a hectic time, with months of back-to-back courses all over the Republic. I was working hard, as were my course instructors. To reward them I arranged a special night, hiring the gallery of wildlife artist Martin Koch, where I had the caterers transform the place into an elegant private restaurant.

It was a superb evening, and after the excellent meal I gave my first ever after-dinner speech, thanking every individual in turn for their help in making Kontact so successful, saving for last Wessie, the man who, above all others, had given me my start in South Africa.

I concluded with, 'The last time I said thank you to Wessie he called me a *rooinek* and said he'd prefer it if I never did it again. Well, I'm sorry Wessie, but ...'

I had commissioned a Martin Koch painting, which was hanging on the nearby wall. I lifted it down. 'Wessie, this picture is a token of my appreciation for the risk you took in putting your trust in my program and me. Thank you.'

I think I detected tears in Wessie's eyes; to be frank, I was feeling pretty emotional myself. This celebration was the culmination of years of hard work; I felt I'd achieved what I'd set out to do.

A week later, I received a request from the Honolulu Police Department, offering me an all-expenses-paid trip to Hawaii to make a presentation of Kontact. It put a smile on my face: for the first time I was washing ashore at someone else's request and expense.

My work in Hawaii brought me to the attention of the US Federal Bureau of Investigation, who requested I fly to Los Angeles to conduct a basic course for the Bureau's SWAT team there. And so in LA I met Doug Able, the team commander, a man of the same independent and supportive ilk as Wessie and Andy Chalmers. After the basic course, Doug wrote a detailed article about Kontact for *The Tactical Edge*, the official journal of US National Tactical Officers Association. The article generated even more interest and Doug requested an advanced Kontact course — part of which involved me going along on drug raids with the squad.

Which, I reflected, while sitting in the passenger seat of Jerry's car, is how I'd come to be in Hollywood, crashing around in a drug dealer's van racing to a drug bust.

CHAPTER 21

Johannesburg

I'D BEEN away for over a month, first taking down heroin dealers in parking lots in Los Angeles with Doug Able's SWAT team, then back in London, presenting at Chelsea Barracks in the City. Not having seen any of my friends for a while I called them on my return and suggested lunch at a favourite restaurant in Sandton.

It was good to be back in South Africa; the weather was perfect, Wessie, Fred and Fryk were in a good mood as always, and we were celebrating with a few bottles of wine and a lot of laughter. Glancing around the busy, noisy restaurant I suddenly lost interest in my food. 'Hell.'

'What's got into you?' Fred asked.

'That woman over there. She has to be one of the most beautiful women I've ever seen.'

The others eyeballed her. 'Yeah, she's beautiful all right.'

'I'm going over to talk to her. See if I can get a date.'

They laughed. 'Forget it, man. What would a gorgeous creature like that see in an ugly bastard like you? She's going to tell you to *voetsek*.'

Ignoring them was a decision that changed my life; I stood up and threaded my way through the crowded tables to where the woman was lunching with a couple of girlfriends. I introduced myself, then added, 'but everyone calls me Red.'

'Red? Why?'

'It's a long story but I'll be happy to tell you it over dinner one evening. If you give me your number I'll call you tonight.' She smiled and said nothing, considering me with clear, cool eyes. I was aware of her girlfriends appraising me critically. 'So, what's your name?' I asked.

'Natasha.'

'Really? Do you know, that's my favourite name.'

She laughed, a deep, throaty chuckle. 'You'll have to do better than that.'

'It's true.'

'Even if it is, I'm not giving you my phone number. I only give that to my friends.'

'Well, I'm a friendly guy.'

'I'm sure you are, Red,' she said levelly, 'but so is my neighbourhood dogcatcher. Doesn't mean to say I'll be giving him my phone number.'

I could see she was someone who knew her own mind and to push for her number wouldn't lead anywhere worthwhile. I wondered if I'd made a connection; she had used my name and there was something in her eyes that told me she might, perhaps, be a little intrigued.

'Okay, then let me give you *my* number.' I slipped a business card from my pocket and proffered it.

She took it reluctantly. 'Why would I want your number? It's not as if I'm going to call you.'

'Well, you never know. You might. You could change your mind and decide that I would be a good bloke to go out with; that you'd actually enjoy having dinner with me.'

She shook her head. 'Don't hold your breath, Red.'

I returned to the table where the others were waiting in expectation.

'So, did you get a date?'

'No.'

They laughed.

'What about her phone number? Did you get that?'

'No. But I gave her my number.'

They laughed louder. 'Did she tell you to *voetsek*? I bet she did. I bet she said *voetsek*.' I knew they were pulling my leg, but what they didn't appreciate was that, even in the few seconds I'd stood at her table, something about Natasha had got to me. I tried to take my mind off her. 'So what is this *voetsek*?' I asked. 'When I first came here it's all anyone ever said to me.'

'It's a word you use when some annoying little dog starts snapping at your ankles,' Fryk told me.

'Or a pesky Pekinese starts humping your trouser leg,' Fred added, laughing.

'Or when an irritating Australian interrupts your lunch,' Wessie chuckled. 'Hey, maybe that's why she wouldn't date you. Because you're Australian.'

'Yeah, and that's another thing, while you're all opening up. When I was first trying to sell my program, whenever I told a cop I was Australian, he practically threw me out of the station. What was that about?'

'They would have thought you were a Wallabies supporter and you know how Rugby is a religion here. We hate being beaten and the Wallabies have beaten us. They wouldn't like you for that reason alone.'

'But I've never watched a game of rugby in my life.'

'Just as well you didn't tell them that, man. They'd have marked you down as a homosexual Australian and thrown you in the cells.' Again they burst into laughter.

I laughed too. These guys were good friends, but, like mates everywhere, when it came to women they were bound to give me a hard time. It was a natural law of the universe.

I glanced across at Natasha's table and caught her eyeing me. She looked away quickly.

I never forgot her.

I went back to the restaurant a few times in the hope she might be there. She wasn't, and my disappointment was much sharper than it had any right to be. Why should I care so much? I had only spoken to her for a minute. But it looked like I'd have to live with it. She wasn't going to call me.

I'd travelled north, accompanying Fred and Derrick — another senior SAPS officer — on a semi-official South African Police Service tour of goodwill to Zambia, Zimbabwe and Botswana.

We'd cruised down the Chobe River by ferry, enjoying the sight of elephants grazing majestically in the distance, giraffes feeding on acacias and crocodiles concealed in nearby mud flats.

At the end of a long day, we set up camp in the Savuti Marshes. Feeling a little stiff after unpacking our gear from the four-wheel drive, I decided to go for a jog. Fred and Derrick were happy to stay in camp and prepare the evening meal over a couple of Botswana beers — which we all agreed were surprisingly good — so I jogged along the river bank alone.

I'd gone about a kilometre when I caught a flash of movement over to the left of me. Whatever it was, it was reasonably large, brownish in colour, and fast. Knowing it was probably stupid to keep going, I kept going. About fifty metres on, I caught another flash of movement, this time to my right, and closer. I scanned the area and was just starting to hope I was imagining things when, looking straight ahead, what I saw made my legs go rigid. Sitting in the middle of the track, staring intently and directly at me, was a very large baboon. It was less than twenty metres away. Maybe it was just being territorially aggressive, but I had never seen such molten hostility and blatant contempt pouring from a set of eyes. I could actually *feel* the ape's loathing, as if it were a physical weapon.

To my left, I caught a glimpse of movement. To my right, another flash of fur and limbs. I quickly glanced over my shoulder; four more baboons were circling behind me.

The fear I felt at that point was, quite simply, primeval. It went far beyond being scared; it was something else altogether. My throat contracted, my heart rate spiked, my legs shook, and I started to sweat; not the clean healthy sweat that comes from a good workout, but a sickening, viscous sweat that consumes and inhibits.

The large baboon blocking the path was clearly the troop leader. Not only did he have an overwhelming air of regal arrogance, but the other baboons — of which the number seemed to be growing by the second — were clearly deferring to him with head bobs and furtive glances. It was as if they were minions humbly requesting his royal consent to rip me to pieces.

Fear riveted me to the ground.

I could hear the blood thumping in my temples.

Motionless, the baboon stared.

And stared.

What seemed to be an eternity slowly ticked by.

Still the baboon stared.

Suddenly, the creature burst into action; in a single bound it sprang forward, bared its teeth and *yelled* … it did not growl, or howl or make a noise you would expect from an animal; it *yelled*.

I have no idea what prompted me to do what I did next; it did not conform to the Kontact principle of *not* matching your opponent's mode of attack, but it did demonstrate the value of non-compliance and not easily submitting. I sprang forward, bared my teeth and yelled too.

The effect was instantaneous; the baboon's eyes widened in shock — we were now less than four metres from each other and I could see his eyes clearly. He seemed to stop in midair.

I yelled again.

Reluctantly, and with a hatred that was palpable, the baboon withdrew a few paces. I yelled again. I spent the next twenty minutes slowly walking backwards to camp.

Every few paces I would have to stop, bare my teeth and growl at the closest baboon. They followed to within a hundred metres of the camp. It was the longest twenty minutes of my life.

Arriving back at camp, Derrick — lounging on a canvas chair, with an iced beer in one hand and a cheroot in the other — casually remarked, 'You took your time. Another couple of beers and I was goin' to start thinking about seeing if you were okay.'

When I eventually got back to my flat in Pretoria, the little red dot on my answering machine was flashing like a strobe light. It was late and I was half tempted to leave the messages till morning, but I grabbed a pad and ballpoint, and sat by the machine.

Natasha's call came halfway through the sequence. I recognised her voice instantly.

She left a number. I glanced at my watch. Damn … damn … too late to call her now. I went to bed feeling as if I'd won the lottery and called her early the following morning.

She sounded a little reticent but said she'd thought about it and had decided she might have dinner with me, though only if she chose where and when. She wasn't used to dating, she said, which surprised me. I'd have thought someone as beautiful as she would have been fighting them off with a flamethrower.

Her choice of restaurant was small and unpretentious with good food and friendly staff. She'd had her share of tragedy: though young, Natasha was a widow. Kevin, her husband, had been killed in a car accident when she was five weeks pregnant with their second child, Cuan. Kevin's family and her own, both extensive, had rallied round and seen her through the nightmare. It had taken her almost four years to recover but now, she told me across the candlelight, she was emerging, getting ready to face life once more.

By the end of the evening I knew I was in love.

Twelve days later we were married.

In a simple, flower-strewn ceremony at which Albertus Wessels was best man, I was adopted by Natasha and her children, Reilly and Cuan.

A few days later, as I was finishing a training session on the garden lawns, I noticed a Presidential aide hovering close to the beloved flowerbeds. Grabbing a towel I jogged across the lawn.

'Is it true you have recently married a South African woman?' the aide asked.

'Yes. Why, is that a problem?'

The aide shook his head. 'No. The President wishes to congratulate you. He asks if you and your wife would have lunch with him at Government House. Next Friday?'

Our names were announced as we were ushered into an enormous dining room where we were surprised to find we were the only guests. As the double doors closed silently behind us, Mandela stood up, his eyes on Natasha.

'Natasha,' he said in his gravelly voice, 'you are truly beautiful. Tell me, why did you marry *him*?'

The light-hearted remark set the tone for what was, for me, one of the most memorable lunches of my life. Natasha was a seventh-generation South African, with a vast network of relatives, and she and Mandela had a surprising amount of history and personal experience in common.

Close up, I saw that I was about the same height and build as Mandela who said that in his youth he had been a serious distance runner and boxer. Cross-country running, Mandela told me, had taught him the valuable lesson that training counted for far more than natural ability.

That discovery — that diligence and discipline could compensate for a lack of natural aptitude — had stood him in good stead in everything he had done since. He had, he said, seen countless young men with outstanding natural ability who had not had the patience or self-discipline to maximise their advantages. Being in Mandela's presence and listening to him speak was exhilarating. At last I'd found someone who could truly lay claim to the title of guru; though Mandela would probably be the last man on earth to actually claim it.

When the time came for us to leave, I said, 'Thank you, sir. We've had a marvellous time.'

He placed a hand on my shoulder and said, 'I do not like to be called sir, especially by my guests. Why don't you call me Madiba? Everyone else does.'

Walking away I reflected on how often I'd been forced to address some snobby subaltern or pissed punter as sir. I'd always hated it.

It seemed ironic that the only person I'd met in my entire life who I'd have been happy to call sir, should refuse it. It was a lesson that true greatness comes quietly and with humility. It's the wankers the world over who scream for recognition and honorifics. In a chapter entitled Correct Carriage and Warrior Attitudes, in *The Book of Five Rings* by Miyamoto Musashi, Japan's greatest swordsman had written: *'The true warrior does not go around telling everyone he is a great warrior. He permits his actions to govern other's responses ... you must understand this basic lesson.'*

In the house of Nelson Mandela — Madiba — I was in the presence of a true warrior.

* * *

Natasha fell pregnant almost immediately and we moved into a big house complete with a swimming pool and separate maid's quarters, hiring both a maid and a garden boy to take care of the domestic chores.

It was, without doubt, the good life. My business was now firmly embedded in a score of South African agencies and though I still made trips away to run courses, in my newfound domesticity I limited my overseas visits. For a whole lot of reasons I didn't like being away from Tash and the kids; most critically because of security concerns.

Though South Africa had been good to me, it was, undeniably, a violent country — and getting more violent every day. Car-jacking, home invasion, murder and rape were all common. Within a few kilometres of our new house, five men, armed with AK47s, had broken into a home and, in the process of robbing the place, had shot and killed the mother and father of an eleven-year-old girl who they had then proceeded to rape on the floor beside her dead parents. The incident was considered too commonplace to make the national news.

The country seemed to be descending into chaos and the violence that previously had been a peripheral concern to me was now central to my life. I was a married man with a wife and the responsibility of children; a responsibility that hugely increased with the birth of our son Liam.

So much of our life was concentrated on security. Despite the continuing risk of car-jacking I drove the children to school through fifty-five minutes of rush-hour traffic rather than send them on a school bus that had been hijacked by men with machine-guns three times in three months. And, coming home every evening, Tash and I followed a ritual that would have been laughably neurotic if it hadn't been so necessary.

And so deadly serious.

Driving into our street I'd check the footpath, fence line and gates for anything unusual while listening for the Dobermans to start barking, thereby confirming they were still alive. Arriving in front of the eight-foot gates I'd check the rear and side mirrors for anyone behind the car before leaping out, locking the door and opening the gates while Tash climbed over the central console and put the car into reverse, ready for a quick getaway. All being normal I'd open the gates to allow Tash to drive in quickly before slamming them shut. I hated the whole ritual, especially as Tash, pregnant with our second child, found it increasingly difficult to climb around in the car.

We were living like mediaeval barons walled up in our castle, afraid to venture into a world filled with danger. Our home was a cage; gilded on the inside, ugly on the outside with high fences and gates; every window barred, every wall splattered with alarm boxes. What was worse, whole sections of the population were descending into a sea of hysteria over security. People were paranoid, trigger-happy, primed to explode at the least provocation.

Returning to my car in a car park, I watched a guy zoom into a bay that a woman, waiting in her car, had been indicating she wanted. It was the kind of shitty, bullying behaviour I had no time for, made worse by the fact that the guy and his mate were openly laughing at their cleverness. Without thinking, I went up to the guys' car and tapped on the window. The man burst out of the vehicle like a tornado, crashing his door open and slamming me backwards before bulldozing me against the side of the next car with his heavy gut. The guy was big and had a long reach. He threw a punch, which I jammed with my briefcase before driving my elbow into his head. He went down unconscious.

The woman driver seemed both grateful and impressed, saying repeatedly, 'No one wants to get involved or help other people any more.' A minute later the police arrived — and I was arrested for assault. Some days later I received a writ from the guy I'd dropped, suing me for damages for the sum of a million rand. In the end the charges were dropped and the claim for damages came to nothing, but not before the woman's solicitor had written to me telling me that his client did not wish to be involved and not to call her as a witness in any court proceedings.

It gave me something to think about. Supposing the guy had had a gun in the car? I was a husband and a father who had risked himself — for what? For the sake of decent behaviour and a woman whose commitment and integrity went no deeper than her make-up.

I talked it over with Tash.

'I want this family to live in a place where the kids can walk down the street to buy an ice cream without the very good chance of being murdered or raped,' I said. 'Last year, this country had seventeen *thousand* recorded murders. Australia, with half the population, had three hundred.'

'Australia.' She didn't sound very enthusiastic.

'Yes. I think we should consider emigrating there.'

I knew it was a hard ask. South Africa was Natasha's home, her family part of its warp and weft. To go to Australia would be dragging her and the older children up by the roots, taking them away from close-knit families that had seen them through the death of their father. And Australia would cost. While we were pretty affluent in the Republic, with the exchange rate and the comparative price of property, migrating to Australia would mean starting over again from well behind the line.

But things were changing. Mandela was coming to the end of his term and had announced he would not run again for President. I had a notion that when he stepped down life might be different. I would miss Madiba, who occasionally stopped in the gardens to talk, chatting about anything from his personal philosophy to the days when he had boxed.

And then, as if on cue, Andy Chalmers called me from Stirling Lines at Hereford. He had a contact, he said, an Australian SAS major who was one of the senior security managers for the 2000 Sydney Olympic Games. The Olympic committee wanted me to teach Kontact to the police and military instructors assigned to Dignitary and Athlete Protection. It was a big, prestigious contract. And very tempting.

What finally settled matters for me was being woken one night to the sound of screaming. The screams were coming from out on the street, from what sounded like a woman in fear of her life. I leapt out of bed and rushed towards the front of the house, checking on the children as I went. The woman's screams had woken them, and as I scuttled from room to room they too began screaming. Reaching a front window I peered into the sickly glow of the streetlights to see a hysterical woman running the length of the street. Racing after her was a man, bellowing abuse and waving a piece of timber over a metre long.

My instinct was to rush outside, scale the gates and deck the guy. I turned — and stopped. Was it a set-up? A classic ruse to lure me out of the house so five men with AK47s could get in, murder Tash and rape the children? But supposing the woman was an innocent victim? I could help. But should I? I had a family. Surely, they had to come first. I wanted to help the woman but ... I moved from foot to foot, torn one way and then the other.

Finally I decided, turning back to the window to watch the man and woman disappear into the gloom at the far end of the street.

It was the right decision, I told myself; I was a husband and father now. I couldn't take unnecessary risks.

But, if it was so right — why did I feel like such a total arsehole?

It was a terrible feeling, and I had an idea that if I stayed in South Africa it was one I'd experience a lot.

Jointly we made the decision to leave. It was the right thing to do. In Australia we could stop living behind high walls and barred windows. In Australia we could raise our children free from fear and the ever-present threat of violence. Australia was the land of opportunity. And if I could be successful in South Africa ... imagine how well I could do in my own country. Already I had a lucrative contract to go back to. It was *definitely* the right thing to do.

Madiba invited us to the Presidential Estate to say goodbye and I asked one of the bodyguards to take a photograph of us: Madiba, grinning and holding Liam in his arms, Natasha, the older children and me.

He noticed Natasha was pregnant again and talked about children and family life. 'You must remember, Aussie,' he said, 'there is only one thing a child owes its parent.'

'What's that, Madiba?'

'Nothing. A child owes a parent nothing. A child does not owe a parent respect. A child does not owe a parent gratitude. These are gifts the child *chooses* to give. But only if the parent deserves them.'

There were many things I was going to miss about South Africa: Nelson Mandela was definitely one of them.

DUAL WORLDS

1999–2005

A STRANGE WALK IN TWO
DIAMETRICALLY OPPOSED WORLDS.

CHAPTER 22

The Lucky Country

EIGHTEEN YEARS after escaping Bairnsdale I was back. Tash and I wanted to spend some time with my parents and give the children an opportunity to experience rural Australia while we got ourselves on our feet financially.

It was great to be away from the pressure of life in Johannesburg but even so, Bairnsdale was hard to take. Everything I had done, all I had learnt over almost two decades, didn't count for much in that particular shire. The most common question I encountered was, 'So, what are you going to do now?'

The unvoiced attitude was that I had my head in the clouds and ought to come down to earth like ordinary folk. It reminded me of an incident immediately after our lunch with Madiba. Blown away by the fact that Natasha and I had just been in the presence of one of the world's greatest leaders, I had wanted to tell someone, to share the experience. I rang my eldest sister, Julie, a school teacher in Bairnsdale.

'You'll never guess who Tash and I had lunch with today,' I'd announced. I knew I sounded like an enthusiastic schoolboy, but it had been a big event in my life — in anybody's life. 'Nelson Mandela. Imagine that? We actually had lunch with Nelson Mandela.'

'Yeah? So you and who else?' she had said.

'No, there was nobody else. We were the only ones. Just him and Tash and me.'

There had been a silence on the other end of the line, then, 'But why would Nelson Mandela want to have lunch with you?' Even at six thousand miles I heard the bewilderment in her tone.

'He wanted to congratulate us on getting married.'

'Nelson Mandela wanted to congratulate *you*?'

With that my mood had evaporated.

For me, every day in Bairnsdale was surreal, a waking dream of incongruous images and forgotten memories. I was in a constant state of unsettling *déjà vu*. It was odd, in the extreme, introducing Tash and the kids to people I'd once gone to kindergarten with; triple-chinned, nicotine-stained strangers who we bumped into when shopping or just taking a walk.

We were marking time until the Olympics contract came on line. Andy Chalmers had worked hard to get me the deal and Andy's counterpart, Greg Shaw, the Australian SAS Major, now a senior security manager for the Games, was a good bloke, and supportive, but the whole issue of Olympics security was beset by politics and vested interests. I lost count of the number of times I travelled to Sydney on my own money to be told, yet again, that the start date had been postponed; the extent of the training I was to provide, reduced.

In the meantime I needed to develop Kontact in Australia.

This was easier said than done.

I had new brochures printed up outlining my program and sent copies off to state and federal police authorities, the military and other target groups. Their response reminded me of my early days in South Africa, with the added twist that not only was there disbelief in what I was offering, but also a weird kind of jealousy.

Time and again I was told there was no record of any Australian training Mandela's bodyguard, the British SAS or FBI SWAT teams. I didn't get it; why *would* a cop or soldier in Australia be aware of what I'd done overseas? Nelson Mandela or Doug Able was hardly going to phone up some suburban constable and inform them of my history. And though I supplied contact details for Fred Blaaue, Doug Able and Andy Chalmers, not one Australian bureaucrat contacted these people to verify my claims.

Back in Bairnsdale, my brother found me a way to fill the time waiting for Sydney. A regular at Steve's pub, a guy I'd gone to school with, coached a local Aussie Rules football team and asked me if I would train the squad midweek. I thought it would be a bit of a lark to train some local guys so I said yes.

Sixty blokes turned up, and though they were almost all younger than me, from what I could see under the floodlights of the muddy, rundown oval of the team's training ground, none of them looked especially fit. Many were overweight and at least half, after a few minutes warm-up in the cold, bleak, misty Gippsland evening, were coughing nicotine.

I worked them for sixty minutes, careful not to overdo it with guys so patently out of condition. Even at half pace, several of them went staggering to the sidelines to throw up. At the next session twenty of the original sixty turned up; at the session after that, seven. There was no fourth session.

The guy who'd hired me told me that my training was just too hard for his men to take. I didn't point out that he was paying fifty bucks a session for the same training the FBI had paid thousands for, but I couldn't resist asking if his team was at all interested in winning. It was a remark that didn't go down very well.

That night, for the first time ever, I felt like I needed a beer. It wasn't a burning desire, but I didn't like it; surrounded by beer-bellied slobs I was tempted to take solace in a few ales myself. Instead I read Harry Potter to the kids and went to bed early with Tash. A little before midnight the phone rang. It was Steve, calling from the local pub, drunk and asking for help.

Walking into the bar, nothing had changed; the floor was sticky with spilt beer, the air thick with cigarette smoke and the sickly-sweet stench of stale grog. Clean-shaven and sober, I stood out like dog's balls.

When Steve spotted me he growled, 'Now you're fucked, you bastards. My brother'll kick yer skulls in.'

Three men turned their heads to look in my direction.

On making eye-contact Punter #1 sneered and said, 'What, that faggot?' His cronies cackled.

Punter #2, a tall streak of pelican shit, stood up menacingly from his bar stool as Punter #3, a pot-bellied fat-boy with no neck, circled behind the pool table. I knew exactly where this was going.

It was a textbook scenario; the blueprint was simple, and proven: *subtract the leader; move to a flank; deliver a good skill on one person, move straight onto another. Aim to finish quickly. Don't stuff around. Keep moving — no matter what. Don't fight them in the way they want to fight. Be aggressive. Win.* It was easy. I'd done it before.

Masking my face with a hint of timidity I positioned myself in front of Punter #1. He was standing now and in a bellow loud enough to drown out the lyrics of a Jimmy Barnes song pumping from the jukebox, was busy describing in detail what was about to befall my brother and I; every second word, predictably, was 'fucking'. The blue and grey squares of his flannelette shirt were just inches from my chest.

Ignoring the dribble coming from his mouth I selected a pre-emptive strike as I watched Pelican Shit take a swig of beer while Fat Boy left my peripheral vision, having fully circled behind me.

I knew what was coming.

The feeling of my elbow driving into the loudmouth's jaw would marry with a sound like wet clay smacking against a brick wall. Then, in the distorted window of time that followed, I'd see Loudmouth stumble back with a look of surprised pain on his face during the heart beats it took for him to decide whether to fight or quit. As that decision was unfolding Pelican Shit would start swinging. He wouldn't aim; he'd just thrash wildly. I'd flinch my hands up to protect my head before closing the gap and clinching on for dear life as I drove my knee into his peroneal nerve. Meanwhile, Fat Boy would be barrelling in without thinking — Fat Boys always barrel in without thinking. His goal would be simple; to take the fight to the ground. That was fine by me; I'd go with the flow and as soon as he made body contact I'd force my thumb deep into his eye-socket. It would be over in seconds.

It was easy. Too easy.

'The car's out the front Steve. Get in the passenger seat.'

Steve looked disappointed. 'What? Aren't you gunna teach these pricks a lesson?'

'Get in the car, now.'

'But …'

'Just get in the fuckin' car, before I break your fuckin' nose.'

My brother looked more shocked than if I'd belted him. He started to speak, stopped, then without another sound drunkenly stumbled away.

Pelican Shit laughed. It was a sound cruel people make when they get what they want without knowing how they got it.

I turned and walked towards the exit. No one followed.

The following Sunday was an unusually fine day and after enjoying a family picnic Tash and I strolled along the riverbank while my parents played with the children.

A few hundred metres ahead of us, a man in some kind of uniform was doing a jig on the riverbank, hopping from foot to foot and running in tight circles. I felt my intuition telling me something was wrong. I ignored the feeling. I didn't want to be bothered by my ferreting instinct. I had things to talk about with Tash, was enjoying myself holding her hand and strolling by the side of the river. I took my gaze off the man for a few moments then switched it back. Even at that distance everything about his body language was screaming that something was wrong. Maybe not, I told myself. The guy could be jigging around like that for any number of reasons, though right then I couldn't think of what they might be. Anyway, there were other people on the riverbank; if there was a problem one of them could handle it.

I switched my attention to what Tash was saying, deliberately fixing my eyes on her. After a minute or so I couldn't help myself and glanced again at the man.

By now we were close enough that I could see the uniform was that of a First Aid Volunteer.

The guy was having some kind of seizure. A small crowd had gathered around him.

'Look, I'm sorry,' I interrupted Tash, 'something's going on up ahead. It isn't good. You stay here; I'm going to see what the problem is.' I jogged swiftly, arriving to find the First Aid Volunteer lathered in sweat, rolling his eyes and clutching his chest. 'What's happening?' I asked one of the crowd. 'Is he ill?'

'No. He says there's some kid in the water.'

'What?' I turned and fronted the volunteer. 'There's a kid in the water? Where?'

The man pointed out into the river with a shaking hand. 'A little girl.' His voice was high and quavering. 'Out there. Under a log.'

'Shit. Well, come on. We gotta get her.'

'No. I can't.'

I stared at him. 'What?'

'I can't leave my oxygen resuscitation kit.' He pointed to a bulky piece of equipment at his feet.

I gazed into the man's eyes. They were all over the place: something inside the man had retreated from reality; he was no longer present, no longer a participant.

I turned and jumped into the river. The water came up to my waist and was surprisingly cold. There was a splash and an older guy with short grey hair was beside me; another splash and a tall, gangling kid in his late teens was on the other side. The three of us eased into the river. We reached the log and began groping around, our feet churning up oozy mud, turning the water black.

The kid ducked under the water and came up rubbing his eyes. 'Can't see,' he gasped. It took us what seemed like minutes to locate the child stuck fast under the log. The older guy and I lifted the log as best we could while the kid pulled her out. Though the girl, aged about ten or eleven, was thin and light, it was a struggle carrying her back. Between us we lifted her onto the bank.

'Quick,' I gasped. 'Give her oxygen.' We dragged ourselves out of the water and made room for the volunteer to work.

'I can't,' the volunteer wailed.

'What do you mean, you can't?' the grey-haired guy growled. 'You're the qualified one here. The most qualified gets the job.'

I was glad to know at least one other person knew the score.

'I can't,' the volunteer repeated.

'Anyone here know how to operate this equipment?' the old guy demanded.

There was a round of shaking heads. 'You've *got* to do it.' He stabbed a finger at the volunteer.

'Forget him, he's out of it,' I murmured. I knelt beside the girl and began CPR.

'No, no, that's not the way you do it,' the volunteer screamed. 'That's all wrong.' I ignored him. 'No, that's wrong.'

I looked up from beside the girl's body. 'Anyone properly trained in CPR?'

'I am,' the grey-haired guy said quietly. He moved beside the girl and took over. Though I could see the man was much more practised than I was, the volunteer continued to wail that he was doing it all wrong.

Then, just as we heard the ambulance drawing up on the paddock of the picnic area, the volunteer snapped out of his paralysis. Moving the older guy aside he bent to the girl and began applying professional CPR.

It was too little too late. I caught the old guy's eye. The girl was dead.

I stayed to give a statement to the police before driving home in a sombre mood. After we had put the kids to bed and I'd read to them, I sat with Tash. 'I am never going to ignore my intuition again,' I told her. 'If I'd listened to what my gut was telling me instead of my brain, that kid might still be alive.'

'You don't know that,' she told me. 'And the point is … you did something. That First Aid Volunteer didn't do anything.'

I wanted to agree, but couldn't. I'd had enough. I needed to get away.

On a theoretical level, I knew there must be plenty of people in Bairnsdale who were participants of life — not mere spectators — unfortunately, on a practical level, I didn't know any. The incompetence of the First Aid Volunteer, the attitude of Pelican Shit and his cronies and the slothfulness of the local footy coach seemed typical of the people I was crossing paths with.

The following day I called Greg Shaw who told me there was still no progress on the Olympics contract. During the call I mentioned my decision to get out of Bairnsdale. Greg said he had a friend with a house for rent in Soldiers Point on Nelson Bay, forty kilometres north of Newcastle in New South Wales. I took it unseen, a few days later driving to a local solicitor's office to sign the lease agreement.

I got home to find my mother in tears. My father had been admitted to hospital — decades of heavy smoking had caught up with him. He died four days later.

It was a hard time.

While grieving for my father, I was joyously looking forward to the birth of my second child; while arranging for my father's funeral, I was preparing to move my family over a thousand kilometres away.

Though I'd never been close to my father I had loved him, and, what's more, I'd respected him for the fact that all his life he had been his own man. He had never drunk alcohol or shown any interest in football (no small feat in a town like Bairnsdale); he'd raised four kids on a basic wage and been faithful to the same woman for forty-four years. He had also tried to make a better life for his family by starting his own business, and though he hadn't succeeded he died at least having tried.

The price he paid for that failed venture undoubtedly sapped his spirit in a number of ways, however it never stole from his responsibility as a father. Several years later, my parents had — through hard work and frugal living — managed to save a small nest egg. Just as they were getting ready to use that money for a deposit on a home, my eldest sister Julie and her husband fell on hard times. Instead of buying their own home, my parents lent the cash to my sister and brother-in-law. It took them years to repay the loan — during which time my parents were forced to live in cheap rental properties — but not once did I hear my father complain or demonstrate impatience. He trusted that my sister would pay the loan as quickly as possible — which she eventually did. My parents were happy to help and, naturally, they refused any interest.

I didn't express these thoughts to the packed church when I was asked to deliver my father's eulogy, though I did emphasise his independence and individuality, knowing as I spoke that, by implication, I was criticising many in the town for their compliance and inertia. I didn't care. This was my father's funeral and I felt entitled to speak my mind. If that made some people squirm, then so be it. I finished by saying, 'It is hard to imagine a greater richness or more honourable title than to be called a devoted husband and loving father. My father was both of those things.'

For a moment there was complete silence before the congregation burst into spontaneous applause.

A week later we left for New South Wales where my second son, Blake, was born.

CHAPTER 23

Soldiers Point

'I THINK I'm going to write a book,' I said to Natasha. I had just finished my nightly ritual of reading to the children and returned to the lounge carrying the kids' copy of *The Power of One*.

Natasha, feeding the baby, looked up. 'What about?'

'Just some of the things I've learnt over the past few years. How to compete, how to perform in any situation with confidence. I think a book would help to promote Kontact.'

'It sounds like a good idea but I don't think it's all that easy to write a book.'

Tash was right, of course. It wasn't easy getting my thoughts down in a logical, readable order, but as hard as writing the book was, it was nothing compared to trying to sell it. I approached over a dozen publishers with my manuscript. Most took months to respond with a terse, dismissive two-line rejection; some wrote a few extra lines to tell me there was no demand for a book like mine. Some didn't reply at all. Yet the more I was rejected the more I believed in my book. I'd called it *Perform with Confidence*, and now I'd written it I was even more determined to see it in bookshops. There seemed to be only one option.

'We're going to have to publish it ourselves,' I told Tash.

'That sounds expensive.'

'It is. But I've got a pretty good idea of who'll want to buy it and how to get it to them. So why use a publisher? In the end this book will make money.'

'And in the meantime?'

215

'In the meantime, we use our savings to cover the cost of printing.'

'The money that's our deposit for a home?'

'Yep.'

Tash had her concerns, but one of the many reasons I love her is that she is not a fearful person — of course, like any sane person, uncertainty can intimidate her but she is prepared to embrace a challenge and give it her best shot. Together we managed the project of publishing the book; we were the editors, the typesetters, the proofreaders, the graphic designers. We sourced the paper, selected the printer and began marketing the book, selling it into bookshops in Queensland and New South Wales. Most outlets demanded fifty per cent of the cover price and when I crunched the numbers I saw that, even though the book was starting to sell well, I was never going to make money out of it. It looked like the best I could hope for was to break even.

More by luck than design, I managed to get myself some slots on local and national radio stations talking about both *Perform with Confidence* and Kontact. I discovered, happily, that media people are the biggest media feeders and that once I'd been noticed by one media outlet, others were eager to take me up.

Attention from the radio stations triggered interest from the *Today Show*, which filmed me running a Kontact course in Sydney at the University of New South Wales. The exposure not only helped sales of the book but also prompted interest from the prime-time *60 Minutes*. The program, which had been looking at the security aspects of the Sydney Olympics for months, initiated investigations into how Kontact fitted into the overall security of the Olympics.

I was delighted, and I enjoyed the irony. After more than twelve months since being approached for the job, I was still waiting for the committee at SOCOG to give me the go-ahead to start my training. Now, still without a firm start date, Kontact was becoming the focus of media attention.

Not being a political animal I didn't appreciate the position I was in. Not yet contracted to SOCOG, I was a free agent and therefore at liberty to talk about security training at the Olympics. Somebody at the top realised this and suddenly there were urgent moves to sign me up, the unseemly urgency flushing out the hidden bias that had been holding the contract back. When it was reported that I was about to be signed, a middle manager with the New South Wales police apparently fell out of his tree, demanding to know, 'Who is this character? I've never heard of him. Our instructors are the best in the world. What the hell is Kontact anyway? Can't this moron even spell?'

Yet despite middle-ranking policemen throwing their toys out of the cot, I was finally signed to provide training for the Sydney Olympics to instructors from the Federal Police, the SAS, the State Protection Group and the New South Wales Police. The contract specifically prohibited the media from filming the training.

A couple of days before the program was due to start at a commando base in Randwick, I took a call at home from a producer of a national current affairs television program interested in running a feature on my training routine. I explained that I couldn't talk about training for the Olympics and nor could the guy film it.

'Yeah yeah, that's okay mate,' the producer said. 'I want to do a feature on you. I think you've got potential. You and your self-defence stuff might make a good three or four minute piece. Get you to do a few fancy moves, that kind of thing.'

'I don't do fancy moves.'

'Well, mate, whatever you do, I need you to do it big. Smash a few bricks. You can do that, can't you?'

'I don't know. I've never smashed a brick in my life.'

'You haven't?'

'I don't get a lot of call to hit a brick. I've never been attacked by a brick, so why would I hit one?'

There was a moment's silence.

'Look mate, I don't think you understand *television*.'

He said the word as if it was the secret of the cosmos and the

Ruler of the Universe combined. 'You've got to impress the viewers. Make them go wow, mate.'

I was getting irritated at this unknown, pushy spruiker calling me mate. 'Look, I'm not presenting martial arts training. I'm concerned about improvement. I provide honest and realistic training. It's supposed to *do* good, not look good.'

'Yeah, but you've still got to put on a show, mate.'

'I think you've got the wrong stooge, *mate*.' I put the phone down.

Afterwards, I wondered if I'd done the right thing. It would have been marvellous exposure. But to have done what the guy wanted would have been a sell-out, more than a contradiction of everything I believed about my program; it would have been a slap in the face to people like Wessie who had taught me so much. And yet … it would have been a big boost to my business. I shook my head. What the hell. I'd made my decision. There was no going back on that now.

Only there was. The guy's production assistant called me the next day, telling me her boss was still willing to do a piece and that she needed to see my uniform. 'If it doesn't look right we'll get one specially tailored. Something that looks really good.'

I told her my 'uniform' was a pair of bush-walking boots, jeans and an old T-shirt. For a moment the PA seemed at a loss before she said, 'Well, all right, we'll get something made. And we think it would be better if you smashed some roof tiles.'

'What happened to the bricks?'

'Roof tiles are better. They'll look more impressive.'

'I don't get it. What the hell have you people got against building supplies?'

I caught the irritation in the PA's voice. 'Look, we're trying to help you,' she snapped. 'If you don't want us to run a story about you, there are plenty of other punters we can give national exposure to.'

'Fine. You do that.'

I put the phone down, again experiencing that swift, sneaking moment of guilty regret. Then I shrugged. Forget it, I told myself.

I had plenty else to occupy me. The Olympics training was due to start the next day.

If I had been a fatalist I would have sworn the SOCOG contract had been cursed from the beginning. On the afternoon of the first day I was wrestling with a guy from the SAS. The guy made a move and I countered, I made a move and the guy countered, I moved in as the guy pivoted, and I fell — awkwardly. The moment I hit the ground I knew I'd damaged myself. The pain in my shoulder and along my right arm was excruciating. Lying on the grass staring up at the sky I did what I'd instructed other injured men to do, I focused on my breathing, forcing the part of my mind screaming at the pain to concentrate on the slow, rhythmic movement of my lungs. At the Emergency Department of the Prince of Wales Hospital, Randwick, X-rays confirmed what I'd already guessed; my arm was fractured, my shoulder dislocated.

The next morning, with my shoulder heavily taped and my arm in a padded sling, I was back at the commando base where the guys made a lot of jokes about their unarmed combat instructor being a one-armed combat instructor. I laughed with them — I could see the funny side of the situation, though the nature of Kontact made it difficult to teach with one arm in a sling. Fortunately I was being assisted by my friend Graham Kuerschner, a forty-year veteran of martial science; with his help the course went well and feedback from the majority of participants was extremely positive.

The opinion of the doctors at the hospital in Newcastle was not so encouraging. My shoulder and arm were permanently damaged, they told me. My days of teaching unarmed combat were over. It was not good news, especially as Natasha was pregnant once more. Soon I would have six mouths to feed while my profession, my only source of income, looked as if it was going down the toilet.

'What are you going to do?' Tash asked me.

'Get better. Get my arm working again.'

'You think you can do that? The doctors seemed pretty sure you'd never get the strength back fully.'

'What do doctors know? They don't know me.'

'But they do know medicine. They know about damaged limbs. You could make it worse by trying to make it better.'

'Maybe. But if I'd listened to experts all my life I'd be living on the dole in Bairnsdale.'

She laughed. 'Don't tempt fate. It may come to that.'

I gave her a look. She laughed louder.

The trouble with being married to Natasha was … well … nothing.

I started rehabilitating my arm and shoulder straight away. When I came back from the local swimming pool a few days later, Tash was waiting with a message. 'A man called Geoff Crewe wants you to call him back.'

'Who is he?'

'He says he's a businessman from Melbourne. He's read *Perform with Confidence* and wants to talk to you about a presentation.'

'What kind of presentation?'

She shrugged. 'Why don't you call him and find out?'

The guy sounded businesslike and to the point. 'I liked your book,' he said, 'and was wondering if you would be prepared to deliver a keynote presentation at a conference I'm organising.'

'A keynote presentation?' I had only the haziest notion of what a keynote presentation was.

'Right. You'd need to talk for about fifty minutes.'

'Where?' I asked cautiously. Though Crewe sounded okay there was always a possibility he was some nutter who had got hold of my phone number.

'Just off the Gold Coast.'

I did the sums in my head. Travel to Queensland; accommodation for one, maybe two, nights; meals … it sounded as if the deal might cost me a lot of money.

'Are you … err … what are you thinking of paying?' I asked tentatively.

When Crewe told me, I had great difficulty in not screaming,

'What! How much?' Instead, in a neutral tone I said, 'Yes, that sounds acceptable. When?'

'Well, first I'd like you to come to Sydney to meet me and my business associate.'

'Well?' Tash asked when I got off the phone.

'That bloke just offered me a shed load of money to talk for fifty minutes.'

I liked both Geoff Crewe and his associate, Peter Drake, straight away. We met in a suite of plush offices in the CBD where I was clearly being vetted for my fitness to perform on a platform.

I passed the interview and a few weeks later I gave my first corporate presentation at an island resort off the coast of Queensland. I was a little nervous but compared to teaching and selling Kontact, public speaking is a walk in the park; there is no risk of physical injury and by that stage I'd worked out the keys to effective group communication; *do not learn a speech verbatim*; speak from the heart, not from notes; maintain eye contact with the people you want to convince; inject humour when possible; say what you believe is true. Never swear ... unless it's absolutely bloody necessary.

That first engagement led to another, and another. Pretty soon I was averaging at least one keynote a week for industries as diverse as telecommunications, real estate, finance and IT. And so began a strange walk in two diametrically opposed worlds: high-risk reaction and corporate speaking. Curiously I enjoyed both. Each was so obviously different from the other, yet also subtly similar, and I enjoyed the physical and intellectual contrasts ... in fact, I found it quietly amusing to be chauffeured to a five-star resort one day and then a few days later to be sweating it out with a SWAT team in some grubby gymnasium.

Life took on a sense of balance and security which was comfortable and fun. Despite the negative predictions, my shoulder recovered well; business was booming and, most importantly, my family was happy and healthy.

In what seemed no time, Natasha reached full term and was

admitted to the John Hunter Hospital in Newcastle where she gave birth to Brontë, our daughter, in the same room where eighteen months earlier, almost to the day, Blake had been born. It was a happy, joyful time. Our family seemed complete. Now we had two girls, the eldest and the youngest, like bookends, complementing and balancing the three boys.

Four weeks later the unimaginable happened. Little Brontë contracted a viral lung infection that rapidly multiplied its fatal potential by also developing into a bacterial infection. Rushed to John Hunter, she was connected by serious-faced nurses to life support and assigned round-the-clock supervision. From the other side of the sterile glass Natasha and I stared wide-eyed and numb with fear at our baby, her small, vulnerable body attached to machines by grotesque tubes as she alternated between fits of frighteningly violent coughing and a drugged unconsciousness that so closely resembled death.

Only twice were Natasha and I, wearing sterile gowns and masks, allowed close to her. On both occasions, placing my finger in the palm of her tiny hand and bending to brush my masked lips against her ear, I whispered, 'It's me, your daddy. I love you.'

Not once had I faced a situation as frightening as this. I had never felt so ineffectual. Like the wound opening before the knife, I was coming to understand the first horrific rule of parenthood; the worst thing that could possibly happen to me was never going to happen to *me*. It would happen to my children; it was happening to my daughter.

On the morning of the third day, pandemonium broke out in the ward where Brontë was being monitored: her tiny lungs had collapsed and, exhausted, she lacked the strength to take another breath. With six nurses in tow, she was rushed to Intensive Care where the on-duty specialist managed to revive her — for the time being.

'I have to be frank with you,' the specialist said, 'two days ago we had another baby with exactly the same symptoms. Sadly, that baby died. I don't want to be the bearer of bad news, but your little girl isn't going to make it.'

These were truly devastating words — words which my wife refused to accept. 'He may be a doctor,' Natasha said, 'but that doesn't mean he can predict her future!' There was no anger in Natasha's voice when she said this — just incredible love. And faith.

I wanted to help her but how could I? I wanted to be strong, to hold up for her and the children. But how could I be strong when I was so powerless? 'For God's sake,' I wailed, 'I wish there was something we could *do*. Anything. Something.'

'There is,' Tash said.

'What? Tell me. What?'

'We can pray.'

'Pray?'

'It's doing something, isn't it? As a matter of fact, it's doing a lot.'

First we prayed with the children and then, later, we prayed together in our room. Afterwards, she said, 'There, we did something.'

Curiously, I felt lighter, less weighed down. Nothing, absolutely nothing, had changed. Brontë still hovered between life and death, yet I felt better. I had done something. Natasha had made me do it.

We prayed at every opportunity for nine days. On the tenth day Brontë turned around. She began to recover.

We brought Brontë home two days later; she was gurgling and seeking to suckle. Carrying her into the house with my tired, smiling wife and happy, noisy children I thought … *this is living.*

That night I crept into Brontë's room. She was asleep, breathing peacefully. Placing my finger in the palm of her hand, I whispered close to her ear, 'It's me, your daddy. I love you.'

* * *

Since my first speaking engagement, Peter Drake had been introducing me to a whole spectrum of business contacts, one of whom was the CEO of a major British company with extensive property and financial interests in Australia. The company impressed me: unlike the indifferent bureaucrats in Australian government agencies I'd been trying to negotiate with, this company took the initiative and used its resources to check out my credentials in Britain and elsewhere. After a couple of presentations to executives of the company, the CEO offered me a major contract to train and develop his people in teamwork and what he described as 'streetwise leadership'.

The price we negotiated for one year's work was more than I would have earnt in ten years as an officer in the army. Returning to the house in Soldiers Point I burst through the door waving the contract. 'We're outta here,' I yelled.

Natasha and the children came running from the kitchen. 'What do you mean?' she laughed.

'I mean we're going to find a nice place to live and we're going to buy a house. Our own place.'

We finally settled on a place on a nine-acre block in the hinterland of the Gold Coast with a creek, plenty of bird life and the regular appearance of frilled-neck lizards, green tree frogs, and even the occasional wallaby. The main verandah was huge, with a westerly view overlooking a broad valley filled with eucalypts and acacias.

'So what do you think?' I asked as we surveyed it.

'I love it,' Natasha said. 'But it's a lot of money. Can we afford it?'

I laughed. 'No, we can't. But who the hell ever can afford their house?'

We moved in a few weeks later.

* * *

After 9/11, public interest in all things related to security increased dramatically. A New South Wales government organisation contacted me to conduct an evaluation of the personal defence training of its people. I spent several weeks working in the field with operators, looking at what they did and how they did it. To describe their training syllabus as woefully inadequate wouldn't even come close to indicating how truly ineffective — to the point of being downright dangerous — it was. I wrote a detailed report dissecting exactly what was wrong and what needed to be done to correct the problems. It was a long report. I learnt later I'd been hired to validate their program, not actually critique it. The organisation had no intention of changing anything; what they wanted was a tick in a box, a pat on the back and a hearty, 'Well done and keep up the great work.' Not getting the result they wanted from me, they paid a local martial arts guru to tell them what they wanted to hear and then kept on doing exactly what they had been doing — oblivious to Einstein's definition: *'Insanity is doing the same thing over and over again and expecting different results.'*

Having already proven the value of Kontact to groups like the Federal Bureau of Investigation and the British SAS, I had no desire at all to battle bureaucratic insanity. Apart from having some technical articles published in *Security Solutions* and the journal of the American Society for Law Enforcement Trainers, I kept a low profile. I continued to teach my program, but only if the group I was to teach seemed interesting. It was an approach that enabled me to provide for my family and still train, travel and learn.

After delivering a keynote presentation in Borneo I decided to recharge my batteries by being a student rather than a teacher. Timm Smith, a former Kontact student, had set up a successful bodyguard school in Hout Bay, South Africa. Internationally respected for its paramedical component, Timm's five-week intensive course included accompanying ambulance crews on emergency callouts. It was the type of real-world experience that appealed to me.

At 165kph the ambulance thundered past the oil refinery on the outskirts of Cape Town.

The unmistakable stench of processed fuel blended mercilessly with the more timeless stench of blood and excrement. Our last patient had been shot in the thigh, at close range with a shotgun, and then stabbed repeatedly with a broken beer bottle, puncturing his bowel in the process. There had been no time to clean the trolley after taking the patient to Somerset Hospital in the city; we had barely begun to unload when the radio crackled into life, demanding we move immediately to a squatter camp just beyond the refinery.

With the siren wailing and the ghostly image of acres of shanties in the electricity-starved camps juxtaposed against the neon opulence of the refinery, we belted towards our destination. How the driver knew where to turn off the main road and enter the darkened labyrinth of tin shacks was beyond me. It was after midnight when we started to crawl through the camp but it may as well have been the middle of the day. Dogs were barking aggressively and an eclectic collection of African music thumped out from distorted battery-powered speakers as children and adults stared intently at the spectacle of a bright white ambulance, red light flashing, slowly navigating the dirt tracks and open sewers of their private world.

Our patient was one of seven people living in a two-room shack; four adults and three children crammed into an area roughly the size of my laundry and bathroom. Sitting on a plastic sheet covered in vomit, urine and faeces was a young black woman who I guessed was only in her late teens, though her ravaged face looked much older. Clutched close to her breast was a small girl. It was impossible to guess the child's age but you didn't need a medical degree to know she was deathly ill; skeletal thin, her sunken eyes were almost lost in a fog of suffering that was beyond my comprehension.

Looking at the paramedic for guidance, I was surprised to see him shake his head and indicate we should leave. Silently he mouthed the single word, AIDS. That one word sent a shiver down my spine. I could feel the blood drain from my face as I took in the sights and smells of the shack.

Mistaking my lack of movement for a determination to offer assistance, the medic shrugged his shoulders in resignation and moved towards the small girl. He gently started to take her temperature as he instructed me to read the mother's blood pressure. As I was in the process of performing this simple task, the mother turned her head towards me and vomited. The force and heat of the contents of her stomach hitting my chest was stunning. The smell was horrific. Committed now, I tried to ignore the sensation of my shirt soaking up vomit like blotting paper soaking up ink as I followed the sad scenario through to its sorry conclusion. There was, of course, nothing we could do.

After that trip, going home to Australia and my family was even sweeter than usual. However, even though I knew there had been no *exchange* of body fluids, the thought that I might infect someone I loved was an ongoing worry until repeated tests indicated I was safe.

Some months after the invasion of Iraq I started getting calls. Some were from people I knew, some from people who had heard about me. They were all about the same thing.

Iraq.

The private security companies, of which there were hundreds, were paying top dollar to experienced people to provide protection to civilian workers. A twelve-month contract in Iraq would earn me enough to make me comfortable in Australia for several years. I said no to all of them. It wasn't solely because my business was doing well — I had a major series of keynote presentations lined up and had just secured a contract to teach Kontact to instructors from the Australian Air Marshal Program and Queensland's Special Emergency Response Team, plus an agreement to run training at the Dutch police academy at Ossendrecht.

Nor was it simply because Iraq was dangerous, although that was a factor.

The reason I refused all the callers was that I didn't agree with the war. It seemed to me — as it seemed to many others — that America had gone in with a hidden agenda, dragging Australia and the Brits with it. There were no weapons of mass destruction in the country, and it was becoming increasingly clear that the Americans had known that before they had invaded.

227

I might have felt differently if the invasion had been sanctioned by the United Nations.

I had no time for Saddam Hussein, and if the world community had said, 'Go get the bastard,' I would have been all for it.

But as it was, I was sorry but ... no.

In the couple of years after the invasion I took maybe a dozen calls related to Iraq. My fortieth birthday came and went, and my forty-first. I was teaching Kontact on a select basis, travelling overseas three or four times a year and making a comfortable living from corporate work in Australia.

Life was good.

And then came the seventh of July and the London bombings.

CHAPTER 24

Baghdad

IT'S FUNNY how little things can change the course of your life; an unexpected phone call; a chance meeting; a passing comment; a moment spent choosing between turning left or turning right.

I'd just finished a sixty-minute keynote address for a group of IT managers.

The presentation had gone well; the audience had laughed in all the right places, taken notes and generally had a good time. The conference organiser was happy with the result and was in the process of briefing me for another event when one of the delegates approached. I could see that the delegate was 'on a mission'.

'I liked your talk,' she said.

'Thanks.'

'But, don't you think you're a bit young to retire from the real world?'

'What do you mean?' I asked, though I had a feeling I knew what was coming.

Every now and then my talk would arouse strong personal feelings in a listener.

'If you've really got something to offer, what are you doing at a conference at a five-star resort?'

'You're at a conference at a five-star resort,' I said, keeping my tone light.

'Yes, but if I had your background and skills, I'd be helping aid workers in Africa or something like that.'

'Last month I spent two weeks in Kenya providing training for volunteers from UNICEF and World Vision.'

'You did?' She looked sceptical. 'You never said that in your speech.'

'There are lots of things I didn't say in my speech.'

'Well, even if that's true, I bet you were well paid for it.' The mix of avarice and envy in her tone was almost tangible.

'My trip to Kenya was completely voluntary. I didn't get paid a single cent.'

That stumped her. I guessed she was the kind of person who rarely, if ever, did anything without financial return. She looked like she was searching for a reply, started to speak, stopped and then stormed off.

Whether she believed me or not was irrelevant to me. Everything I'd said was the truth.

Very early in my speaking career I had made the conscious decision that I would always 'walk my talk'. Determined to avoid the traps of plush five-star conventions, business class travel, mini-bars and free luncheons I gave up alcohol completely. Maintaining a strict personal fitness regime I was also strict about the type of speaking engagements I took on; if the brief was relevant to my background, skills and beliefs then I accepted the job. Otherwise I would decline. This approach allowed me to stand in front of my bathroom mirror without encountering a hypocrite looking back at me.

On the flight home I thought about the delegate's comments, but not for long. It's simply not possible to please everyone.

The next day was the seventh of July. I watched the newscasts for hours; it was the longest time I'd sat in front of a television since I was a boy. I saw the bodies stretchered into the ambulances, the walking wounded shocked and bloodily bandaged, helped by the emergency services.

I've never been a flag-waver of any description. To me the best causes are those carried out in the absence of cameras or trophies. When I look at a fireman or a paramedic the word that frequently comes to mind is hero — not hero in a glittering sporting sense, but hero in that more honourable, humble sense. Watching the emergency workers dealing with the devastation of Tavistock Square, Kings Cross and Edgware Road, I was inspired. Unaccompanied by any bolt of lightning, I decided that I would go to Iraq. I would go to Iraq and provide close personal protection to aid workers in that country.

It's likely the conversation with the delegate the day before had contributed to my decision, but it's probable I would have reached the same conclusion anyway. Sometimes — not often, but sometimes — following a particular course of action just *feels* right. That doesn't mean that it feels *nice* or *easy*, but it does feel *right*. It would be possible to over-analyse that type of rationale, but for me it's a formula that works.

I shared my feelings with Tash, who gave me a worried look.

'But you don't agree with the war,' she said.

'No I don't, that's true. But there are thousands of people in Iraq who don't agree with the war. All those aid volunteers trying to help the Iraqis rebuild their country — they're not there supporting the war. They hate violence.'

'But you're not an aid volunteer.'

'I know that. But those people need protection, Tash.'

'And your family needs you alive,' she said.

'If I was still in the army and I was asked to go to Iraq, then I would. Lots of Aussie soldiers have been sent to Iraq. Many of them have families too. They don't go because they want to — they go because that's what they're trained to do. There's a contribution they can make. I think I can too. That's it.' I shrugged. 'That's how I feel.'

She gazed at me for a long moment. 'You've made up your mind about this, haven't you?'

I nodded.

'How long for?' she murmured.

'Three months maybe. I couldn't afford to go for much longer. I'll be giving up a lot of work here as it is.' Then she did one of the ten thousand things that make me love her without boundaries. She smiled.

'Well then, you'd better get packing,' she said as she wrapped her arms around me.

Months earlier I'd received an email from Greg Shaw saying that he was managing a security company in Iraq and offering me a job running advanced empty-hand training for his operatives. It was Greg who got me the SOCOG work, and with one of his men I had broken my arm on that first day of training. I called his mobile number. He seemed pleased to hear from me.

'Where are you?' I asked.

'Sitting in a compound in northern Iraq listening to small arms fire and a few mortars going off,' he laughed. 'Situation normal.'

'I was thinking if you have a job for me I might come out there for a bit.'

'Yeah? That'd be great. Right now I could offer you work training Iraqis as bodyguards for the new raft of Iraqi magistrates. The money's good; our training budget is healthy and I could make it worth your while.'

'Actually, I was thinking of something more like running defence for civilian aid-workers.'

'Really? Well, I should tell you the money's nowhere near as good and it's considerably more dangerous. With the training job you'd spend most of your time inside the compound. As part of a protection unit you're out there — on the streets.'

'How dangerous is dangerous?'

There was a moment's silence. 'We lost our first man last month.'

'What happened?'

'Suicide bomber. We were conducting an escort from Baghdad airport, sandwiched between two US Embassy convoys. Our guys were in the middle of the fleet and bore the brunt of the blast. One was killed on impact; one has both his legs broken, another has serious burns to thirty-five per cent of his body.'

I thought about it, picturing the scene. After what must have been a while I heard Greg's voice, 'Hello, hello, you still there?'

'Yeah, I'm here. So who are your men?'

'Aussies mainly, ex-SAS and state cops. Good blokes. We've also got a dozen or so former French Foreign Legionnaires along with a handful of Brits, some Yanks, a few other nationalities. They all know their business. So, what do you think?'

It took another long moment for me to decide. 'I'd like a short-term contract, say three months with a front-line protection group. I don't care about the money, just so long as it's enough to live on and I can send some home.'

Greg's tone grew serious. 'Are you fit? How's your arm?'

'Fine. I clocked up three kilometres in the pool this morning.'

'Good.' His tone was dark. 'Because you'll need to be fit; as fit as you've ever been. Physically and mentally. Nothing you could possibly imagine is going to prepare you for this place.'

It took me a couple of frenetic weeks to organise my affairs, some of which was painful as I needed to return advance fees I'd received for speaking engagements I was now having to break. Most clients understood that I had security commitments which had to take priority, but a few were irritated and couldn't see why I would risk my neck for a lot less money than I could earn as a speaker. I wasn't entirely sure I understood myself; all I knew was that there was a cost to what I was doing and it wasn't only pecuniary.

There was an emotional price too.

The night before I was due to fly out I lay on the bed with our youngest children reading them a story. To finish I turned out the lights and, in the darkness, recited some of *The Man from Snowy River*. Confident that they were all asleep I was about to creep away when out of the blankness a voice whispered, 'You will come back, won't you Daddy?' The innocent directness of the question no one else dared ask punched me in the heart, taking my breath away.

Before I could speak another small but confident voice came out of the darkness. 'Of course he will. Daddy loves us. He always comes back.' Gulping, I bent to kiss the owner of the second voice, smelling the warm sweetness of a child falling asleep, sensing the movement as the little body nestled itself for the night. 'You *will* come back, won't you Daddy?' the first voice whispered plaintively.

'Of course I will,' I murmured. 'I always come back.'

I stumbled into the bathroom, sat on the edge of the bath and breathed deeply, barely holding back tears. Had I told the truth? Would I come back, or would those words turn out to be the worst lie I could ever tell my children?

After a while I stood up, splashed cold water on my face and walked as nonchalantly as I could into the lounge. Natasha looked up from her place on the sofa. 'You look upset,' she said.

It was the beginning of a long conversation. Afterwards we both felt better.

* * *

The connection from Dubai into Iraq was on Ishta Airlines flight XV101. I stared down as the plane came in over the city, spiralling down in a series of tight corkscrews to confuse the aim of insurgents with ground-to-air missiles. All I could see was sand, a few drooping date palms and a sea of box-like houses, some big, some small, each one painted the same dull, drab colour; a colour which, as we dropped lower I realised was not paint but dust. Not the sienna-red dust of the Australian desert but a flat, lifeless dun-grey.

A pall of smoke hung over the city, in the centre of which I glimpsed the winding Tigris flowing north to south and shining like a silver snake.

Greg was waiting for me in the arrivals lounge. 'Welcome to Baghdad,' he said, shaking my hand warmly.

I grinned. 'It's great to see you again.' I glanced around, mildly surprised. The place was better than I'd anticipated; the floor well polished; the rows of plastic seating, that somehow reminded me of McDonald's, clean and, apart from a few cigarette burns, well maintained. As well as a few uniformed soldiers there were close to a dozen clusters of private security contractors standing around and smoking while waiting to collect clients.

Outside, the heat hit me like a hammer, the dust immediately getting into my eyes and mouth. 'This place is *bloody dusty*,' Greg said. 'It's a bugger, but you learn to live with it.'

I blinked rapidly, noticing the airport walls and entrances heavily sandbagged, the windows taped, the ground littered with discarded plastic water bottles swirling about in the wind. Staring through the dazzling sunshine I saw concrete barriers and rolls of razor wire everywhere.

One of Greg's guys handed me a Kevlar jacket murmuring, 'There you go, buddy. You gotta be armoured up for the trip.' I put it on.

Greg briefed me.

'Okay. We'll be travelling the first few kilometres in relative security as the roads leading to and from the airport are well protected and act as a kind of buffer zone. Then we pass a checkpoint and after that we are on the most dangerous stretch of road on the planet. It's sixteen kilometres east to the Green Zone in Baghdad and the score so far is about two dead for every hundred metres. Plus dozens badly wounded. It's not a road, it's a battle zone. Insurgents open up on us with armour-piercing grenades, missile launchers, machine guns, mortars, landmines, plus a lot of VBIEDs.'

'VBIEDs?' It sounded like veebee-i-e-dees.

'Vehicle Born Improvised Explosive Devices. What the media calls car bombs. One of which killed our bloke halfway along the road. So, we drive fast, like we're in a hurry. Intimidation, that's the name of the game here. Something gets in our way, we drive over it or through it. Okay?'

'Yes.'

'Good.' He led the way into a concrete-covered parking lot also liberally scattered with dust and plastic water bottles, stopping at three armoured Land Cruisers, two of which, with their tailgates fixed in the open position, were adapted to accommodate rear gunners. There was something attached to the back of one of the

235

vehicles and I stepped around to take a look. It was a big sign in English and Arabic: DANGER! STAY BACK 100m. DEADLY FORCE AUTHORISED.

I shot an enquiring glance at Greg. 'It means what it says,' he said simply. 'Standard rules of engagement; if any vehicle comes within a hundred metres we flash a spotlight at it. If that doesn't deter it, we fire a warning shot into the road a few metres in front of the vehicle. If that doesn't do it, the next round is fired into the vehicle's grille. The round is armour piercing, it'll go through the engine block.'

'And if that doesn't stop them?'

'The protocol is to shoot the driver in the head.'

'Ever had to do it?'

He shook his head. 'Never had to do more than fire into the road. Most vehicles get the hell out of the way when they see a convoy. Why wouldn't they? They can't exactly miss us — matching SUVs, obviously armoured, darkened windows, driving fast and in formation. We're high profile and hard-core. We stick out like dogs' balls.'

'What about other convoys?'

'The American and British military convoys apply the same rules. A hundred-metre bubble — no exceptions. Out on the road everyone enforces the exclusion zone. They stay away from us. We stay away from them. Same with most of the other PMCs.'

I had just landed in a war zone. I realised I'd need to get up to speed on the jargon. 'PMCs?'

'Private Military Companies — also known more euphemistically as PSCs: Private Security Companies.'

'How many of them are there?'

'About three hundred.'

'That many?'

'And we're all busy. Twenty-six million people in this country, mate, and it's half the size of New South Wales. Five million just in Baghdad. That's a million more than Sydney. There's a lot to do here and there's a lot of people who don't want us to do it. Prepared to kill us and themselves to stop us. Anyway, we'd better get going.'

He reached into the back of the vehicle and came out with an AK47 which he proffered to me. 'You checked out on this weapon?'

I nodded. From somewhere in the distance came a drum roll of dull explosions. I cocked my head. Mortar fire. No one else took any notice.

I got in the back of the middle vehicle with the guy who had handed me the body armour. Greg climbed in beside the driver. The vehicle had a left-hand drive. Greg turned in his seat. 'We drive on the right here. You'll need to practise changing gear with your right hand. You stay here long enough, sooner or later you'll have to do some fancy defensive driving.'

Peering through the front window I watched the rear gunner in the lead vehicle scramble into position and wedge himself in, a Kalashnikov PKM across his lap. Moving slowly, the convoy negotiated the concrete barriers, Greg acknowledging the US soldiers guarding the airport approaches. We drove in a normal fashion for a few minutes until we passed what was evidently the airport's final checkpoint. The moment we were on the open road the driver shoved the pedal to the deck, forcing me back in my seat with the acceleration.

I gazed through the front window at the highway, a light dusting of sand blowing across the dark, pitted bitumen. Everywhere there were bomb craters and burnt-out cars, some of the craters in the road itself, the drivers swerving at speed to avoid them. I felt sorry for the rear gunners, facing backwards and swerving like this must be a great way to get carsick.

Greg was reading my mind. 'It's usually too dangerous to repair the road.' He indicated the groves of flattened palm trees on either side of the highway, beyond them a bleached landscape of scrubby desert, white cement walls and washed-out, Saddam-era housing blocks. 'The Yanks bulldozed the trees. They were providing cover for snipers and mortar crews.'

I nodded, surveying the ugly landscape. No airport road was

attractive but this was both grotesque and menacing, made more so by the occasional tank-like Bradley fighting vehicle parked by the side of the highway. On the other side of the median strip I watched an American convoy of Humvees, bristling with machine-gunners, rocketing towards us like artillery shells. It passed in a storm of dust and noise.

The guy beside me, an American, caught the look on my face and chuckled. 'Not too pretty, eh? The Yellow Brick Road this is not. But then, this ain't Kansas, Dorothy.'

I laughed. I couldn't think of anything better to do.

CHAPTER 25

The Green Zone

AFTER ABOUT twenty minutes the convoy turned north and crossed the river, cruising over a pockmarked, shell-scarred bridge that Greg announced was the Fourteenth of July Bridge, the main route from the airport into the Green Zone.

Inside the Land Cruiser I felt the tension wind down. Gazing out of the windows I could see why. Surrounded by four-metre high reinforced blast-proof concrete slabs that Greg called T-walls, the area was defended by long coils of razor wire, chain-link fences and earthen berms, its armed checkpoints monitored by M1 Abrams tanks, Bradley fighting vehicles and Humvees, topped off with .50 calibre machine guns. The place looked under siege — the ultimate gated community. The convoy raced through the streets to Camp Freedom, the headquarters of the US Army's 3rd Infantry Division situated on the banks of the Tigris.

'Okay, this is home for the next week,' Greg told me as we alighted from the vehicles. 'You'll be undergoing refresher training here.'

'Training?'

'Pistol, rifle and machine-gun assessment. Plus of course tactical driving, first aid, radio communications … the whole bag of tricks. Actually, the week is more in the nature of an evaluation. Everybody who arrives here is expected to possess good skills already. But you'll need to pass. Everyone has to pass evaluation, otherwise their life-insurance cover is invalid. For you it'll be a piece of cake.'

'Who's doing the evaluation? The Yanks?'

'No, our own people. We merely get to live on Uncle Sam's real estate and use the facilities — the weapons range, gymnasium, canteen and so on. Beyond that we're self-sufficient.'

Greg showed me to my bungalow before taking me on a quick tour of the camp's facilities. That afternoon I was issued with a Serbian-made CZ99 pistol and the Swiss SG552 assault rifle. As I was examining the weapons the armourer said, 'We'll be evaluating you on your handling skills tomorrow morning.'

I glanced up in alarm, Greg's nonchalant faith in my competency flying out the window. Weapons handling was essentially a question of familiarity and practice, and both the pistol and the assault rifle were new to me. And although I had maintained marksmanship skills since leaving South Africa, I had neither handled nor even seen the particular weapons now in front of me.

'Tomorrow?' I repeated in a hollow tone.

The armourer's face was stony. 'Yup.'

That evening I returned to my bungalow with the weapons and spent most of the night teaching myself how to strip and assemble them as well as practising stoppage drills. By the time I got to bed in the early hours my fingers were bleeding. At the evaluation the following morning, the instructor said, 'I'll show you once, then you do it with me. Try to keep up.' In fact I beat him, both on the pistol and the assault rifle.

My final test was to strip and reassemble the SG552 blindfolded. As I was trying to join the connecting pin with the trigger housing and the stock, I fumbled and dropped the weapon. 'Oops,' I said.

'Oops? What the fuck is oops?' The instructor snarled. 'What are you, some fucking poof?'

I smiled to myself. I'd become used to having my children around me and modifying my language. But this was a war zone, and when you dropped your weapon, the thing that might conceivably save your life, it was probably not typical to say oops.

Eating in the canteen surrounded by US soldiers was a new and revealing experience. The last time I'd been in a confined space with so many American troops had been in a bar in Seoul where the men had been loud, arrogant and condescending in their attitude towards the Koreans and everyone else non-American. Here the men were restrained, friendly and helpful, with no sign of arrogance towards the Iraqis or anyone else.

It was a shock, and a lesson I had to think about, realising I'd been guilty of one of the things I most hated — bigotry. I had expected a certain behaviour from these men because they were American soldiers. I should have known better. The difference was nothing to do with nationality; it was the difference between talk and action. None of the men in that Seoul bar had ever been shot at, seen action, or fired a weapon with the intention of hitting another human being. It was the old story. The macho, action-man heroes could always be found in a bar behind the lines. The real warriors were on the front line. I knew these men were the real warriors because they were quiet and respectful with wary eyes and a line in mordant humour.

I watched them preparing to go out on patrol, knowing it would soon be my turn to leave the comparative safety of the Green Zone. On a map of Baghdad the Zone was scarcely three kilometres square, nestled in a curving loop of the river's west bank that looked exactly like the belly of a pregnant woman. Which was appropriate, I thought. There was a safe, womblike quality to the Green Zone. Here it was almost Little America; I could get take-away pizzas, Burger King fries and Baskin Robbins ice cream. Outside, the rest of the city was a cruel, threatening, frequently fatal world.

Not for nothing was the outside called the Red Zone.

My instructors took great pains in schooling me in the rules of engagement, especially as they applied to suicide bombers, reinforcing the subtle signs that telescoped the rules into shooting into a vehicle's grille followed, within seconds, by shooting the driver in the head.

Like all risk, the level of threat from possible VBIEDs had to be assessed — as in any war, resources were scarce and the enemy obviously considered suicide bombers a finite commodity, not to be wasted unnecessarily, so any car containing only the driver was reckoned a higher-level risk than one with passengers. Similarly, because bombs and their metal casings were heavy, cars travelling low to the ground were considered risky, as was any vehicle driven by a female in traditional headdress. Women almost never drove in Iraq and the risk level immediately ratcheted up on the assumption the driver was a bomber seeking to allay suspicion by dressing as a woman.

Other things I was told to watch for were drivers handcuffed to the steering wheel. Apparently not all suicide bombers were volunteers. I didn't believe it at first so they showed me photographs, the most gruesome I'd ever seen. Sure enough, what was left of the body was manacled to what was left of the steering wheel. I was also told to treat with extreme caution any driver who was clean-shaven. Though most Iraqi males sported at least a two-day growth of beard, it seemed martyrs in a jihad had a much better chance of entering paradise if they were clean-shaven.

I wasn't exactly sure how I was meant to spot the last two clues from a speeding SUV; besides, bombers had been known to put manikins in their cars and to fit heavy shock absorbers to mask the weight of their vehicles. So, though I listened intently to the briefing sessions and took careful note of the signs to watch for, I knew much of my decision would come from my instinct. Not just my eyes but my gut would tell me when something wasn't right.

They showed me a video of a recent small-arms ambush by insurgents. The footage had been recorded with a camcorder attached to the dashboard of the second SUV — a common practice by most convoys. I watched it dispassionately, listening to the instructor's critique. Bereft of any Hollywood treatment — perfect lighting, loud colourful explosions, sustained machine-gun fire — the video's poor quality made it seem amateurish, almost boring.

Except that it was real and I was watching an event in which men had been shot to death. The footage showed the lead SUV, about eighty metres ahead, being hit. Rounds were kicking up the tarmac around it and, when I looked closely, smacking into its side. They were coming from a clump of date-palm stumps and grass off to the right. The lead vehicle was stopped, presumably incapacitated, and the operators inside had, the instructor intoned in his low, steady voice-over, 'cracked the doors,' which meant they had chosen to open the vehicle doors in what may have been an attempt to drag a body out to administer first aid while others tried to return fire. As this was happening the second vehicle, now stationary, was also taking fire; above the loud noise of the idling engine, I heard sporadic, three and four round bursts of gunfire, followed by what seemed a long pause before another burst. Someone in the second vehicle, possibly the driver, was shouting, doing his best to reassure one of his team who, I guessed, had 'cracked a door' to engage the insurgents and been shot.

Moments later I saw a man, probably the driver, entering the frame in front of the bonnet from the left, bend down and begin dragging what had to be a wounded man backwards. I watched the driver's face contort and his shoulders hunch as he took up the weight and started shuffling backwards, alternately looking down to speak to the wounded man and looking up towards the incoming fire.

Moments later something or someone bumped the camera and it fell on its side, giving the rest of the sequence a weird perspective. Then, before the ambush was over, the camera was knocked again and everything went black. Like death.

The sequence lasted no more than three or four minutes and when the screen went dark I heard the instructor murmur, 'There but for the grace of God go I.' I shot him a glance. The guy didn't seem like a religious person.

But then, maybe in the presence of violent death …

They made me watch the video repeatedly, analysing the footage, learning what had gone wrong, and by the time I'd watched it for the eight or ninth time I had come to know every date-palm stump and shell hole in the tarmac surrounding the area of contact. It was the most disconcerting training video I'd ever watched. At the end of the week, after I had passed all the evaluation tests, Greg took me to the US Embassy, which, in the heart of the Green Zone, had formerly been one of Saddam's palaces. In what turned out to be a lengthy process I was photographed, fingerprinted and issued with a US Department of Defence Contractor ID card, which allowed me to pass US military checkpoints in both the Green and Red Zones, enter US military bases throughout Iraq, receive emergency medical treatment at US field hospitals, fly on US helicopters, and buy tax-exempt goods from the US military PX stores.

I felt like I had come full circle and was a soldier once more.

I was briefed on my first assignment, told my radio call sign — *Redman* — and convoyed to a compound in Karadah in the Red Zone. As the driver channelled the four-tonne armoured vehicle past the gates I surveyed the place. It looked like a medieval fortress. Surrounded by the ubiquitous, blast-proof, four-metre T-walls, it was protected by a set of huge metal gates, watchtowers with heavy machine-guns, and machine-gun nests on many of the roofs.

Sleeping accommodation was in a three-storey villa in the heart of the compound.

I chose a room weirdly reminiscent of my hutch in Korea. Once a normal-sized room, it had been partitioned down the centre to create a storeroom on the other side. There was a mattress on the floor, a desk, a chair and a cupboard. There were no curtains. I chose it because it was tucked around a couple of odd corridors, which meant if the compound was stormed in the early hours, I'd have more time to respond to the sound of a gun battle. About a dozen guys slept in the villa with two bathrooms between us.

After settling in, which took no more than a couple of minutes, one of the guys on my team showed me the canteen where I had a quick meal. Afterwards the same guy led me downstairs to the Pit, the compound's pub located in the basement of the hotel where the clients stayed. I admired the clients, mainly for their bravery. I knew that a lot of the time they were scared and that some of the time they were petrified, but, like the aid-workers in Kenya, they didn't let their fear stop them from being participants rather than spectators.

I ordered myself a soft drink and stood at the bar with some of the guys from my PMC. The Pit reminded me of the Shat back in 3RAR at Holsworthy. I liked its friendly atmosphere, the air buzzing with that unique sense of excitement generated by a random mix of expats thrown together in a foreign country. There were teams from several different PMCs — from the US, Australia, New Zealand, South Africa, Canada and practically every European country, East and West, I could name. There were even operators from South America, the Philippines and Fiji.

The Europeans seemed to divide into two camps; those from the West, especially the Brits and Irish, but also the Dutch, French and Swedes, appeared professional and alert, drinking cautiously or, like me, not drinking alcohol at all. On the other hand, some of the men from the countries of the old Eastern Bloc were drunk and noisy. I eyed them speculatively. There was something about them that made me wary; it wasn't so much the drinking as an attitude.

I undertook my first convoy the following day. Kitted out in my Kevlar body armour, over which I wore a fishing vest to which I'd attached my smoke grenades, spare clips of ammunition, trauma kit, radio and torch, I looked like something out of a Hollywood action movie. The convoy's mission was to return a group of aid-workers to the airport along BIAP (Baghdad International Air Port) the sixteen kilometres of road the US military called 'Route Irish'. I never knew for sure why; the best explanation I heard was that, supposedly, the *Guinness Book of Records* had named it the most dangerous stretch of road in the world.

Returning from the airport, I was riding in the lead car next to the driver. Suddenly, over the sound of the big V8 engine, I heard the dull thump of mortars somewhere to our left. I peered past the driver, a French ex-Legionnaire. The guy glanced at me and shrugged as only a Frenchman could. The shrug said it all.

Back in the compound I went to my room to check for emails on the laptop I had bought at the PX. Many of the other teams had also returned and there was a cacophony of music coming from every room on my floor: Country ... Techno ... Pop ... Rock ... the place was vibrating with loud, clashing dissonance. Keith, the Kiwi in the room next to mine, played Heavy Metal; Ted, the Yank on the other side, was into Classical, with Beethoven playing at mega decibels. Under other circumstances I would probably have considered the racket an irritating assault on the ears. But here I liked it. It was a sign of life.

That afternoon I went out on another convoy, the following day two more; within a week I was adapting to the rhythm of my new life.

What I found most difficult was adjusting to the country itself.

First, the place was bloody hot. The Americans measured temperature in Fahrenheit and I had arrived on a cool day — 90°F, or 33°C. Since then the thermometer had risen to 46°C and stayed there, every day the same, a dry, blistering heat. Though I preferred a dry heat to the humidity of PNG, it brought its own problems — a choking, sandy dust that got everywhere. Outside dust covered everything; inside there was a thin film of it over the floors, tables, chairs, bottles of drink ... it even managed to get under the covers of my bed. I spent a lot of time stripping my weapons and cleaning them.

Added to the dust was the fact that the city was one giant garbage dump. Apparently before the wars and sanctions, Baghdad had been a sophisticated city, but those days were long gone. The Iraqis threw their domestic rubbish out on the road in front of their apartment blocks and when the giant heaps of plastic water bottles, disposable nappies and used sanitary towels got too big, someone doused them with petrol and set light to them. There were fires burning all the time, not only from the garbage but from bombs and from the sabotaged oil pipelines that burned for days. A permanent pall hung over the city, smudging the sun in noxious smoke.

Apart from the constant smoke and dust, noisy and smelly generators made Iraq a difficult place to even breathe in. The city appeared to have no state-run power company or electricity grid;

instead there were thousands upon thousands of diesel generators ranging from the size of eskies to some the size of trucks, every one belching out billows of black exhaust fumes.

Baghdad, the fabled city of the Arabian tales I had read to my children, was smashed and wasted, with bomb craters too dangerous to repair in the roadways, shrapnel scars defacing buildings, enormous holes puncturing the roofs and walls of once magnificent homes and palaces. Everywhere there was razor wire; everywhere sandbagged gun emplacements; everywhere the four-metre, blast-proof concrete T-walls. There were rows and rows of T-walls, like some maniacal gigantic maze.

The city was ugly, toxic and perilous, the danger continually reasserted by the *boom* of bombs, the *crump* of mortars and the almost constant *whump-whump-whump* of helicopters — medical helicopters transporting the wounded, Blackhawks moving troops, even AH64 Apache gunships on combat missions. And always there were incidents — sixty-seven a day on average — small-arms and mortar attacks on BIAP; an Iraqi suicide bomber blowing up a fuel tanker at a crowded market, killing himself and ninety-one other people while wounding a further hundred and sixty; another suicide bomber targeting an American army patrol that stopped to hand out candy to the locals. The body count from that one included twenty-four dead Iraqi children.

Years before I had struggled through Dante's *Divine Comedy.* Now, I told myself, I needn't have bothered. I was getting firsthand experience of the seven circles of hell. Iraq was its own Inferno.

Yet after a couple of weeks in country, like most operators I had settled in. I had learnt more lingo and discovered that, as a member of a PMC, I was a PSD or Personnel Security Detail, which meant I was a non-uniformed security contractor. PSD was practically a rank; all freelance security operators were members of a definite tribe. I began recognising a few faces, coming across blokes I had once trained.

There was a lot of talk about the good money some of them were making, but for all that, I never had the impression that money was the prime or sole motivator for their presence in Iraq. Not one freelance security contractor I met there, at least not from Australia and other Western countries, could have been called a mercenary. Most had left secure jobs in the army, in Special Forces units or police tactical response teams to come to Iraq and put their skills and knowledge to use in an environment where they could do some good. To my mind these men were professional and disciplined team players with unique skills; guys who genuinely cared about doing a good job and who were in Iraq because they believed this was where a job needed doing.

I was proud that I never saw an Australian or Kiwi speak disrespectfully or abusively to an Iraqi — which is more than I could say for some of the Eastern Europeans. This was an observation, not prejudice, but some of those guys would have been better off staying home and cleaning toilets. Most of them were ex-Legionnaires though you wouldn't have known it. The French Foreign Legion was a top military unit, with high standards and good discipline; now these guys were out of the Legion some of them clearly didn't believe that ongoing training was necessary; they seemed incapable of understanding that under pressure a combatant would never rise to his level of expectation but always default to his level of training.

It wouldn't matter, except I was going out on convoy with these people.

One afternoon, returning from the airport on Route Irish, one of them, a Bulgarian ex-Legionnaire called Mick who reminded me of Milo in Alice Springs, tried to persuade me that if a convoy was ambushed from its right and the vehicles could not be driven away, then the PSDs should get out on the *right hand side* of the vehicles to return fire, thus proving they were not scared of the enemy.

Concentrating on keeping tight formation with the SUVs ahead, I told him that was bullshit. 'It'd be much smarter to get out on the *opposite* side and move into position where we could return fire using the vehicle as optical and to a lesser extent, ballistic cover,' I said. 'Tactically, that's the only thing to do.'

'Ha,' the Bulgarian sneered, 'that shows you fucking scared.'

'So?'

I wasn't about to waste my breath explaining. This idiot was not only a piss-head, he was childish with it. Sitting up front next to me he had the extremely annoying habit of resting the muzzle of his AK47 on the toe of his boot and playing with the trigger with the safety off and a round up the chamber. Watching him out of the corner of my eye I was disappointed he didn't pull the trigger. But, the Bulgarian was an exception. Most of the blokes I found myself serving with were competent professionals. Two men I especially liked were a couple of Fijians, Stan and Lance, both family men who neither smoked nor drank. They were quiet and polite yet sufficiently self-confident to make me feel they could perform under fire. One lunch time we were chatting, along with Keith, the Kiwi from the room next to mine.

The big Kiwi was telling a story of life in Iraq.

'I was at the airport,' he said. 'Had just seen some NGO aid-workers off when I spotted this civilian woman getting off a flight. She was on her own.'

'Alone?' I repeated.

'Right. You *never* see that here. She was wandering about the place like she was at John F Kennedy or Heathrow ... not bloody Baghdad airport. So I went up to her and asked how she was planning to get to the city. She said she was going to take a taxi. She thought she could take a cab like she was in New York. Anyway, I told her how that was about the most dangerous thing she could do in Iraq. But she wouldn't believe me, seemed offended even that I should be telling her that. She said all the media hype about violence was just American propaganda. I offered to take her in the convoy. I mean I *begged* her. 'Please', I said, '*Please*'. She wouldn't have it. Fuck knows why. Women's lib? Some stupid cocked-up notion of what's going on here? I dunno.'

He stopped and looked up. Two Apache gunships in combat

formation were coming in low over the rooftops about a kilometre away. We watched as the rear chopper opened fire, the smoke trails of two rockets — one red, one green — shooting down towards the hidden target. We waited, listening for a secondary explosion. None came. For a few moments the gunships hovered, then they banked and headed north. Keith waited for the noise to die away before continuing. No one commented on the action. It was too familiar.

'Go on,' Lance said.

'Well, she must have left the airport before we did because about ten minutes down Route Irish we came across her taxi. It had been ambushed and the woman was standing beside it. In flames. She was melting in a ball of flame. She was screaming and melting … screaming and melting.' He stopped.

We were silent, listening intently. 'I've got two regrets,' he said. 'One, I didn't force her to join our convoy. Two, I didn't put a bullet in her head as I watched her melt and listened to her scream.'

I was watching his face when a convoy came roaring through the compound gates, slewing to a stop in a billowing cloud of dust. Startled, we brought our weapons to bear. The driver of the lead vehicle, along with two PSDs in the back, jumped out. Carefully they began lifting a figure out of the front passenger seat. It was Bulgarian Mick, squealing like a pig.

'What happened?' Keith called.

'The tosser just shot his big toe off.'

I couldn't help myself. I began to laugh. The three men chair-lifting the bawling Bulgarian were trying hard to suppress massive grins. Though Stan and Lance looked concerned, Keith too was laughing fit to burst.

'Couldn't have happened to a better bloke,' he chuckled.

CHAPTER 26

The Red Zone

IT WAS a busy day. In the morning we had escorted some people from the State University of New York from the Red Zone into the Green Zone; in the afternoon a group of NGO personnel along BIAP to the airport. The NGO people were pleased to be getting out: they had been in the country for months.

One young guy, his face grey and with dark rings under his eyes, was talking about the mitigation of risk and the Pareto principle: eighty per cent of the risk in Iraq was located in twenty per cent of the country, he explained to us PSDs in the vehicle, while a hundred per cent of the risk came from less than ten per cent of the population. I got it, or at least the basics of it. It was pretty much the formula I'd applied in the fight in the bar in Penang. By dropping one-third of the people I eliminated ninety per cent of the risk.

The client had a whole raft of mathematical formulae concerning risk and its mitigation. Time was also a factor. Risk moved in positive correlation to both time and exposure: the longer the exposure the greater the risk.

Which was why he was glad to be getting out. He had worked out that with the time he had been in Iraq, he was now at maximum risk. Of course, he would have been at no risk of being killed or maimed if he had never come here, he said. But having come, his chances of being killed increased every day.

Danger came closer with time.

I thought of mortar bombs creeping closer and closer to their target and wondered where I was on the risk scale. In the time I had been in

Iraq one security operative from another PMC had been killed, two others wounded.

On the return trip in the afternoon, I took up position as rear gunner, wedging myself in as best I could and settling the PKM on my lap. A few kilometres along BIAP I noticed a blue sedan containing a lone driver join the freeway from a slip road. I figured that the sedan would have to have gone through at least one Iraqi police roadblock to get on to Route Irish. But that wasn't much comfort to me. I watched it carefully. It closed on the convoy rapidly and within seconds was just outside our hundred-metre exclusion zone.

I waved the driver off, pointing to the warning sign attached to the Land Cruiser and energetically flashing a white strobe light at him. The sedan kept coming. Now it was inside the bubble. I waved another couple of times then raised the machine-gun in an obviously threatening manner. At seventy metres the driver must have seen me but still the sedan failed to slow down. I fired into the bitumen in front of the vehicle, the round kicking up a spout of black tarmac, easily visible to the driver. He took no notice.

I felt my heartbeat notching up.

The car was fifty metres off and closing fast. I raised the weapon and fired an armour-piercing round into the grille in line with the driver's hips, immediately sighting the weapon for the next shot. Through the driver's head. At this range I wouldn't miss. The car spun off the road on to the sandy shoulder, disappearing in a storm of dust. The convoy kept moving.

I peered into the dust. Had I hit the driver? The projectile would have penetrated the engine block and blown the engine, but would it have got beyond that? I didn't know.

The question that really consumed me was whether or not he was a bomber.

If the guy wasn't a suicide bomber, why had he not heeded the blindingly obvious warnings? I had been prepared to kill him. Another two seconds and I would have squeezed the trigger. I got no pleasure from that thought, nor did I feel any other emotion. I had felt almost nothing as I raised the weapon for the head shot; nothing except a slightly accelerated heartbeat and the cold, implacable demand of necessity. I would have killed the man because it was necessary. Killed him to save my own life and the lives of the people with me. No more, no less. I would have killed as I had learnt to fight. Out of necessity.

Back at the compound I wrote up an incident report for the duty-watch keeper. When I'd finished I stared at the bald statement of the facts. Incident reports, I reflected, were not about feelings, and duty-watch keepers, like today's ex-Royal Marine Sergeant, were definitely not interested in the philosophical reflections of their authors. Yet making out an incident report was one measure of the changing magnitude of risk.

Two days later I completed another one.

Travelling back on Irish, I was driving the lead Land Cruiser. I found my side of the highway blocked by a US army convoy of Humvees responding to an explosion a few hundred metres ahead. I slowed to a crawl and had to stop — the hairs prickling on the back of my neck. The last thing anybody ever wanted to do on BIAP was stop. We were now sitting ducks for any sniper or mortar crew hidden in the suburbs beyond the road. And traffic was coming up behind us.

Getting on the radio to the other drivers, I initiated the standard tactic for a blocked BIAP, the convoy driving aggressively forward for thirty metres then reversing the same distance; forward again, then back, forward and back, thus presenting at least a partially moving target to any insurgents. For a couple of minutes it worked, though a couple of minutes of BIAP time seemed to stretch into half a lifetime of heartbeats.

But oncoming traffic was edging forward, reducing our room to manoeuvre down to twenty metres ... fifteen ... ten. It was no good. We were wedged in.

I glanced about, desperately trying to figure the next course of action. The scene outside the vehicle was the same as it was everywhere; pitted, potholed tarmac and truncated date-palms. Nothing remarkable. Except …

A chill went down my spine. Surely this was where the ambush had taken place. I'd watched the video enough times and since then had driven BIAP enough to know every sawn-off date-palm, every hole and crevice in the road.

Suddenly, through the windscreen, I saw flickering, poorly lit images of an SUV eighty metres ahead taking fire from a clump of date-palm stumps to my right. I jerked back in my seat, shocked and disorientated. I felt my hands go clammy, less from fear of what was happening outside than from what was going on inside my head as I recalled the video footage I'd watched in training. Already in a dangerous situation that was completely real, I was being sucked into one that was unreal; one that had already happened. I watched men crack the doors in the vehicle in front; heard the short bursts of gunfire smacking into my own vehicle. Yet that wasn't happening. *This* was happening — I was wedged in on BIAP. Two dramas were occurring simultaneously.

It was as if I'd moved through the windscreen of the SUV and *into the video*. I wasn't here; I was there. Yet I was also somewhere else, somewhere high and mystical and elevated, *watching myself not being here*. It was like watching a dramatic news event and then stepping through the screen into it. I wondered if this was what happened before you died.

Did you watch the events unfold as if you were watching television? The feeling was so ethereal, so bizarre and surreal, it made my skin crawl.

Or was that common or garden fear generated by what was *really* happening? I shook my head, forcing myself to focus on the reality, the here and now. I needed a solution — a way out. Now.

'Plan B,' I bellowed into the radio and yanked the steering wheel, savagely, peeling the SUV out of the traffic and on to the median strip — leading the convoy into yet another danger zone.

BIAP's median strip was no more than a broad strip of dust, sand

and the sawn-off stumps of date-palms on which some locals kept goats and even sowed a few crops. Crops were not the only things sown; insurgents planted landmines there and a few PSD and military convoys had been blasted crossing the strip. The blockage on BIAP may have been a deliberate ploy, a strategy to induce a convoy to do what I was now doing — drive across the strip and over a landmine powerful enough to destroy a four-tonne armoured SUV and either kill me or, at the very least, blow my legs off. And all I could do was drive, hoping like crazy I didn't hit a mine while the two following SUVs followed *very* carefully in my tracks. I gripped the steering wheel tightly.

We made it, bouncing off the strip and onto the opposite side of the highway, driving *into* the stream of traffic. I switched on the siren, palmed the horn and started flashing the lights. The traffic coming at us was thick and fast; above the sounds of the siren and our own horn I could hear the approaching cars' angry klaxons. I was swerving from side to side to avoid bomb craters.

Sean, the guy up front beside me, had been a marksman with the British paras. He was Irish, with an accent so thick that most of the time I had no idea what he was saying; the only word I recognised with any certainty being 'facking'. There was a lot of facking now, with Sean screaming through the loudspeaker at the traffic barrelling towards us, '*Gitootdafackinwee, gitootdafackinwee.*'

My heart hammered as the adrenalin rocketed through my system. At any moment I was about to have a head-on collision.

Suddenly Sean opened his door and leaned out into the rushing air, hanging from the vehicle by a strap he had looped around the hinges of the door. 'What the fuck are you doing?' I screeched. I watched Sean raise his weapon and fire off three rounds.

The weapon was a Heckler & Koch G3, loaded with 7.62 tracer. Despite myself, despite the pumping rush of adrenalin and the need to focus on the road, I stared at the red tracers languidly flying over the roofs of the approaching vehicles. I was always captivated by tracer — manufactured with a phosphorescent coating they burn brightly and allow the shooter to follow the flight path of the projectile to aid in the aiming process. Sean fired more warning shots, this time in front of the vehicles. I was irresistibly drawn to following their graceful flight, seeing their brilliant prettiness turn into something far more vicious as they exploded into the bitumen and ricocheted out of sight into the distance.

The traffic in front of us slewed on to the shoulder of the highway.

I felt my palms damp and spongy on the steering wheel. Though tracer fired into the roadway was effective for most oncoming traffic, it would never deter an American convoy of Humvees or Bradleys. The Yanks would immediately assume we were insurgents and apply the first principle of defence against an oncoming vehicle. They would shoot the driver, me, in the head. The Humvees carried .50 calibre machine guns. Just one round would take my head off. The Americans never fired just one round. And there were always Yank convoys on BIAP.

My sphincter clenched as I thought about it, my eyes straining for the familiar sight of Humvees approaching at speed, realising they might be the last thing I ever saw.

We drove on the wrong side of Irish for over a kilometre before I decided we could safely cross back to our own side of the highway. I indicated my intention and bounced onto the median strip, taking the convoy back into the potential minefield. I drove as carefully as I could, desperately scanning for any sign of mines.

We reached our own side of the highway where, with one hand on the wheel, I leaned over and dragged Sean back inside the SUV. He slammed his door. '*Datwosfackingreet,*' he laughed.

We got back to the compound in the middle of the afternoon. The villa was quiet so I took advantage and had a long shower, the water, as usual, whether from hot or cold tap, no more than lukewarm. Then I called Tash and the children from my room on my mobile.

Later, I came down and was making my way across the dusty compound towards the canteen when a convoy from another PMC drove in. I watched them clambering out of the armoured Range Rovers, the men carrying AK47s and encumbered by flack jackets and vests festooned with radios, smoke grenades and ammunition clips, and did a double take at the guy getting out of the passenger side of the lead vehicle. There was no mistaking that squat figure or that ravaged face. After twenty years, pug-ugly was still pug-ugly.

'Jocko?'

The little guy spun around. 'Red? Fookin' hell, is that you?' He frowned, his face as ugly as a troll's. 'What the fook happened to your hair, ya bald prick?'

My world was suddenly filled with crazy Celts. 'Hello, Jocko. It's nice to see you too.' I crossed to the vehicles and shook his hand. 'How are you?'

Jocko grinned. With his crooked teeth it wasn't a pretty sight. 'Okay. Should have known you'd be here.'

'Yeah? Why's that?'

'This is your kind of place.'

I was surprised. What kind of person did Jocko think I was if he thought Iraq was my kind of place? 'So, you want a drink?'

'Aye, a quick one.'

I took him downstairs to the Pit where I ordered myself a 7Up. Jocko asked for a light beer. He too, in his own way, was being cautious. He had been in the country eighteen months, he told me.

I asked whether, in that time, he thought things had got any better. That morning an Australian politician had been reported in the media as saying, 'The situation in Iraq is improving.'

'Fookin' pollies, what do they know?' Jocko snarled. 'Things might be improving when you're sitting behind a desk in Canberra. But here it's getting worse.' He told me he had been involved in High Profile convoys since arriving in Iraq. At first, incidents had been rare. Now he and his mob were writing up incident reports too often for comfort. During his time two of the guys he'd worked with had been killed, four others seriously wounded.

'Sounds like you're pushing your luck, Jocko,' I said seriously.

He looked unfazed. 'Nah, I'll be right. Anyway, what about you?'
'Me?'

'Last time I saw you was in the Alice. How come you fetched up here?' I told him about PNG, Kontact, South Africa, marriage, and the speaking circuit.

'You've done all right. I reckoned you might. Just so long as you didn't become an officer, eh.' He cackled.

I laughed with him. 'We've both come a long way since then, that's for sure.'

'Yeah, but you got further.'

'I don't know about that. I don't want to make comparisons. All I did was make the most of my personal experiences. The bad ones as well as the good.' I shrugged.

'That, and a willingness to learn. That's all I've ever had going for me, Jocko.'

Jocko grunted and gazed at me reflectively. 'You remember that recon we did on the island?'

'You kidding? I'll never forget it.'

'Well … I never told anyone this before, but I was scared shitless that night. And you know what made it worse?'

'What?'

'You. You weren't scared at all. As icy as this fookin' beer you were.'

I stared at him. 'Is that what you think?' I laughed. 'You're wrong, Jocko. I was scared out of my head. In fact, if I remember rightly, I wanted to smack you in the gob because I thought *you* weren't scared. I wanted to know how come I was just about shitting myself while you didn't give a toss.'

Jocko laughed along with me. 'Looks like we both got it wrong.' He glanced at his watch. 'I'd better get back. We've got a mission.'

We shook hands at the bar and quickly exchanged contact details. When Jocko wasn't in Iraq, he lived in Thailand and I fully intended to catch up with him if I ever found myself in that part of the world. It surprised me, but I realised I actually liked the little ferret. 'Good luck. And take it easy, mate. Stay safe.'

He smiled. 'Same to you, ya bald prick.'

I watched him scurry out of the bar before ordering another soft drink. The meeting had put me in mind of my months of bouncing in Alice Springs and of one of the things I'd learned there. High Profile invited trouble. It was true there and it was true in Iraq.

Here, in this country, HP was hard core. Three or four armoured SUVs driven in tight formation like bats out of hell by clean-shaven Caucasians tricked out in flack jackets and vests like extras in a *Rambo* movie was about as alien as it was possible to get in the Middle East. It was a dog and pony show, designed to send out a very clear warning: 'Don't fuck with us.'

And, I was forced to concede, most of the time it worked. Most of the population stayed the hell away from a HP convoy. And yet, as in the Alice, it invited the attention of the hard men on the other side, the guys with experience, skill, and cunning. The guys who knew how to fight. HP convoys were the preferred target of suicide bombers, whose mobile spotters used the simple tactic of sitting at busy crossroads or driving around looking for a fat target into whose vicinity they would order the poor sod who was about to blow himself up.

Of course, tactically, HP and the necessity of killing anyone who breached the security of the hundred-metre bubble made perfect sense. And yet it was so 'in the face' I could see how the locals, even the peaceful locals, would resent it. I knew I'd be the first to get extremely pissed off if I was driving along a road in Australia and some foreigner began pointing a weapon at me and telling me how and where I could drive.

HP was not the way to win friends and influence people, but it was greatly favoured by most of the ex-SAS and Police Special Ops types. In fact, almost all the very experienced people preferred HP.

I went in search of Greg, finally running him to ground a few days later in the Green Zone, and asked him to schedule me for more Low Profile operations.

Greg looked surprised.

'Do you know what you're asking? Most blokes ask to *stop* doing LP.'

'I know, but I think it's the way to go. At least for me.'

I didn't voice the moral quandary I felt about enforcing something as extreme as the HP hundred-metre bubble.

'You know what's involved?'

I nodded. 'We travel in split convoys. Different makes and models of not-very-clean, not-very-new sedans, though they're all armoured.'

'Hopefully the insurgents don't know that. Hopefully they don't notice the cars.'

'And we dress like locals. Maybe wear a flack jacket, but it's under the long shirt ...'

'The *thobe*.'

'Plus everyone has a few days growth of beard and wears the head dress.'

'The *keffiyeh*, yes, that's right.' Greg gazed at me. 'Well, you could pass for a local at a distance. You're the right height and build. And you're dark enough.' He paused. 'How you ever got the name Red, God alone knows.'

'It's a long story. But can I get on to LP?'

'Of course. It won't be only LP, but it'll be mainly what you do. We have a contract to provide security for a bunch of Iraqi legislators writing the new constitution. I need men for that. You'll be assigned. Okay?'

In old clothes, my body armour under my shirt, and with four days stubble and a little skin toner, I could pass for a local. At least I could in the car driven by Rassim, a former Lieutenant Colonel in Saddam's army and now my guide and interpreter. Outside the car I wasn't so sure. It wasn't because I was toting an AK47 — there was nothing extraordinary about that in Baghdad. It was more in the way the locals moved and walked. I tried to duplicate it so I could blend in on the streets.

Most LP missions included providing close security on foot, accompanying VIPs from their vehicles to conferences and meetings in government buildings, hotels and private residences. I learnt the rules fairly quickly. I'd had experience of it with the Royalty Protection Group in Britain and been taught the basics by some of the best in the world. It was not unlike watching over my kids at the beach, being always aware of where they were as I monitored the surf for rips and scanned the crowd for that one small 'something' that was out of place. Scanning the crowd … scanning the kids. Scanning the crowd … scanning the clients. Always searching for the absence of the normal and the presence of the abnormal.

But this wasn't the beach, nor even the streets of London, and I was continually trying to figure out what the hell, in this madhouse, was normal. Here, what passed for normal was so far into abnormal it was totally off the wall.

Low Profile missions were not helped by the attention of the press and television crews, who often turned them into High Profile media events. One morning, accompanying my Iraqi legislators to a conference of hundreds of delegates at Baghdad's Palestine Hotel, we were mobbed by scores of media crews just inside the lobby of the hotel. It was a struggle pushing through the mob, and though the hotel had been turned into a virtual citadel, protected by a bulwark of T-walls and the presence of manned Humvees and Bradleys, it was still in the Red Zone and the noisy scrum was a perfect opportunity for a suicide bomber or mortar attack.

Deeper inside the hotel I felt slightly more secure. The delegates filed into the conference room and the media drifted away while the rest of the LP crew and I remained in the lobby, alert and on guard. Both conditions had their own set of difficulties. Being alert in a place with no air-conditioning and the temperature at 47°C was not easy, while being on guard wasn't helped by the fact that the place was a functioning hotel and people were coming and going all the time.

I noticed one guy enter the lobby and immediately my alarm bells began ringing. He was young, athletic-looking and clean-shaven. He didn't approach the check-in desk, nor did he seem interested in any of the lobby shops; instead he wandered around looking lost and, to my eyes, subtly dangerous. I asked Rassim to find out who the guy was and what he was doing in the hotel. When Rassim approached him the man became agitated and aggressive, whipping out a scrappy photocopy of a letter that stated he was a police officer. There was no photograph on the letter and the guy had no other ID.

Rassim returned and reported this as I watched the guy continue his aimless wandering around the lobby. I positioned myself on a sofa out of the man's line of sight, the AK47 on my knees, the safety off, my whole system keyed up and watchful for any sign of violent intent.

If they arose, I intended to shoot the man in the head.

It was a surprisingly easy decision to make even though I recognised it was bizarre. I was sitting in the lobby of a modern hotel, prepared to shoot to kill. At this point, I realised one of the drawbacks of LP missions: this man was not some faint, ill-defined face behind a car windshield. I could see him clearly; would see his brains splatter if I was forced to shoot him. It was not a pretty thought, yet I knew I was prepared to go through with it. Surprisingly, it was an easier decision to reach than it had been in many of the instances when I'd decided to get physically involved and hit someone. Here there was no macho posturing, yelling, empty threats. My thought processes were clinical, rational, almost detached. I was clear in my head and, most surprising of all, calm.

I watched the man like a hawk, knowing with certainty that, if I judged it necessary, I would kill him.

After about twenty minutes a uniformed Iraqi policeman walked into the lobby, greeted the guy and they left together. I relaxed.

Two days later I was pointing my assault rifle at a policeman.

CHAPTER 27

Rubicon

THE POLICE in Iraq bothered me, as they bothered many people. They were incompetent and, because they were so frequently the target of insurgents, incredibly trigger-happy. It was well known that the police had a fifth-column in their ranks and that insurgents stole police uniforms and weapons to set up false roadblocks to kill or kidnap foreigners. Like most PSDs, I tried to avoid the police.

Rassim was away and I had a new driver, a young Iraqi called Tariq whom I didn't know. Returning from an LP mission I was sitting in the back seat travelling in the Red Zone when we were pulled over at a random police checkpoint. It was one of the disadvantages of LP missions. Rassim had always handled it well enough for us to have no hassle and to be on our way in a few moments. Tariq was not Rassim. He was too young or too dumb to realise that, though nowhere in the world was it advisable to argue with a uniformed cop who stopped you in your car, it was especially inadvisable in Iraq. Tariq was nervous and arrogant and soon he and the cop were in a heated argument.

I had an uncomfortable feeling and slowly eased the safety off my AK47, moving it stealthily behind the seat so I could train on the 'policeman' without him knowing. I would need to shoot through the seat without hitting Tariq who by now was yelling at the cop who was angrily yelling back. Pressing the muzzle of the weapon hard against the vinyl upholstery, I carefully angled the shot so the bullet would miss Tariq's ribs and hit the cop's pelvis. It was like angling a pool cue in a game of billiards — except it wasn't a game. Slowly my finger started taking up the slack on the trigger, deciding that if the cop made a move for the machine pistol slung across his chest, I would fire — though I had no idea what I would do after that. The checkpoint was manned by about a dozen supposed policemen and if I shot one, then God knows what would happen.

Suddenly the cop stepped back and Tariq accelerated away. I breathed a quiet sigh of relief.

That afternoon a dust storm hit the city. It blew for three days and two nights, shutting down the airport and reducing visibility in the compound to less than fifty metres. The wind was neither dramatic nor violent; there were no howling vortices as there were with the Sirocco in North Africa, but it blew steadily and unceasingly, covering everything in a gritty, sand-coloured layer of dust like a light fall of snow. The dust got everywhere; in my nostrils, my eyes, my lungs, even in my mouth though I kept it tight shut. It caked itself on my hair, my eyebrows, my eyelashes. Some guys — clearly not Jewish — even complained of it getting under their foreskins.

I noticed the old hands were edgy. 'Everyone seems keyed up. What's happening?' I asked a big, gregarious, cigar-smoking, ex-Special Forces Swede I knew by his call sign, Gladius.

'The storm gives the insurgents optical cover to lay their mines. There's a much bigger risk of ambushes with IEDs after a dust storm,' Gladius told me. 'And they launch attacks under cover of the storm. In this country, dust means death. In fact there's only one good thing about a dust storm.'

I spat speckles of dust, wiping the grit off my lips. 'Yeah, what's that?'

'It sharpens you up. Makes you more watchful.'

I knew what he meant. Life, even life in Baghdad, had become routine. My days had become weeks and my weeks had morphed into more than two months, while my experience of individual convoys had blended into a memory of all convoys, just as the heat and dust of one Baghdad day had merged into a seamless memory of every Baghdad day.

What had once been extraordinary was now commonplace; the sudden chatter of small-arms fire in a nearby street, a heavy machine gun opening up from a rooftop, the *crump-crump* of mortar fire, the *whumping* of US helicopters overhead, the quick arching flashes of red and green rockets fired from gunships; even driving the wrong way on BIAP, though notable, failed to command any degree of respect. My system had adjusted to the intensity of the experience so the adrenalin-fuelled rush of a Low Profile mission through the streets of the Red Zone was not as sharp as it had been. The human system could adapt to almost anything and mine had. Life in Baghdad had become routine. And what the big Swede, whom I respected, was telling me was that routine could kill.

It was a good reminder and I purposely psyched myself up to be more alert. It was curious; the first thing I noticed in my newly focused state was that the sound of small arms and explosions were much closer than I'd previously thought.

I shook my head, shrugging off the notion. It had to be my imagination.

In the early hours of the second morning of the dust storm I was awakened by an explosion somewhere to the south, followed almost immediately by another, then another and then by the rattle of small-arms fire that went on for several minutes. It was a major action, though by whom and against what I had no way of knowing. I found out the following morning in the canteen. I was having breakfast with Keith when Gladius joined us at our table.

'You hear what happened last night?'

'The explosions?'

The big Swede nodded. Unusually for him, he seemed subdued. 'Insurgents stormed a compound a few kilometres from here. A suicide bomber drove a VBIED into the gates. Of course, the bastards knew that wouldn't gain access, so they had a second suicide bomber drive another vehicle in straight after. Then, to make sure, they drove a *third* VBIED into the gates and that did it. Four truckloads of insurgents stormed the compound and massacred everyone in it, aid-workers and PSDs.' We gazed at him, our faces betraying none of our thoughts.

'Only a few kilometres from here,' he repeated.

Maybe, I thought, it wasn't my imagination. Maybe incidents and explosions *were* creeping closer.

I was due to revert to High Profile convoys for a couple of days. It wasn't my choice, but I was an employee and tactical decisions were made by other people. Sitting in my room around noon and waiting for the next mission, I was emailing Tash with the news that I had less than three weeks to go in the country when, with a roar, an enormous explosion shook the villa, rocking the walls and shaking plaster and dust down on to my laptop.

I leapt up, my chair going over as I grabbed my Kevlar vest, my AK47 and rushed out, joining the other guys crashing down the stairs. In the courtyard, pieces of twisted shrapnel speckled the ground and I could see holes in some of the roofs where shards of flying metal had punched through the tiles. Several windows were broken, the glass held together by shredded white tape hanging like bunting at a fair. Gladius was already there, standing next to the compound manager. Seconds later, Keith, the big Kiwi, charged up. 'What happened?' he gasped.

The manager ignored him, talking rapidly into his cell phone, ordering the compound into lockdown. I watched groups of Iraqi guards moving into position at the heavy machine guns on the watchtowers and roofs as PSDs began shepherding the clients out of the exposed courtyard and back into their rooms. The big metal gates were tight shut, no vehicles were permitted either in or out; okay for those inside, I thought; not so hot for those caught on the outside with nowhere to go.

From the direction of the blast we heard a flurry of small-arms fire. Gladius stared at the manager who was listening intently to someone at the other end. The manager finished and signed off. 'It's the hospital,' he growled. 'Car bomb. The place is under attack.'

The hospital was less than five hundred metres away.

'There're women and kids in there,' Gladius said.

'*Their* women and kids,' said the compound manager.

'Bastards.'

We stood silently in the dusty courtyard listening to the sound of machine guns and grenades.

Unable to keep my mouth shut any longer I snapped, 'So what do we *do*?'

'We do what we're paid to do, and maintain security here,' the manager said.

'While women and kids come under attack in a hospital? For fuck's sake!'

'*What*, you think I *like* it?'

I backed off a little.

'Okay, okay. But we can't just do nothing. Look, there's enough of us here. I'm willing to lead a fighting patrol out there to see if we can kill whoever's doing the shooting. Or, get one of the others to lead it. It doesn't matter — so long as we do something. And if we can't kill the bastards, maybe at least we can give some emergency medical aid.'

'Don't be fucking stupid.'

'We're already stupid,' Gladius chimed in. 'We're in Iraq, aren't we? How stupid is that?'

'Right, better to be stupid and useful than clever and fucking useless,' said Keith.

'No, you don't get it,' the manager said. 'You go out there without company sanction and your life insurance is invalid. You get killed or wounded and your family gets nothing. That's why it's stupid.'

We were silent, glancing at one another before staring at the ground. Though our hearts said one thing, our heads were telling us something else.

'Fuck,' Keith exploded. 'This place is shit. A total, fucking shithole.' He turned and stormed towards the villa and his room, savagely kicking at a lump of metal on his way.

The heads had won.

For a moment I was tempted to go out on my own. There were a few ways out of the compound and it was only five hundred metres to the hospital. But I thought of Tash and the kids. What could one man do? Yes, that was another rational argument. Rational thinking got me off the hook. It made inaction acceptable — no — it made it compulsory.

Rationalisation could always excuse cowardice.

I sloped back to my room and called Tash on my mobile. I needed to hear her voice.

She asked how things were. 'Pretty quiet,' I lied. She was looking forward to me coming home, she told me; the kids were counting the sleeps. Only twenty more to go, she said.

I didn't sleep well that night. The next day, when we heard there had been several women and children killed at the hospital, I felt physically ill. Retreating to one of the bathrooms I hovered over the basin, staring at my reflection in the mirror, knowing that this was not my finest hour.

Later I was told I would be staying in the Green Zone for a few days while running High Profile convoys. I was glad to be getting a change of scenery if not a change of assignment: I would be escorting Iraqi magistrates to the airport and to various locations in the Red Zone.

The bullets hit on the morning of the second day, the convoy roaring through the suburbs en route to Baghdad International Airport. I felt the draught, the sudden rush of a vacuum sucking the air close to the top of my skull, as I heard the vicious *CRACK* of a high-velocity bullet ripping open armoured metal. I knew immediately what it was.

I was driving the second Land Cruiser in the convoy and an insurgent with a heavy machine gun had me in his sights. The rounds had to be armour piercing, chewing through the hardened steel at fourteen hundred feet a second.

The second burst of fire was less well aimed; I watched the bitumen a few feet in front of the SUV exploding in chunks as the rounds slammed in. The third and subsequent bursts were in line with the vehicle, but low; I could hear repeated clumps of bitumen hitting my door — at least, I hoped it was bitumen.

I felt my heartbeat rocketing, my palms slick with sweat, my mouth as dry as the dusty street.

I dropped down a gear with my right hand and floored the accelerator, moderating my breathing as I swerved the big vehicle from side to side, radioing to the rear gunner in the Land Cruiser ahead, giving him directions to return fire. The guy either saw something or thought he saw something because he opened up with the PKM. Every third round was green tracer but I had no time to watch. For the next couple of kilometres the convoy drove evasively, swinging crazily all over the road before straightening up and racing for the airport.

At the airport I was still pumped from the ambush, the adrenalin roaring through my system. I wasn't bothered about the return journey; in a perverse kind of way I was looking forward to it. The man who had shot at me knew his business; to hit a vehicle moving at over a hundred kilometres an hour he would have to have 'led' the target; easy enough to do in practice, but to accomplish that in action and under pressure showed a high degree of expertise.

And hate. The guy had meant to do more than hit the vehicle — he had meant to kill. Me. Well, that was okay. I wasn't angry about that. I didn't feel any hate towards him; if anything I admired his skill. Yet, if I got the scintilla of an opportunity, I was going to kill him. Killing the man who had tried to kill me seemed as natural to me as night following day. Not as an act of revenge though. Definitely not that. No, my motivation was solely that it was the most permanent and reliable method of stopping the sniper from trying to shoot someone else.

But to kill him would require all my focus and concentration. I couldn't do that and drive at the same time so I persuaded Sean to change places, and I rode up front, staring up at the buildings when we got to the neighbourhood. 'Slow down,' I barked.

Sean accelerated. *'Wit? Fackdat. Yuwannasheetdisfacker yudoitonyereenteem, bejaysus.'* I saw no sign of my would-be assassin.

Back in the Green Zone I filled in yet another incident report before going to the Liberty Pool to swim a couple of kilometres. Afterwards, I drove to the US Prosperity camp where, in the army mess, I had a delicious T-bone steak, followed by a double helping of Baskin Robbins ice cream. I felt good. I was alive.

The adrenalin turned sour and rancid in the early hours of the morning when, instead of sleep, came a succession of morbid, pathological thoughts as long and as dark as a funeral cortège. What if the guy hadn't missed?

What if, instead of killing me, the bullet had taken off half my head and left me a vegetable? What if the next round had turned me into a quadriplegic?

By an odd twist of fate the mission had been my last scheduled HP convoy; in the morning I was due back on LP. Lying there in the darkness I was glad. No more HP. I settled down to sleep. I had been close to being killed, had got away with it and wasn't going to be undertaking HP any more.

But sleep wouldn't come. Something was gnawing at me. My original decision to switch to LP had been based on a tactical preference for the low-key approach. But now I found myself looking forward to LP for a more visceral reason. I was suddenly afraid of HP. In fact, rather than do another HP I began scheming how I could hitch a ride on a US military chopper to the airport and fly out of Iraq, ASAP. Other people had done that. Why not me?

But I knew why not. If I did that, I would have let fear master me. Fear wouldn't stop at one thing. It never did. As sick as the thought made me, I knew I had to get back on the horse. The short-term pain of facing my fear would be better than the creeping, long-term agony of letting fear control me.

The following morning I went in search of Greg. 'I don't want to come off HP just yet,' I told him.

'Yeah, why not?' he said. 'I thought you preferred Low Profile work.'

'I do, but I'm not ready to move on just yet.'

Greg gazed at me for a moment. I wondered if he would quiz me further. I needn't have worried. The bloke had been around the track too often to start probing why people did things. People had their reasons.

He shrugged. 'Okay. Suits me.'

The next convoy on BIAP was hard to take; so was the one after that, and the next one. That night there were a thousand more 'what ifs'. The following night, after two more HP missions, there were only hundreds, the night after that almost none. My mind had got tired of listening to them. It wanted sleep. I had not conquered fear; no one did that. It would always come back. But I had mastered it, at least for now. I had also learned first-hand Seneca's dictum: *'A man who suffers before it is necessary, suffers more than is necessary.'*

A few days later I was ordered back to the compound in Karadah in the Red Zone. Now I was ready to return to LP for the right reasons. I was also counting down the days to go home.

This time we knew about the dust storm before it hit. The forecast had said it would blow for at least three days and, in readiness, compound security was ramped up with more men crewing the watchtowers and rooftops. On the afternoon of the storm's second day we heard an explosion close by; insurgents had launched rocket-propelled grenades at an Iraqi police roadblock. The compound went into full lockdown with clients escorted back to their rooms and most of the PSDs, armed and ready, in the canteen to get away, at least partially, from the dust.

Frustrated by the inactivity and irritated by the dust, even inside, I slipped on my armour and vest, took my AK47 and stepped outside into the courtyard.

The wind, laden with dust and as hot and as thick as soup, was blowing steadily, the dust reducing visibility to no more than thirty metres. I was wearing a traditional *keffiyeh*, having come to appreciate there was nothing better to cover my head and mouth during a dust storm. After a couple of minutes I asked myself what I thought I was doing. I sure as hell wasn't getting any fresh air.

I turned to make my way to the canteen when I heard the boom of a single explosion, outside yet relatively close to the compound walls. I ran to the closest watchtower and shouted up to the Iraqi lookout, 'What can you see?' I hoped his English was up to telling me.

The wind caught his words, '... not big ... one explosion ... hard to see but maybe vehicle turned over ...'

I hesitated. The vehicle was not one from the compound; they were all accounted for. If it had been an attack by a suicide car bomber it would have rammed the gates on the other side of the perimeter. Since that hadn't happened, it might be a roadside bomb intended for a passing vehicle from another PMC. Which meant there would be PSDs out there, exposed and calling for help on their radio. In real terms they'd have quite a wait: it would take long minutes before a Quick Response Force was mobilised. And then what? Would the compound manager stand around in the courtyard and debate the efficacy of rescue like the last time? Meanwhile, what about the poor sods outside?

I knew I had to act. I didn't want this job, but it was sitting in my lap. I had about a four-minute start on anybody else coming to the aid of those who may have survived the explosion. I could participate. Or I could walk away. It was make-your-mind-up-time.

I loped around to the opposite side of the compound. The secondary access point was manned by two Iraqi guards. With their focus on sheltering from the storm, they asked no questions when I motioned for them to let me through beyond the T-walls.

Outside the world was different. It blew dust and shimmered with hate.

I scampered close to the foot of the external wall as far as the first corner and then circled around to the parallel street. Looking over my shoulder I could no longer see the watchtower. The dust was thick; all I could make out was the dark outline of an SUV on its side. I moved forward with maximum caution, the metallic taste of fear in my mouth. Insurgents often had stand-by teams ready to move in to the kill-zone to execute survivors or take them hostage. If they were there and there was fighting it would be at close quarters, maybe hand-to-hand.

Hunched low I shuffled through the dust, the sand stinging my eyes, the safety of my AK47 off, my finger inside the trigger guard.

I reached the vehicle, a Range Rover, and sidestepped around it carefully. It had taken a rocket-propelled grenade, which had thrown it on to its side. I peered down to look through the shattered windshield. The two men in the front were dead. I straightened up. The flames spurting from the engine were dying, smothered by the cloying dust. I looked around, the muzzle of my rifle following the sweep of my vision. A figure was lying in the dust on the far side of the vehicle. I scuttled towards it.

A large puddle of dark arterial blood had formed around the man's hips and despite the dust the flies were gathering. I bent to the figure, conscious of the smell of blood and cordite and burning rubber. Everywhere there was dust and filth and more dust. The man was on his side, clutching at his femoral artery, clearly in great pain.

Gently I eased him over. The face was ashen but there was no mistaking the crooked teeth, the tombstone look, the pitted skin.

'What the fook you lookin' at?' Jocko groaned.

'You, you ugly bastard.'

Recognition flared in the dying eyes. 'Red? Is that you?'

'Yeah, it's me, Jocko.'

'Whatcha doin' with a tea-towel on your head?'

I whipped the *keffiyeh* off. I could use it to staunch the blood. 'Lie still. Help's coming.'

Jocko's head moved imperceptibly. 'Nah.'

I watched the bravado peeling away with each weakening heartbeat. After a moment Jocko sighed.

'You know that recon on the island?' he whispered.

I bent closer to hear him. 'Yes.'

'Were you really scared?'

'Shitless.'

There was another long moment before I heard the faint, final whisper, 'So maybe we are the fookin' same. You an'. me.'

He died moments later.

* * *

The body of Iain Jack McKenzie was moved by truck to a US military base where it was unceremoniously stuffed into a vinyl body bag before being buried in a communal grave near Basra. There was no church service and there was no one to mourn his passing. His was just another name in a long list of names; casualties in something that wasn't even called a war.

Three days later I left Iraq, taking the last hair-raising ride on BIAP and shaking hands with Greg at the airport.

'If you want to come back for a second stint, just let me know,' Greg said with a smile.

'Not bloody likely, mate.'

I went out the same way I came in; a connecting flight to Dubai and then Qantas to Brisbane. As the plane made its big sweep out over the ocean before coming in to land, I felt that huge surge of warmth and contentment I always felt when arriving back in Australia.

Immigration and Customs took forever. After collecting the mandatory rubber stamp, I caught a train to the Gold Coast and from there a taxi home. It was bizarre and intoxicating to drive sedately on smooth, orderly roads lined with lush green trees. When my taxi-driver complained about the traffic I burst out laughing. His bitching was the funniest thing I'd heard in ages.

As far as my family was concerned, I wasn't due back until the following day. I wanted to surprise them, and I had a plan.

When Tash and the children arrived home from school, they let out a collective exclamation of surprise when they spotted the very large parcel on the verandah. It was Brontë's fifth birthday and she was the first to rush over and try to open it. She held her ground well as the older kids bustled forward, clamouring to read the notice attached to the box.

'What does it say Mum?' they chorused.

Tash read the words out loud: 'Caution. Contains Wildlife. Open Under Adult Supervision.'

Just then a scratching noise came from inside the box, followed by a low growl.

Brontë screamed. So did her sister. Everyone stepped back from the box.

With that wonderful mix of total dread and sheer delight that young children have in abundance, one of the boys declared there was a lion inside. That theory was quickly dismissed by his brother, who thought the box was too small.

When I burst out of the box I was greeted by the sight of six stunned, happy, smiling faces, Tash's mixed with a fair measure of relief. I pulled her close to me, kissing her, breathing in the scent of her hair. There was a moment's silence before a barrage of excited children pressed in on me from all sides, enveloping me in a cocoon of laughter and life.

There was nowhere else I wanted to be.

POSTSCRIPT

LOOKING BACK IS FINE,
BUT LOOKING *FORWARD* IS BETTER.

POSTSCRIPT

South East Queensland

FOR THE first few months after my return from Iraq I didn't want to go anywhere. It just felt incredibly good to stay home and work on our property, take the kids to school, spend time with my wife, read and relax.

It was great to be home. It was great to be in one piece. It was great to be *alive*.

With plenty of time to think, I reflected on my particular journey as I've ridden different waves and came to the conclusion that I have nothing to complain about and a great deal to be thankful for. And then something unexpected happened: I received a call from Lisa — my old Melbourne girlfriend. She had done a search on *Google*, found my website and decided to phone. We chatted for quite a while. It was nice to hear from her, but her call reminded me of a period when I had seriously questioned the value of where I was headed. No one I knew at that point in time respected my choices — not just Lisa's pot-smoking friends, but also the people I spent the first fifteen years of my life watching television with.

Since then I've been very fortunate to have crossed paths with dozens of outstanding people who have generously given advice and encouragement. Their support has more than compensated for the exposure I've had to small-minded, small-hearted people along the way. Friends like; Seb Alexander (deceased), Fred Blaaue, Dean & Kylie Clifford, Sue Davies (nee Kellie), Brian & Joan Goldrick, John & Abbe Harman, Hydor Honiball, Christine Maher, Lance Mans, Barry Markof, Mark & Carol McKeon, Ray & Mary Ninnes, Tom

O'Toole, Marty & Chris Stone, Fryk Strydom and Albertus Wessels have allowed me to advance in ways that would have been impossible if I'd never ventured beyond the town where I was born.

Around the time of the call from Lisa, I started doing corporate presentation work again. I found that after the break in Iraq (if 'break' is an appropriate word to describe spending time in Iraq) I really enjoyed speaking to corporate audiences again.

The vast majority of people I came to work with were a pleasure to speak to and interact with but, as always, a few weren't.

In any industry, town or city there are always people who, in various ways, try to drag you down to their level. They resent people who dare to grow and make a dent in the world; seem affronted by non-conformity. They treat life as if it goes on forever. Focusing on irrelevancies such as the type of car they drive and the brand name on their sunglasses, they passively watch their marriages deteriorate and the relationship they have with their children fade into the distance.

These are the *spectators* of life. Their outlook has nothing to do with culture or how much, or how little, they have experienced or travelled. Like everyone, they choose their attitude.

On the other side of the coin there are the *participants* of life. These are the people who accept there are no guarantees and realise that mistakes are also opportunities to learn. In a myriad of ways they embrace life and empower the people around them. They understand that looking back is fine, but looking *forward* is better.

A few weeks before this book was due to go to press, I was returning from a conference in Cairns. My wife had picked me up from Brisbane airport and we were travelling south along the M1. I'd only been away for forty-eight hours, but with five children there was plenty to talk about.

We were chatting and laughing until our conversation was suddenly interrupted by a loud *clunk*. I looked behind me to be greeted by the spectacular sight of a medium-sized transit van — airborne! At least three metres off the ground, the underside of the vehicle was leading the way. My wife, genius that she is, had the presence of mind to pump the accelerator, not the brake. Barrelling forward, the spinning van catapulted off the highway, did a complete 360-degree flip, landed back on its wheels and then crashed onto one side.

Just a few moments before I'd been relaxed, enjoying the company of my wife. Now I was out of the car and sprinting northwards along the southbound lane of the M1.

Incredibly, *miraculously*, the three occupants — one adult and two children — had been thrown clear of the wreckage, unscathed. Standing wide-eyed and in shock, they clustered together, hugging and in tears.

The driver, clearly amazed to be alive, kept repeating: 'I fell asleep! I fell asleep!'

The image of the underside of that transit van, travelling at 110 kph three metres above the tarmac, is one of many which illustrates to me how very quickly one's circumstances can change. It doesn't matter where you go or what you do, there is risk, uncertainty, in *everything*.

But this fact shouldn't hold people back. On the contrary, it should encourage them to move forward, to embrace it. The alternative — complacency, and subsequent atrophy — is such a poor second best. **R.R.**

PPS: *Just as* Waveman *was being readied for its second print run, there was a highly publicised case of rocket launchers being stolen from the Australian Army and then, supposedly, onsold to terrorist organisations. In relation to this, a news program invited me to give an interview outlining my views on the situation. I decided it might be an interesting experience to go live-to-air on national television so I said yes. To my surprise, within minutes of completing the interview, my phone was ringing and emails were being received. My favorite response from one viewer was: 'Saw you on TV this morning. Nice work. You were factual, realistic and the voice of reason. I assume we will never see you on TV again.'*

DISTRIBUTED BY Macmillan Publishing Services, Courtney Ballantyne Publishing is an Australian-based publishing group keen to promote quality writing based on personal experience. If you have a manuscript which has the ability to; inform, educate, entertain or amuse, we would like to consider your work for publication. For submission details visit:

www.cbpublishing.org